Let's Vote!
The Essentials of the American Electoral Process

Daniel M. Shea

Allegheny College

Boston   Columbus   Indianapolis   New York   San Francisco   Upper Saddle River
Amsterdam   Cape Town   Dubai   London   Madrid   Milan   Munich   Paris   Montreal   Toronto
Delhi   Mexico City   São Paulo   Sydney   Hong Kong   Seoul   Singapore   Taipei   Tokyo

Executive Editor: Reid Hester
Editorial Assistant: Emily Sauerhoff
Senior Marketing Manager: Lindsey Prudhomme
Production Manager: Fran Russello
Full Service Project Management and Composition: Ravi Bhatt/PreMediaGlobal
Cover Design Manager: Jayne Conte
Cover Designer: Axell Design
Cover Art: Fotolia
Printer/Binder: Courier Companies, Inc.

Credits and acknowledgments borrowed from other sources and reproduced, with permission, in this textbook appear on appropriate page within text.

Library of Congress Cataloging-in-Publication Data

Shea, Daniel M.
    Let's vote: the essentials of the American electoral process / Daniel Shea.
        p. cm.
    Includes index.
    ISBN-13: 978-0-205-83123-4
    ISBN-10: 0-205-83123-0
        1. Elections—United States.   2. Voting—United States.   I. Title.
    JK1976.S55 2013
    324.60973—dc23   2011041866

10 9 8 7 6 5 4 3 2 1—CRW—16 15 14 13 12

ISBN 10: 0-205-83123-0
ISBN 13: 978-0-205-83123-4

*To All Those Teachers and Activists Who Help
Others Understand the Importance of Elections
and the Necessity of Involvement.*

BRIEF CONTENTS

CONTENTS

PREFACE

When 18-year-olds were first given the right to vote, in 1972, 50 percent of those under 30 years old came to the polls. By 1996, participation among that group had dropped to just 32 percent. As for midterm congressional elections, one in four in this age group was making it to the polls by the end of the century. A 2002 study of younger Americans, commissioned by the Center for Information and Research on Civic Learning and Engagement (CIRCLE), found that only about two-thirds of the 18- to 25-year-olds had even registered to vote; 49 percent of those under 25 said that voting is "a little important" or "not at all important" to them. Roughly 40 percent, which was twice as many as a decade earlier, suggested that it did not matter who was elected president.

The problem ran much deeper than nonvoting. In the 1960s, about 35 percent of those under 30 "tried to influence how others voted," but by the end of the century, that figure had dropped to roughly 20 percent. The percentage of young citizens "very much interested in campaigns" stood at roughly 30 percent from the 1950s to the 1980s, but declined to just 6 percent by the 2000 election. In 2002, 67 percent of all Americans cared "very much" or "pretty much" about the outcome of congressional elections in their area, but only 47 percent of those less than 25 felt the same way.

The withdrawal of young citizens from politics appeared deep and broad. Robert Putnam, in *Bowling Alone: The Collapse and Revival of American Community*, summed up the issue this way: "Very little of the net decline in voting is attributable to individual change, and virtually all of it is generational."

Yet, the response over the last decade to this decline was equally swift and comprehensive. The number of youth-centered political efforts, like Rock the Vote, Redeem the Vote, Choose or Lose, and HeadCount, took root or dramatically expanded their influence. Hefty philanthropic initiatives were launched, most notably the Pew Charitable Trusts' "New Voters Project." A number of college and university pro-grams were also created, including the Vanishing Voter Project at Harvard; CIRCLE at University of Maryland (now at Tufts University), and the Center for Political Participation at Allegheny College, where I teach, to name only a few. Both the major parties, but especially the Democrats, allocated unprecedented resources to youth engagement efforts—likely due to the shrinking number of persuadable older voters.

Things seemed to improve. Although a direct causal connection to these efforts would be difficult to verify, interest in politics among young citizens swelled in the 2004 and 2008 elections. By 2008, the turnout for those under 30 rose to 51 percent. Many other indicators of political behavior, such as participating in campaign events, talk-ing about politics, and paying attention to the news, also saw improvement. Given the role that young voters played in several of the early presidential nomination contests, it seemed to make sense that *Time* would dub 2008, "Year of the Youth Vote" (January 31, 2008). Young citizens, it seemed, had rediscovered the potential of electoral politics.

Or had they? The first indicators of a reversal were the 2009 gubernatorial elec-tions in New Jersey and Virginia; exit polling found that voters under age 30 accounted for just 9 percent of voters in New Jersey (compared with 17 percent in 2008) and

10 percent in Virginia (down from 21 percent in 2008). Young citizens also stayed home in the critically important special election to fill the Massachusetts Senate seat vacated by the death of Ted Kennedy, the so-called 60th seat. Overall, turnout was high for a special election—a robust 54 percent. For those *older* than 30, turnout was 60 percent; for those under 30, it was a scant 15 percent.

By the 2010 midterm election, it appeared quite clear that the youth engagement bubble had burst. Turnout for those under 30 reached just 22.8 percent—a decrease from the previous midterm election (2006). Coming off of the surge in 2008, the drop just two years later ran against a long line of scholarship that suggests once a citizen starts voting, it becomes habitual.

So what happened? Why would so many citizens sit on the sidelines even though the nation faces daunting policy questions? Shouldn't there be heightened interest in politics, given the massive amounts of political information and a deepening partisan divide? Why haven't social network sites and other online organizing tools helped bring young voters to non-presidential elections? For all the money being spent, shouldn't candidates expect higher turnout? What's happening in the myriad civics and government courses taught in high schools and colleges? Have young folks simply grown too cynical and lazy?

Another possibility, the rationale for this book, is that the growing complexity of modern electoral politics pushes many to the sidelines. Few aspects of American politics have changed more in the past half-century than the way Americans pick their leaders. New laws, regulations, norms, customs, practices and much else can be daunting to anyone—much less citizens just wetting their toes in the skills of democracy. Young people are not turned off and lazy; they care and are ready to give their time, energy, and money for causes they believe in. At the same time that a generation turned away from electoral politics, the numbers who volunteer in their communities skyrocketed. They are not indifferent or turned off. For many, electoral politics is just too distant, too complex.

Thus, the aim of this book is to help readers, particularly younger citizens, appreciate the importance of elections in the United States and their potential to play a meaningful role in the process. Sure, modern elections are complex, but each individual can make a difference—that is, if he or she really understands how the system works.

Understanding that history and context matter, I have opened each of the chapters with background information, and from there moved to current information on how each element shapes modern elections. Rather than offering an encyclopedic approach, my hope is that the reader does not feel overwhelmed by the material. That is to say, I have done my best to offer the essential nuts and bolts. Finally, to help students truly comprehend information and to spur discussion, a list of critical thinking questions is noted at the end of each chapter.

Will this book or any text on electoral politics draw young Americans back to the electoral process? Likely not. But as with any private or civic endeavor, getting started—that first step—can be the toughest hurdle. Many believe that elections are byzantine and certainly not for them. My sincere hope that is that the pages to follow might convince a few readers otherwise.

Daniel M. Shea

ACKNOWLEDGEMENTS

My earliest memories of elections are of late nights, smoke-filled rooms, crowds, lots of beer, a bit of joy, and a heavy dose of tears. My father, Dennis Shea, was a political science professor and my mother, Rosemary Bowers Shea, a true political activist. They believed in elections and the power of engagement. I learned at an early age that democracy should not be considered a spectator sport; you cannot sit on the sidelines and complain about the course of government. Those in the trenches—doing the hand-to-hand combat of making calls, knocking on doors, and licking envelopes—chart the course of public policy, as they should. Victories are sometimes fleeting, but individual effort matters.

I took this passion for electoral activism to college, where I became *that* student who organized campus events, helped the local party committee, and hit the road to help presidential candidates. Few at the State University of New York at Oswego were surprised to hear that I would go to graduate school to become a campaign consultant and that my first career move would be, once again, in the electoral trenches. As an academic, my foremost interest has been the electoral process. I have come to better understand the nuances of the process, but always at the center, regardless of prevailing forces and momentous changes, lies my admiration for the efforts of average citizens. Elections still matter, and individual engagement is still critical.

And yet, many Americans, particularly young Americans, have come to doubt the utility of elections. There are many reasons for their skepticism, topics discussed in the pages to follow, yet at least some of this indifference (or even hostility) might be explained by the complexity of the process. Future activists might feel better about joining the fray if they understood the numerous moving parts of contemporary elections. That idea has been the guiding principle behind the creation of this book.

Numerous friends and colleagues have helped. At Pearson, Political Science editor Reid Hester was instrumental in fine-tuning the manuscript and in developing the pedagogical elements. Many undergraduate student assistants at Allegheny College—including Julie Cain, Lynn Burke, Robin Lyle, Alex Sproveri, and Richard Shafranek—helped pull together charts, figures, and graphs, and in editing some sections. Student Megan McNally deserves special mention, given her diligence and skill in reviewing material and pulling together important data sets. My colleague and good friend at the Center for Political Participation, Mary Solberg, helped copyedit parts of the manuscript, and my pals in the Political Science Department have been very supportive of this project, as well as all of my writing and research.

Finally, as always, this book would not have been written without the love and encouragement of my wonderful wife, Christine, and our three darling children, Abigail, Danny, and Brian.

1

Democracy's Feast

After reading this chapter, you should be able to understand these core concepts and explain their significance:

- Role of Elections in America
- Framer Intentions
- Themes of the Book

- Clash of Election Theory and Conduct
- Institutional and Cultural Barriers to the Process

Let's vote on it! As simple and as common as these words are, one would be hard-pressed to bundle four other words to say as much. Voting—the simple act of raising a hand, checking a box, pushing a lever, hitting a button, or touching a video screen—carries profound implications for citizens, government, and society. It signifies that each person matters and that everyone is an important player in the decision-making process. It denotes equality, and the right to discuss preferences and to direct the course of policy. Characteristics that too often define one's standing in society, such as race, gender, affluence, education, and social connections, are invisible in the voting booth. On Election Day, the powerful CEO must stand in line with the factory worker, the teacher, the nurse, and the farmer. Moreover, voting is an opportunity, a powerful nudge one might say, for people to step beyond their private world into the civic realm and to become informed and engaged in public matters. Everyone has a seat at the table of what H. G. Wells dubbed our "democratic feast." "Democracy's ceremonial," he wrote. "Its feast, its great function is the election."[1]

Voting is often proclaimed to be the fundamental ingredient of any democracy. One might argue about the frequency of elections, constituents per legislator, requirements for voting (such as age and residency), and how much attention to pay to ballot initiatives, but few would suggest that a political system can be democratic if it denies its citizens the right to vote. The more robust the electoral process—the more citizens that are engaged and the more frequency of contests—the healthier the system, many assume. It is certainly no surprise that traditionally disenfranchised groups, such as women and African-Americans, throughout much of American history set their sights on voting as a requisite of equality and liberty. "Suffrage," noted Susan B. Anthony, "is the pivotal right."[2]

To some, voting and elections *themselves* can help create a democracy. Many assumed that Iraq would leap toward a democracy after the fall of Saddam Hussein just by having elections. At the very least, it would signify a "turning point," and a "commitment to democracy," as George W. Bush argued in January 2005.[3] People who assumed that Iraq is taking a turn toward democracy didn't think it would matter that other core democratic freedoms and institutions were yet to be established (if they thought about it at all). They believed that by allowing average citizens to vote, democracy would take root, and once a citizenry is enfranchised, retracting this "pivotal right" becomes unlikely.

As we will see in chapters to follow, voting gives legitimacy to the ruling elite in most systems. Although wide segments of the population may dislike the outcome of a particular election or official policies, rarely do they challenge the system of elections so long as they think the elections are open and fair. Iranian protesters took to the streets in the summer of 2009 not because they lost their national election but because they perceived the results to be fraudulent. Likely, this does not bode well for the long-term stability of the ruling elite in Iran, a point well illustrated by an anecdote of the ancient Chinese philosopher Confucius. Confucius was asked about the forces that promote stability in a government. "People must have sufficient food to eat," he replied. "There must be a sufficient army; and there must be confidence of the people in the ruler." But if a system were forced to give up one of these, which would Confucius suggest? "I would go without the army first." And next? "I would do without sufficient food. A nation cannot exist without confidence in its ruler."[4]

For Americans, elections build confidence in the system, as they seem the perfect mechanism to merge three core beliefs, elements of what people sometimes call the "American creed": egalitarianism, populism, and majority will.[5]

---

[1]H. G. Wells, *Democracy under Revision: A Lecture Delivered at the Sorbonne, March 15, 1927* (London: Hogarth Press, 1927) published in *The Way the World Is Going: Guesses and Forecasts of the Years Ahead* (Garden City, NY: Doubleday, Doran, 1928), 51–77.

[2]"Susan B. Anthony Quotes." Accessed at: http://www.ushistorysite.com/susan_b_anthony_quotes.php

[3]President George W. Bush, "Remarks by President George W. Bush at the 20th Anniversary of the Nation Endowment of Democracy" (November 6, 2003). Accessed at: http://www.ned.org/george-w-bush/remarks-by-president-george-w-bush-at-the-20th-anniversary

[4]Christian Science Monitor, "Confucius Gives Reagan Some Advice," *Beaver County Times*, January 11, 1981, A-7.

[5]Alan Abramowitz, *Voice of the People: Elections and Voting in the United States* (Boston: McGraw-Hill, 2004), 2–3.

Egalitarianism is the doctrine that holds that all people are created equal and have a right to participate in the conduct of government. Populism maintains that average folks have a great deal of wisdom (and, conversely, that there is much to fear about elites). Majority will is the idea that from a basic tabulation fair and just outcomes can be reached.

Indeed, Americans place such faith in elections that enfranchisement is often viewed as the panacea to the problems confronted by groups in society. As noted by a prominent student of elections:

> The established American response to social discontent is the extension of the ballot. The protests of women led to their enfranchisement, but not to the end of sexual discrimination. Antiwar sentiments of the young facilitated the enfranchisement of eighteen-year-olds, even as fighting continued in Vietnam. Black discontent was answered by passage of voting rights laws, but not by any fundamental economic legislation. Elections themselves are seen as the basic solution for social problems.[6]

It is not surprising, then, that Americans use elections to fill many, many government positions. Some would suggest that America is the most election-crazed nation in the world, boasting roughly 500,000 elected positions nationwide. It elects a president and members of the national legislature, of course, but also state governors, thousands of state legislators, county officials, mayors and other city officials, town trustees, justices in many states and counties, sheriffs and other law enforcement officials, assessors, attorneys general, comptrollers, auditors, and scores of other government officials. In some communities, even the choice of animal control officer (i.e., dog catcher) is put to a ballot, and in many places coroners are also elected.

Not only do Americans rely heavily on elections to fill government positions, the frequency of these events far outpaces that found in most other nations. Some Americans believe that elections occur only every four years, given that this is when they select their president, but elections are, in fact, held every year. State and some federal legislators are selected every two years, and most municipal posts are filled in odd-numbered years. Moreover, given that party organizations now nominate candidates to run in the general election through primary elections, it is fair to say that Americans are called to the polls at least twice every year—once for the primary and once for the general election.

Americans use elections not only to select candidates but also to directly change government policy. Referenda and other ballot initiatives allow citizens to vote on policy matters, essentially sidestepping the legislative process. In some states, voters may even remove elected officials from office in a special election; this is called a recall. As we will discuss in Chapter 10, polling data suggest that interest in these sorts of opportunities is growing. Many believe this process is a better reflection of public will than candidate-centered elections, but others are quick to point out its numerous downsides, also discussed in Chapter 10.

---

[6]Gerald M. Pomper, *Elections in America: Control and Influence in Democratic Politics*, 2nd ed. (New York: Longman, 1980), 3.

Our faith in the election process springs from numerous sources, not the least of which is childhood socialization—the way younger citizens learn about appropriate modes of behavior. By a young age, perhaps just 4 or 5, American children have discovered that voting is a good way to resolve disputes. Want to play kick ball or dodge ball? Dress up or play house? Watch television or go on a sleigh ride? Put it to a vote! And when the "powers that be" establish unpopular public policies, such as mandatory vegetable-eating or limitations on video games, the citizenry often calls for a vote. How surprising and frustrating it must be for these future civic leaders to hear that they do not always necessarily live in an election-based democracy—at least when it comes to eating broccoli!

It is widely assumed that elections are the sole means of expressing the public will. One might argue that some other mechanism, such as group activism, direct lobbying, or the careful assessment of public opinion, might be a better way of directing the course of government. And, as will be discussed in chapters to follow, there are many ways a government might yield to the will of its people without holding elections. But such possibilities would not get very far in America. Americans believe that elections are the fuel of democracy. Some would say that elections are, by themselves, inadequate, but at the very least they are necessary.

FROM THE BEGINNING?

The breadth of elections in the United States would come as a surprise to the framers of its system of government. Most of these men were ambivalent about popular elections. On the one hand, they sought to create a limited government—meaning that they worked to create a political system where public policy would be directed, in broad terms, by average citizens. The governed, they reasoned, should be allowed to instruct the governors—the people they elect. This was a radical idea for its time; a bold experiment. Citizens of the new system would have the duty—indeed, the obligation—to instruct their leaders. Leaders, for their part, would heed the wishes of citizens. "[T]he government," wrote James Madison in his essay "The Federalist No. 52," "should have an immediate dependence on, and [be] in intimate sympathy with, the people. . . . Frequent elections are unquestionably the only policy by which this dependence and sympathy can be effectually secured."

On the other hand, the foremost concern of the framers was with creating a stable republic. Many worried about excessive democracy, or "runaway democracy." Even James Madison suggested that legislators would do well to "enlarge and refine the public will,"[7] meaning that *some* instruction from citizens would be fine, but a direct connection between the wishes of citizens and public policy would be unwise. His lengthy discussion of factions in "The Federalist No. 10," for example, is a warning about how human nature can sometimes push citizens to place their own interests ahead of the nation's interest.

A number of mechanisms were created in the Constitution to limit the weight of public opinion in the development of public policy, thus limiting the importance

---

[7]Alexander Hamilton, James Madison, and John Jay, *The Federalist Papers,* with introduction by Clinton Rossiter (New York: Signey, 1961), Number 10.

of elections. The Senate is a prime illustration. Not only were senators to be drawn from state legislatures (this changed in 1913, with the Seventeenth Amendment), but just one-third of the body could be changed every two years, a system called rotation. The unstated goal of rotation was to decrease the likelihood that angry citizens could push state legislators to change the national government quickly. It would take at least two election cycles to change a majority of senators. (A clear example would be the 2010 election, where anger catapulted Republicans to the majority in the House, but limited their gains in the Senate because only 33 of these seats were up for election that year.) Alexander Hamilton was rather direct in his concerns about the wisdom of average citizens. Speaking about the importance of keeping parts of the new government removed from public opinion, such as the Senate, he noted the following at the Constitutional Convention in 1787:

> The voice of the people has been said to be the voice of God; and, however generally this maxim has been quoted and believed, it is not true to fact. The people are turbulent and changing; they seldom judge or determine right. Give therefore to the first class a distinct permanent share in the government. Can a democratic assembly who annually revolve in the mass of the people be supposed steadily to pursue the public good?[8]

Another part of the Constitution that reflects concerns of the framers about public opinion and direct elections concerns the electoral college. The rationale for this rather odd institution is complex, and it will be discussed in depth in subsequent chapters. Part of its justification, assuredly, was to limit the role of citizens in the selection of the chief executive. The voters would have a say in the process, but only indirectly—through their state legislatures. (By the 1840s, all states changed their rules so that voters would directly choose electors.)

Federal judges are not elected, nor are members of the federal bureaucracy. And of course the Constitution does not allow for ballot initiatives, referenda, or recall elections. Once again, the framers wanted to create not only a system where the governors would heed the wishes of the governed, but also a stable system where change would be incremental.

So, for a nation seemingly smitten with elections, it might come as a surprise that the plan for the national government granted citizens few opportunities to choose national leaders. Only one piece of the huge federal government was to be put directly to voters: members of the House of Representatives. Given the complexity of the legislative process (approval by both chambers is needed to shift public policy, for instance), it is fair to say that the framers created a system where direct elections were only marginally important, at best.

To be fair, Madison and his colleagues believed that elections might be used extensively at the state and local levels. The new federal government was granted only vague powers concerning the conduct of elections, the intent being to leave these matters to the states. States could levy voting restrictions and regulations as they saw fit. In

---

[8]Alexander Hamilton and Thomas Jefferson, "Hamilton versus Jefferson on Popular Rule." Accessed at: http://www.pinzler.com/ushistory/hamjeffpopsupp.html on June 1, 2011.

the early years, for example, states imposed rather burdensome residency, religious, and property qualifications for voting, and several states even charged a fee. The outcome was that relatively few residents were allowed to vote. All told, although the framers set out to create a system that would reflect the will of the people, that was, for the most part, to be done only indirectly.

Beyond their uncertainties regarding the capacities of voters to act with good judgment, the framers were also unsure about the mechanics of voting. They were heading into new, uncharted territories. How would elections work? How many candidates would run for a particular office? Would candidates actively pursue office, or would others speak on their behalf? How should candidates or their advocates persuade voters? How long should election contests last? And perhaps most importantly, how would violence during heated contests be averted? All of these questions, and many others, were left unanswered.

Likely the single greatest misapprehension in the early years centered on the role of political parties. The framers worried that political parties would threaten their democratic experiment. Madison noted, "The friend of popular governments never finds himself so much alarmed for their character and fate, as when he contemplates their propensity of this dangerous vice."[9] The problem with parties (also called "factions") was that they would rally self-interest and greed, rather than promote the long-term public interest. John Adams bemoaned the drift of the country's elites toward party politics in the 1790s: "There is nothing I dread so much as a division of the Republic into two great parties, each arranged under its leader and converting measures in opposition to each other."[10]

The framers were also students of the Enlightenment, an 18th-century European philosophical movement that believed all difficult questions, whether scientific or social, could be solved through the application of value-free scientific principles. Answers to all policy questions could be discerned through careful investigation and deliberation. Conversely, parties promoted alternative solutions (thus implying self-interest over the public interest). As for the conduct of elections, parties would surely enflame the passions of citizens, pushing them to discard civic ideals in favor of selfish ends, and maybe even to violence.

As momentous policy questions arose in the first decade of America's history, parties emerged, nevertheless. It was a time of great anxiety. As George Washington stepped down from the presidency, he warned the nation about the dangers of emerging political parties. He was especially critical of partisan demagogues whose objective, he claimed, was not to give people the facts from which they could make up their own minds, but to make them followers instead of thinkers. In an early draft of a speech renouncing a second term (not used in 1792), Washington maintained that "we are all children of the same country . . . [and] that our interest, however diversified in local and smaller matters, is the same in all the great and essential concerns of the nation."[11] Determined to make good on his intention to leave office in 1796,

---

[9]Hamilton et al., *The Federalist Papers.*

[10]Quoted in David McCullough, *John Adams* (New York: Simon and Schuster, 2001), 422.

[11]Quoted in James Thomas Flexner, *Washington: The Indispensable Man* (New York: New American Library, 1974), 263.

Washington issued his famous farewell address, in which he admonished his fellow citizens to avoid partisanship at any cost:

> Let me . . . warn you in the most solemn manner against the baneful effects of the spirit of party. . . . It exists under different shapes in all governments, more or less stifled, controlled, or repressed; but, in those of the popular form, it is seen in its greatest rankness and is truly their worst enemy. The alternate domination of one faction over another, sharpened by the spirit of revenge natural to party dissension, which in different ages and countries has perpetrated the most horrid enormities, is itself a frightful despotism . . . [The spirit of party] agitates the community with ill-founded jealousies and false alarms; kindles the animosity of one party against another; ferments occasional riot and insurrection. It opens the door to foreign influence and corruption, which finds a facilitated access to the government through the channels of party passions.[12]

Observing the effects of partisan attacks on her husband, John Adams, during his presidency, which followed Washington's, Abigail Adams wrote: "Party spirit is blind, malevolent, un-candid, ungenerous, unjust, and unforgiving."[13]

Despite these warnings, elections soon became partisan contests. In 1800, Thomas Jefferson ran for the presidency as a Democratic-Republican, and John Adams sought reelection as a Federalist. Many people at the time believed the nation was coming apart at the seams. But it endured. There were a few minor disruptions and a bit of violence, no doubt due to the gravity of the issues, but the election proved to be one of the high points in American history. The Democratic-Republicans swept into power, and one group of rulers was peacefully replaced by another. This was heretofore unprecedented in world history. Because of this, many, including Madison and other framers, had a change of heart about political parties. The term "legitimate opposition" emerged, meaning that in a democracy it makes sense that there should be an "out-of-power" group vying for public support, checking the actions of the "in-power" group; it became another important limit to the power of rulers in a democracy. If the voters believe the current group is doing a good job, its members are reelected. But if there are problems, another group is waiting in the wings, ready to change course. Time and again in American history, the voters have changed the course of public policy by changing which political party controls the reins of government. This, as you will soon read, will be an important theme of the book.

The election of 1800 further demonstrated that political parties, in their drive to rally public support, did much to organize the election process. For example, party nominations serve to limit the number of choices afforded voters on Election Day. One might be frustrated by two major party candidates, and yearn for viable alternatives, but can you imagine dozens, perhaps hundreds, of candidates to choose from?

---

[12]"Washington's Farewell Address 1796." Accessed at: http://avalon.law.yale.edu/18th_century/washing.asp

[13]Quoted in A. James Reichley, *The Life of the Parties: A History of American Political Parties* (New York: Free Press, 1992), 29.

The winner might net just 20 percent of the vote, as is seen in many systems across the globe. But parties screen candidates and simplify the job of voters. They also educate citizens about issues, bring new voters into the process, recruit candidates, combine like-minded citizens into a unified group, and much more. They even allow voters an efficient way of making rational choices. All of this and more will be discussed in the pages to follow. The point here is that the framers of our system were uncertain about the mechanics of elections and, much to their surprise, political parties helped smooth the process. In doing so, parties enhanced the democratic character of America.

THE CLASH OF THEORY AND PRACTICE

After the election of 1800, domestic politics in the United States calmed. America entered the "Era of Good Feelings," and the Federalist Party slowly faded into the history books. A dramatic clash of policies, personalities, and what some saw as corruption invigorated the electoral process by 1828. The nation moved into a period dubbed by historians as the "Jacksonian Democracy." Elections and party politics became integral elements in the everyday lives of American citizens. Consider the following quote from Charles Dickens, who traveled around America in the 1840s:

> Quiet people avoid the question of the Presidency, for there will be a new election in three years and a half, and party feelings run very high: the great constitutional feature of this institution being, that [as soon as] the acrimony of the last election is over, the acrimony of the next begins; which is an unspeakable comfort to all strong politicians and true lovers of their country; that is to say, to ninety-nine men and boys out of every ninety-nine and a quarter.[14]

It was during this period, from the 1840s to the end of the 19th century, that American elections expanded to their full breadth. The frequency of elections and the staggering number of elected posts in American system today have their roots in the second half of the 19th century. Americans' current faith in elections as instruments of democracy draws from this period.

Yet the clash between the theoretical value of elections in a democracy and the way they are conducted has often been dramatic. At the very least, recent developments have led many to consider the value and legitimacy of the process. Has the voice of the people been trumped by the weight of money in elections, new types of media, and new-style campaign consultants? Is the process really as open and fair as one might expect? A few anecdotes from some recent elections are worth recounting.

* * *

When Democrat Jon Corzine announced his bid for the U.S. Senate in September 1999, shock waves went through New Jersey politics. The field of possible candidates quickly thinned, and even the sitting governor, Christie Todd Whitman, decided not

---

[14]Charles Dickens, *American Notes* (London: Chapman and Hall, 1842), p. 149, as cited in Howard Reiter, *Parties and Elections in Corporate America* (New York: St. Martin's Press, 1993), 6.

to seek the Republican nomination. It was not his long career of public service, good reputation, or even powerful celebrity status that made Corzine a formidable opponent. He was not an ex-governor, a former New Jersey Nets basketball player, or a movie star from Hoboken. Quite the contrary. Corzine had never held elective office, and very few citizens of New Jersey would have recognized his name. What he did bring to the table was more than $400 million in personal resources and an intention to spend as much of it as necessary to win.[15]

Corzine quickly demonstrated his resolve. His only opponent in the Democratic primary, Jim Florio, had decades of political experience as a former member of Congress and as New Jersey's governor. Because both candidates were considered liberal, Florio made Corzine's money the issue, accusing him of trying to buy a Senate seat to bolster his ego. He also attacked Corzine's past as a Wall Street executive. Corzine's response was to spend more money, lavishing massive donations on local Democratic organizations and spending heavily on television. Toward the end of the campaign, Corzine's commercials were especially aggressive, using lines like, "Florio lied about Social Security," and "Why would we ever trust him again?"[16] Florio managed to spend $3 million, an impressive sum for a primary election, but Corzine spent eleven times that much—$33 million. Despite being endorsed by most major New Jersey newspapers, Florio lost the primary by a 16-percent margin.

Corzine's opponent in the general election was Republican Bob Franks. Franks attacked Corzine on a number of fronts, claiming that Corzine was for "the largest expansion of the federal government in American history."[17] The charge seemed to stick; one newspaper editorial called Corzine a "big government liberal" who wanted to spend taxpayers' money "like a drunken sailor."[18] Yet Corzine's—not the federal government's—spending seemed to be the defining issue of the race. Franks constantly accused Corzine of trying to buy New Jersey's voters and wondered aloud what the nation would think of a state that sold its Senate seat to a Wall Street executive. Corzine attempted to turn his wealth into a virtue, claiming his self-financed status meant that, unlike Franks, he did not have to pander to special interests for donations.[19] In its final days, the race got close, with polls showing Corzine only slightly ahead—and in the end, Franks could not overcome his high-spending opponent. Corzine won by a 3-percent margin.

* * *

Polls in the fall of 2000 suggested the election between Vice President Al Gore, the Democrat, and George W. Bush, the Republican governor of Texas, would be close. Other candidates, Ralph Nader of the Green Party and Patrick Buchanan of the Reform Party, posed the threat of drawing enough votes away from Gore and Bush to

---

[15]"Corzine Prevails on $62 Million Senate Bid," *Record (Bergen County, NJ)*, November 8, 2000, A1.

[16]David M. Halbfinger, "The Ad Campaign: Florio's Words Used vs. Florio," *New York Times*, May 24, 2000, B6.

[17]Quoted in Jeff Pillets, "Spending on Campaign and Country," *Record (Bergen County, NJ)*, October 13, 2000, A3.

[18]"For New Jersey, Bob Franks," *New York Post*, October 30, 2000, O48.

[19]Halbfinger, "Florio's Words Used vs. Florio."

determine the outcome of the election. Few were willing to make predictions, and on the second Tuesday in November, the world watched as Americans demonstrated an essential component of democratic government by choosing their next leader.

The parties gave it their all because they believed the outcome would matter; they knew it would shape public policy for years. Some pundits suggested that there was little real policy difference between the candidates, but the voters disagreed. In a poll conducted immediately after the election, some 83 percent of voters suggested that they could easily make distinctions between the candidates.[20] The election was about much more than which of these two men would occupy the White House for the next four years; it was about direction of public policy. It was "legitimate opposition" at work.

Yet less than 50 percent of eligible Americans came to the polls that election. For younger Americans, just 35 percent of those under 30 bothered to show up at the voting booth. Americans had become accustomed to shrinking levels of participation, but the 2000 election seemed to highlight an embarrassingly low watermark—and a continued downward trend.

When Americans awoke the morning after the election, they discovered that the issue of which candidate would serve as the next president of the United States was not settled. Vice President Gore received about 500,000 more votes than Governor Bush, but under the complicated electoral college system for selecting the president, Gore did not gain majority support in enough states to capture the presidency. Despite support from fewer total voters, Bush had won enough states to be neck-in-neck with the vice president in the electoral vote count. The entire decision hinged on the results of the state of Florida, where election controversies and a tight race created a chaotic situation. In several counties, there were problems with ineffective punch-card voting machines, inaccurate voter registration lists, and a ballot designed in a confusing manner. Such problems also appeared in counties of other states, but the race was generally not as close elsewhere, so those problems did not affect the declaration of a winner. By contrast, the outcome of the entire presidential election rested on the resolution of voting disputes in Florida. The nation waited with growing anxiety.

For more than five weeks after the election, teams of lawyers battled in county circuit courts in Florida, federal district courts in Florida, the U.S. Court of Appeals located in Georgia, the Florida Supreme Court, and the U.S. Supreme Court. Finally, in a narrow, controversial 5–4 decision, in the case entitled *Bush v. Gore*, the majority of justices effectively ordered an end to ballot recounts and preserved Bush's narrow victory, by a mere 527 votes in Florida. In a sense, George W. Bush had become the 43rd president of the United States because of one vote on the Supreme Court. Gore's supporters were incredulous.

* * *

By the election of 2006, there was mounting frustration over the war in Iraq. Polls indicated that a clear majority of Americans saw the war as a mistake, and were anxious to change course. They vented their frustration at the ballot box and brought in a

---

[20]The Pew Research Center, "Campaign 2000 Highly Rated," November 16, 2006. Accessed at: http//www.people-press.org/reports/display.php3?ReportID=23

Democratic majority in both the House and Senate. In the Senate, Democratic candidates defeated six Republican incumbents: Rick Santorum (PA), Mike DeWine (OH), Lincoln Chafee (RI), Jim Talent (MO), Conrad Burns (MT), and George Allen (VA). Incumbent Democratic Senator Joe Lieberman (CT) lost a Democratic primary challenge, but was able to win reelection as an independent. In the House, the Democrats picked up 31 seats, enough to bring them to power as the majority. After 12 years of waiting in the wings, the Democrats were given the chance to lead. The voters had spoken and it was time for a change in policy.

Yet public policy changed little in the following years. The Democrats mounted efforts to pull troops from Iraq and to limit resources for the war, but at every turn, they were checked by President Bush or by filibusters in the Senate. The voters had aired their policy preference in the election, which implied a new course. But policies did not change. By December of 2007, a showdown was set over Iraqi war funding, but Bush came out on top. As noted in one news account after the showdown, "Democrats, who took over the US Congress in November 2006 elections fueled by anger at the war in Iraq, have tried without success to use their power of the purse to impose a timetable for withdrawal from the strife-torn country where nearly 4,000 US troops have died since the March 2003 invasion."[21] To many, the election that once seemed so important seemed trivial two years later.

* * *

Americans are familiar with the drama of exceedingly close elections. As noted, George W. Bush ultimately won the 2000 presidential contest by a mere 527 votes in Florida. In addition, the outcomes of several recent congressional, state legislative, and mayoral races have been so exceedingly close that it seems as if they could have been determined by a coin being tossed in the air and landing on its edge.

The intensity and drama of close elections reemerged in the 2008 election. By autumn, many had predicted that the Democrats would score a decisive victory and pick up seats in the House, giving them a comfortable majority. The big question was whether the Democrats would win enough seats in the Senate to reach the "magic 60"—the number of votes needed to override a filibuster in the Senate. On election night, it looked like they would fall short—netting only 58.

However, one race remained too close to call. Former comedian and *Saturday Night Live* regular Al Franken had challenged incumbent Republican Senator Norm Coleman in Minnesota. Initially, it seemed that Coleman would win by a scant 725 votes. But as election officials began the process of certifying precinct totals, Coleman's lead began to shrink—he ended up with a lead of just 215 votes one week after the election. By state law, razor-thin elections like this trigger an automatic hand recount, and when this was complete, Franken was on top by 42 votes. But 933 absentee ballots had somehow been ignored by county election officials. The State Supreme Court was asked to settle the dispute over whether the absentee ballots should be counted, keeping the outcome of the race a mystery throughout the spring of 2009.

---

[21]"US Senate Approves 70 Billion Dollars in War Funds," YahooNews.com, December 19, 2007. Accessed at: http://news.yahoo.com/s/afp/20071219/pl_afp/uspoliticsbudgetiraqmilitary

The importance of the Minnesota Senate seat took on greater urgency in late April, because long-time Pennsylvania Republican Arlen Specter switched parties to become a Democrat. The Democrats now had 59 seats; just 1 more was needed. On June 30, 2009, the Minnesota Supreme Court unanimously declared the absentee ballots valid, giving Franken a 312-vote victory. On July 7, Al Franken was sworn into the Senate—and the Democrats had their 60 votes.

* * *

Or did they? Within two months of Franken's victory, Massachusetts Senator Edward Kennedy died of brain cancer. By state law, the Massachusetts governor, also a Democrat, was barred from appointing a replacement; instead, a special election would have to be held in several months' time. However, in a highly controversial move, the Massachusetts legislature (controlled by Democrats), realizing the importance of the 60th vote, amended the law to allow the governor to appoint a replacement until the special election could be held. On September 25, Paul Kirk, a former chair of the Democratic National Committee, was sworn into office. Democrats had their magic 60 votes again.

A special election was then held to permanently fill the U.S. Senate seat vacated by the death of Democrat Edward Kennedy. The candidates were Democrat Martha Coakley, the state attorney general, and Republican Scott Brown, a state senator.

The contest drew little national media attention at first because most had assumed it would be an easy win for Coakley; Massachusetts was a "blue" state, having gone to Democratic candidates in all but four presidential elections since 1928. Barack Obama had won the state the year before with a whopping 62 percent of the vote. On top of this, it was "Kennedy's seat"; the voters of the Bay State would not hand it to the Republicans.

But as the election kicked into gear, polling data hinted at cracks in Coakley's candidacy. She seemed to represent insider politics; the so-called Beacon Hill crowd. Likely assuming her victory would come easily, Coakley did not campaign hard, preferring to use massive television buys and robo telephone calls. She was lackluster on the stump and seemed unable to connect with blue-collar voters, and she was unable to identify former Red Sox pitching great Curt Schilling—a cardinal sin in "Red Sox nation." Brown was much better on the campaign trail. Traveling from town to town in his old GMC pick-up truck, Brown told ever-growing crowds that it was not Ted Kennedy's seat, but rather the people's seat. He campaigned long and hard, often in cold, rotten weather. He was able to tap into growing populist anger at perceived "Wall Street give-aways" and burgeoning federal deficits. Money also poured in from out-of-state conservative groups and Tea Party activists.

As the election drew near, both sides pulled out all the stops. Prominent figures from both parties rushed to the state, including Barack Obama. All understood what hung in the balance: the all-important 60th vote. With Kennedy, there were 60 Democratic senators—enough to end Republican filibusters (a procedural move that can block legislation). But if the Republicans were to pick up one more seat, the young president's agenda would grind to a halt. The long, hard battle for health care reform would be for naught. It would be a stunning embarrassment for Obama and the Democrats. They just could not afford to lose the seat.

But they did. Brown netted 52 percent of the vote on Election Day. It was a stunning loss—a true game changer if there ever was one. One special election had shifted the balance of power in the Senate, derailing the Democratic agenda.

After the election, Democrats shook their heads in disbelief. What had happened? Why had they taken the race for granted, and why had they nominated such a lackluster candidate? And there was one other bit of data that sent shock waves through the Democratic Party. Turnout for those over 30 was 57 percent, with most supporting Brown. Yet turnout for those under 30 was a scant 15 percent. They overwhelmingly supported Coakley, but with such tiny numbers it mattered little. The youth vote, so important in Barack Obama's victory, had evaporated.

* * *

Even seasoned political observers were shocked in the spring of 2009 to hear that Pennsylvania U.S. Senator Arlen Specter had decided to switch political parties. After 45 years as a Republican, and at times a vigorous, outspoken defender of GOP (a nickname for the Republican Party, which stands for "Grand Old Party") policies, Specter was jumping to the other side. The Democrats in the Senate were still scrambling to reach the 60th vote, so they were only too pleased to welcome the 80-year-old, five-term senator into their ranks.

But why would a seasoned senator switch parties? The answer is at the heart of one of the more important aspects of electoral politics. Beginning in the mid-19th century, state and local political parties introduced a direct primary system for selecting their general election candidates. Rather than allowing party leaders or elected officials from the party to simply choose a nominee, they would let the rank-and-file members (meaning average party followers) make the choice. Thus, for Arlen Specter to run as a Republican in the 2010 general election, he would first have to win the primary. And there's the rub. Specter had developed a reputation as moderate. And although it might be fair to say that his positions fit the outlook of an average Pennsylvania Republican, he was out of step with the Republicans who were likely to vote in the primary election. Specter was clear about his decision: "I'm not prepared to have my 29-year record in the United States Senate decided by the Pennsylvania Republican primary electorate, not prepared to have that record decided by that jury."[22]

As for the timing of Specter's decision, it came at a time when President Obama was actively seeking support for his economic stimulus bill and for an overhaul of the health care system. So in exchange for the senator's switch and support for these two key initiatives, he would receive the backing of the White House in the primary and general elections.

But the direct primary process works the same way for Democrats. Some Democrats were pleased with the senator's convergence, but others, certainly the more liberal members of the party, were furious about the prospect of nominating a 30-year Republican as their party's candidate. An anti-Specter movement began to grow in the Democratic ranks, and their preferred candidate, Congressman Joe Sestak, started to climb in the polls. With two weeks left before the primary election, Sestak

---

[22]Carl Hulse, "Specter Switches Parties," *New York Times*, April 28, 2009. Accessed at: http://thecaucus.blogs.nytimes.com/2009/04/28/specter-will-run-as-a-democrat-in-2010/

released a devastating campaign commercial. Specter was captured on video saying, "My change in parties will enable me to be reelected," followed by a series of clips where prominent Republicans, like George W. Bush and Sarah Palin, applauded his allegiance to the Republican Party. It ended with the line, "Arlen Specter switched parties to save one job—his, not yours." Rarely has a campaign commercial garnered so much attention. It seemed to be the rallying cry for Democrats. The president, the governor, and the party leader might endorse Specter, but the people did not have to vote for him.

Specter was defeated by Joe Sestak. His tenure in the Senate was ended by the Democratic primary election voters in May of 2010. Elected officials and party leaders hold some sway in the nomination process, but direct primaries reflect the will of party followers—in the case of Pennsylvania voters, it appeared that neither party wanted Arlen Specter on its ticket in November 2010.

* * *

With much effort from Republican Senator John McCain and Democratic Senator Russ Feingold, the Bipartisan Campaign Reform Act (BCRA) was passed and signed into law by President George W. Bush in February of 2002. An important by-product of the latest reforms has been the growing number of groups not aligned with a political party but quite interested in certain policies. These groups have been named 527 Organizations (after Section 527 of the Internal Revenue Code, which regulates their practices). They are allowed to raise unlimited sums of money. Most 527s are advocacy groups that try to influence the outcome of elections through voter mobilization efforts and television advertisements that praise or criticize a candidate's record. A great deal of the funds now flowing to 527s previously went to the parties in the form of soft money.

Two prominent examples of 527s in the 2004 election were the Swift Boat Veterans and POWs for Truth and MoveOn.org. The Swift Boat Veterans were set up with the intention of portraying Democratic candidate John Kerry's past military service in a negative light. MoveOn.org, by contrast, was created by a group of Americans who were dissatisfied with George W. Bush. What is most impressive about this list of organizations is the massive sums that these organizations were able to raise. As one observer noted, "Although BCRA cracked down on soft money spending by the political parties, it did nothing to constrain spending by outside groups."[23] Indeed, one estimate is that 527 groups spent some $527 million on television ads alone in 2004.[24]

The most recent chapter in the story of money in Americans elections was a decision handed down by the Supreme Court on January 21, 2010. The case was *Citizens United v. Federal Election Commission,* and it dealt with a provision of BCRA that outlawed explicit campaigning by nonpartisan groups within 30 days of a general election and 60 days prior to a primary election. When the case was first heard by Supreme Court, the issue seemed to center on the prohibitions stipulated in BCRA. But when the justices heard arguments a second time, the topic appeared to be much

---

[23]Marian Currinder, "Campaign Finance: Funding the Presidential and Congressional Elections," in *The Election of 2004,* ed. Michael Nelson (Washington, DC: CQ Press, 2005), 122.
[24]Ibid.

broader: whether prohibitions on corporations and unions from directly spending in campaigns, established a half century before and upheld in several prior cases, were constitutional. In a 5–4 decision, the Court ruled that unions and corporations were entitled to spend money from their general treasuries (without the use of PACs [political action committees]) on federal elections. They could not give money directly to candidates, but they were free to spend lavishly on candidates' behalf.

The decision sent shock waves across the political system. Some suggested the ruling represented a tremendous victory for free speech—a straightforward application of basic First Amendment principles. But others feared that the decision would set loose a flood of money and lead to greater corruption. One thing is for sure, everyone now knows that the amount of "outside money" (money coming from sources located outside the election district) skyrocketed in the 2010 election. Groups were quickly formed to collect massive contributions and to distribute them strategically. The most prominent of these groups was American Crossroads, a conservative unit headed by Bush operative Karl Rove. This one organization, for example, spent over $5 million in an effort to defeat the Democratic Senate candidate in Colorado. It spent $2 million to defeat the Missouri Democratic candidate and hundreds of thousands dollars to defeat House Democrats in dozens of districts. And this was just one of these organizations. Roughly 70 percent of the outside money in 2010 helped GOP candidates, but the Democrats may be on top in elections to come. The key issue is that very nature of candidate spending has dramatically changed in recent years—and there seems to be no turning back.

* * *

It seems, then, that one's faith in elections raises a number of important questions. If one holds that elections are the core of the democratic process, but the actual conduct appears out of order, does that imply that the American system of government is broken? For example, the issue of campaign finance, highlighted in the Corzine anecdote, has stirred a great deal of debate in recent years. The relationship between the amount spent by a candidate and his or her success is strong. Money may not "buy" an election directly, but the more money you have to spend, the greater your chances of success. Did John Corzine buy his election in 1999? To many, elections are no longer about the best candidate but rather the best fund-raiser. How many citizens would be willing to "invest" $200,000, just to start, on a race for Congress? In 2010, California GOP gubernatorial candidate Meg Whitman, founder of eBay, sunk over $175 million of her own money into the race—but lost. Who has that kind of money? Others would argue that a candidate's ability to raise money is an expression of popular support. In other words, the best candidates often raise the most money. Supporters want people to be active in politics, so isn't giving money a way to lend a hand? A related issue is the leverage that campaign contributors have after the election. Are contributors hoping to "buy" votes, or do they simply reward candidates who are already supportive of their policy concerns?

Limited participation by certain groups of citizens would surely be a serious snafu, one might imagine. Much will be said about the slow expansion of suffrage in the pages to follow. At the onset, however, you should understand that despite interest in democracy during the early years of American history, only upper-class, white males were allowed to vote and hold office. Since then, there have been significant institutional barriers to electoral participation, such as those confronted by African-Americans in the South until the passage of the Voting Rights Act of 1965. But what about other, perhaps well-intended, barriers that also restrict who goes to the polls? Residency requirements are an old tune in American history, a condition that the citizen must be a resident of a state, county, or city for a certain length of time prior to the election. In the early years of the republic, several states mandated at least 24 months of residency before being allowed to vote. It is now limited by an act of Congress to no more than 30 days. Registration requirements stipulate that a citizen sign up to vote in his or her community well before Election Day; the cutoff date varies from state to state but on average it is 30 days before the election. Estimates are that only about 70 percent of eligible Americans are registered to vote. Many argue that these two provisions, originally designed to limit voting fraud, are restrictive. Many other democratic nations have no residency requirements and allow same-day registration. They also hold elections over several days, and often on the weekend, but in the United States, the polls are open for roughly 12 to 14 hours on a single day. For the general election, Election Day is the Tuesday after the first Monday in November.

What about noninstitutional barriers? What if swaths of citizen are legally allowed to vote, but for whatever reason decide to refrain? At points in American history, about 85 percent of those eligible to vote turned out on Election Day, but in the past three decades, turnout in presidential elections has hovered at around 55 percent. If turnout had moved just one-percentage point higher in the 2000 election, from 50 to 51 percent, it is likely that Al Gore would have won Florida, and thus the presidency. In 2004 and 2008, turnout increased a bit, but even so only six out of ten Americans found time to cast a ballot, and only about four out of ten 18- to 30-year-olds voted. What happened to the young voters in the Massachusetts special election in 2010, touched upon earlier? Are policy preferences really expressed accurately through the election process when less than half of citizens participate? During non-presidential election years, voter turnout is even lower, generally about 40 percent. In the 2010 midterm election, just 22 percent of those under 30 came out to vote.

Is it really the case that elections produce changes in public policy? In other words, is there a direct connection between the actions of voters and the course of government after Election Day? Support for a candidate is often based upon what direction he or she might steer public policy. What if the connection between a candidate and the course of government is indirect, or nonexistent? Would not people's faith in elections then be misguided? Shouldn't Democratic supporters in 2006 have expected a new course in Iraq? Some argue that the gap between election outcome and policy change has widened over the years.

There are many other concerns. What happens to American democracy if the process of selecting candidates to run in the general election—the party nomination process—is truly flawed? Commenting on the state of the presidential nomination process in 2008, Anna Quindlen of *Newsweek* suggested the system had become "piecemeal, arbitrary, even downright wacky, turning the nation's most important task into a jerry-built mess."[25] Does it matter that American electoral

---

[25]Anna Quindlen, "First Tuesday of Huh?," *Newsweek*, December 24, 2007, 68.

system seems fixed around a two-party model while other democratic nations boast a multi-party approach? When the ideological wings of each party are pronounced and active during primary contests, can moderate candidates even make it to the general election? Should Americans be concerned that PACs, interest groups, and professional campaign consultants have replaced the role of local grassroots activists in conducting elections? Does it really make sense that the media should hold what would seem to be the trump card over which candidates succeed and which candidates fail? Does negative advertising distort the truth and turn off less partisan voters?

Of course, we are only at the tip of the iceberg of controversies surrounding the election process. The initial point is rather simple: Americans believe that elections are the best mechanism for moving government toward the will of the people, the purest democratic tool, and have felt that way for more than 150 years. More Americans use elections—in one form or another—as an avenue for change than any other mode of political action. It is a process that reaches deep into the American psyche. There may be a significant gap between the theory of election-centered democracy and the practice of campaigns and elections in the United States, but the system is here to stay. Some of these problems are minor, whereas others are significant and perhaps getting worse.

THEMES OF THE BOOK

This book is centered on three basic assumptions. The first assumption is that even with all the flaws and shortcomings in the current system, voting and elections matter. They are important events that shape who serve in office, key public policy questions, and the democratic character of the United States. There are numerous ways for citizens to influence government, and a narrow focus on only elections can sometimes stifle other critically important modes of activism. Yet elections can make a difference. One might even argue that elections are the single-best opportunity for citizens to influence the course of government. For all that has changed in American politics, this basic truth remains.

The second assumption is that many Americans, especially young Americans, doubt the utility of the election process and tune out. By sitting on the sidelines, they buttress the probability that elections do not reflect the will of average citizens; that they do not push elected officials to heed the will of the people. Lackluster turnout in elections is a key indicator of this indifference, but there are many other measures—such as the willingness to help candidates, work for a political party, or even talk about electoral politics with friends and family. There has been a modest upturn in modes of participation in recent elections, but most would agree that far too many Americans have shunned electoral politics. Implicit in the pages to follow is the argument that participation in elections matters and that the character of American democracy depends on an informed, engaged electorate.

The third assumption is that a better understanding of the players and the "rules of the game" can help attract citizens to the election process. For many Americans, the process is distant, confusing, and too complex. There have been dramatic changes in the way elections are conducted in recent decades, but the core of the process has remained the same. If more Americans, especially young Americans, better appreciate how the system works, the greater would be the likelihood of their involvement. And the broader the scope of citizen engagement in the election process, the more democratic the final outcome.

Critical Thinking Questions

1. Why do you think elections are so important for a democracy? Why do citizens really need elections?
2. Why do you suppose young citizens are generally turned off by the election process? Might the complexity of modern elections have something to do with it?
3. As you look ahead, do you think transformations in society, such as all the dimensions of new media (social network sites, blogs, twitter, etc.) will push Americans to have more or less faith in the electoral process?
4. As you prepare to read the chapters to follow, what element of the election process is the greatest mystery to you? What do you *really* want to know about elections?

On the Web

To measure how your beliefs fall on an advanced political spectrum, visit **www.politicalcompass .org**, where your results can be analyzed and compared to historical figures and candidates in races all over the world.

2

The Theoretical Underpinnings of Elections

KEY TOPICS

After reading this chapter, you should be able to understand these core concepts and explain their significance:

- Republicanism
- Alternatives to Elections
- Legitimacy of Elected Officials

- Elections as a Check on Government
- Elections as a Means to Fulfill Civic Duty
- Limits of Elections' Effectiveness

T his chapter explores some theoretical issues surrounding elections. As you read you may want to keep in mind a key question: Do elections in a democracy provide citizens all that they promise? Again, Americans place a great deal of stock in elections, but is this faith misplaced? If so, would it be wise or even possible to move the American system away from elections? Are there, perhaps, ways to reform the system in order to make elections better meet democratic ends? Much of this book will explore the conflict between theory and practice, so it would make sense to have a good understanding of theoretical underpinnings. At the very least, this chapter should raise some interesting topics for discussion.

THE THEORETICAL STRENGTHS OF ELECTIONS

Republicanism

The United States boasts a republican form of government; in the American system, a few elected representatives act on behalf of many voters. Americans do *not* have a system where everyone has a say in what government does, but instead a system where they select leaders to run their government, and where it is incumbent upon the leaders to make decisions on citizens' behalf.

Republicanism was instituted in the United States for three reasons. First, the framers of the American system believed discussion and deliberation to be an important part of the policy process, something impractical with too many people. It might be nice to have everyone in a community join the debate over a particular issue, but what if there are thousands of residents? Should they all be allowed a say? How would many issues be tackled when everyone is guaranteed a chance to join the debate? In short, although one might prefer a direct process, where everyone has a voice, there are practical issues that make it impossible.

Second, many people in the early stages of American history believed that some citizens are better suited to head government than others. Government and policy making are complex, so the thought was to let only citizens with education or greater understanding of the issues lead the government.

Finally, many of the framers believed that some mechanism was necessary to curb the visceral, emotional impulses of the public. To borrow from James Madison in "The Federalist No. 10," representatives would "enlarge and refine the public will," meaning that giving the public everything they want, whenever they want it, may not be a good idea. Thus, even if Americans were to overcome the practical issues of space and time, there are reasons to prefer a republic over a direct democracy.

But what is the best way to select leaders? To suggest that the "democratic process" does not suffer when leaders speak on behalf of citizens, which is implied in the "republican principle," begs the questions of who these leaders might be and how they might best be chosen. There are numerous possibilities. One might randomly select members of the community. While some would think this an odd suggestion, something very similar to this occurs in every community and in every state in the union: picking a jury for court proceedings. Randomly selecting would not guarantee a government run by experts, but so long as every citizen has the same chance of being selected, one could argue that it would be a fair system. Perhaps a board could be created to review qualifications of members of the community, and then select the "best" to serve.

Plato (427–347 BC), often considered one of the first political thinkers, had something similar in mind. In Plato's ideal state, or utopia, rulers would be selected based on their superior wisdom. To win acceptance of this person, Plato suggested a scheme: "We shall tell our people in this fable, that all of you are brothers; but the god who fashioned you mixed gold in the composition of those among you who are fit to rule, so that they are of the most precious quality; and he put silver in the Auxiliaries, and iron and brass in the farmers and craftsmen."[1]

Another possibility would be to give an examination to citizens anxious to serve and then fill government with those receiving the highest scores. This would be similar to a merit-based or civil service system. Why not simply give the best qualified and the most intelligent the opportunity to serve? Another option would be to allow public

---

[1]Plato, *The Republic* (New York: Oxford University Press, 1945), 415, as cited in Gerald M. Pomper, *Elections in America: Control and Influence in Democratic Politics* (New York: Longman, 1980), 7.

officials to handpick their own successors. Wanting to preserve their standing with the public, these officials would likely choose citizens who would do a good job.

One of the first attempts at representative government was seen in 17th-century England. Starting in about 1640, a controversy swirled around the role of the British Parliament in the conduct of government. A group known as Tories (dubbed the Court Party) believed that all ruling authority should rest solely with the monarch. Another group, known as the Whigs (or Country Party), held that parliament should reign supreme. By 1689, the parliamentary prerogative question was more or less settled on the side of the Whigs. Parliament, from this point forward, would convene on a regular basis and have concrete powers over most matters of public policy.

Most would be reluctant to label the early parliamentary system in England democratic—even though power to forge policy shifted to Parliament. First, members of the national legislature were selected by the economic and social elite, often based on tradition, custom, arrangement, and family connections. In many other instances, seats in parliament were simply "bought." Second, the logic of representation during the early British Parliament was group based, not individual centered. Members were expected to represent interests, groups, estates, and so forth, not citizens per se. The notion of representation centered on groups, rather than on individuals, lasted until major reforms were made in the mid-19th century.

In summary, there are many ways to select representatives, elections being just one option. Indeed, it can be argued that if you are interested in selecting leaders to "reflect the will of the people," then a jury-like lottery system might be a better mechanism than elections. It would surely be less time-consuming and less expensive. We citizens rely upon pollsters to tell us the "will of the people," so why not use the same type of techniques to select representatives? Finally, remember that a representative-style system of governing does not guarantee democracy.

Elections as an Expression of Popular Will

Not everyone would agree that the core function of elections is to select representatives. Another possibility is that elections serve as an expression of popular will—a means of telling the leaders what is on the minds of citizens. This process can work in different ways.

A "landslide" or "mandate" election, an election where the winners are brought to power with overwhelming support of the public, does more than send a person or group to power. Such an event signals to all the leaders of the system that the policies advanced by the winning candidates during the election are strongly favored. George W. Bush was not up for reelection in 2006, given that he was halfway through his second term as president, but the outcome of the congressional midterm elections sent a clear message: Democrats won an overwhelming majority of contests, which implied the public's dissatisfaction with Bush's policies, mainly the Iraq War. Four years later, in the midterm election of 2010, Republican gains were massive. To many voters, the election was a so-called referendum on Barack Obama's first two years in office, and the results were not good for the president. The public was demanding a different kind of "change." (Barack Obama's campaign slogan two years earlier was "change you can believe in.")

Not all would agree, however, that elections are a reflection of popular will. Perhaps voters pay too little attention to public policy, and therefore tend to vote based on party allegiances, imagery, character-based information, or a host of other idiosyncratic criteria. It is not policy that drives voter choices, the argument goes, because most voters pay too little attention to campaigns and politics in general. Others suggest that voters are a bit more policy grounded than they might seem. One of the strongest arguments along these lines was advanced by the late V. O. Key, a pioneer political scientist during the mid-20th century. In his book *The Responsible Electorate*, Key argues that, in the end, American voters pay close attention to the goings on of government—and structure their vote choices accordingly. "Voters," he writes, "or at least a large number of them, are moved by their perceptions and appraisals of policy performance."[2] Others find this hard to believe. Figure 2.1 and Table 2.1 show the percentage of people who were aware of recent economic and political developments in late 2010. This suggests modest levels of public knowledge. If this is true, can we really interpret elections as policy-based assessments?

What the Public Knows

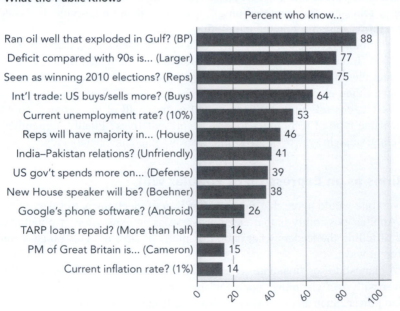

PEW RESEARCH CENTER Nov. 11–14, 2010.

FIGURE 2.1 How Informed Are Americans?

These are the principal findings of the latest News IQ survey by the Pew Research Center for the People and the Press, conducted November 11–14, 2010, in which 1,001 adults were asked a series of 13 multiple-choice questions about events and people in the news.   *Source:* The Pew Research Center for the People and the Press Public Knows Basic Facts about Politics, Economics, But Struggles with Specifics (November 18, 2010). Accessed at: http://pewresearch.org/pubs/1804/political-news-quiz

---

[2]V. O. Key, *The Responsible Electorate: Rationality in Presidential Voting, 1936–1960* (New York: Vintage, 1968), 150.

TABLE 2.1	What the Public Knows by Party

Knowledge of current events also differed by political party, with gaps in knowledge between the parties as high as 18 percent in some categories.

More Republicans Correctly Estimate Unemployment Rate

Economic Items	Repub-lican %	Demo-crat %	Indepen-dent %	Republican–Democrat Difference
Current unemployment rate? (10%)	63	48	54	+15
Int'l trade: US buys/sells more? (Buys)	72	58	67	+14
Seen as winning 2010 elections? (Reps)	88	77	71	+11
Reps will have majority in . . . (House)	55	45	46	+10
New House speaker will be . . . (Boehner)	47	38	39	+9
India–Pakistan relations? (Unfriendly)	45	40	43	+5
Deficit compared with the 90s is . . . (Larger)	81	78	78	+3
Ran oil well that exploded in the Gulf? (BP)	90	90	89	0
PM of Great Britain is? (David Cameron)	14	14	18	0
Google's phone software? (Android)	23	24	29	−1
TARP loans repaid? (More than half)	16	17	17	−1
Current inflation rate? (1%)	14	15	16	−1
U.S. gov't spends most on? (Defense)	28	46	44	−18

Source: The Pew Research Center for the People and the Press, November 18, 2010.
Public Knows Basic Facts about Politics, Economics, but Struggles with Specifics (November 2010).
Accessed at: http://pewresearch.org/pubs/1804/political-news-quiz

Sometimes the expression of public sentiment in America is voiced through a third-party candidate. In 1992, Ross Perot spent most of his time talking about the growing federal budget deficit. The major-party candidates, Bill Clinton and George H. W. Bush, were paying little attention to the issue, possibly because it meant that difficult choices would have to be made (given that many programs would have to be cut or taxes would have to be raised to lower the deficit, why upset a large portion of the electorate?). Perot's hour-long political "infomercials," filled with graphs, charts, data, and statistics seemed out of place and rather quirky. On Election Day, however, Perot netted 19 percent of the popular vote, the second highest third-party vote total in nearly a century (the first being Theodore Roosevelt of the Bull Moose Party in 1912). Perot did not win, of course, but a clear message was sent: The public cares about deficit reduction. By the next election, candidates of both major parties were telling voters about their budget deficit reduction plans.

Still another possibility deals less with which candidates win than with how many people turn out to the polls. Throughout American history, certain elections seem to draw more public attention than others, and while the outcome of the election might not clearly signal a policy preference, these elections tell officials that they should take heed because the public is alarmed. A good example would be the congressional midterm election of 1930, which saw a turnout nearly 5 percent higher than the previous midterm election.[3] What drove voters to the polls was the beginning of the Great Depression, which had begun one year earlier. Clearly, the public was anxious for the government to help ease the blow of massive unemployment and business failure.

Stability and Legitimacy

Although there may be other ways to select government leaders, including means that give every citizen the same chance of being selected and, as such, might be considered more "fair," an important consideration is system legitimacy. This term implies a process of decision making that is perceived to be proper by those who must abide by the decisions. Legitimacy suggests that the mode of selecting leaders is both legal and, in the eyes of citizens, appropriate. In the American setting, elections serve that end. According to James Mason, the denial of electoral power would stigmatize most leaders as "suspicious characters, and unworthy to be trusted with the common rights of their fellow citizens."[4]

When citizens accept the need for representation, and feel that the selection of these leaders is legitimate, the policies that follow are more likely to be accepted. Citizens may not like the direction the government has taken, but they accept the process as lawful and correct. Even the constitutional framers, who believed there was danger in widespread public participation in government, believed elections necessary for this reason. As noted by one scholar, even though many framers of the American system were distrustful of popular participation, they also saw the necessity of elections: "The franchise brought consent even if not ideal policies."[5]

Americans often take the stability that comes as a result of their elections for granted. But simply holding an election does not guarantee that the outcome will be accepted by either the candidates or the voters. For example, Iran's June 2009 elections pitted incumbent President Mahmoud Ahmadinejad against Mir-Hossein Mousavi, a progressive candidate. The Iranian government quickly published results showing an unrealistic landslide victory for Ahmadinejad, prompting charges of fraud from many people familiar with the elections. Prolonged, violent protests followed in which both the legitimacy and stability of the Iranian political system were called into question. *New York Times* columnist David Brooks wrote about the effects of the election on Iranian society, saying, "Recently, many people thought it was clever to say that elections on their own don't make democracies. But election campaigns stoke the mind and fraudulent elections outrage the soul. The Iranian elections have stirred a whirlwind that will lead, someday, to the regime's collapse."[6]

This is precisely why the outcome of the 2000 election was a bit worrisome. Americans usually accept the legitimacy of elected officials; the elected have slugged it out in the battle of ideas and character and have persuaded more voters to support

---

[3]Jerrold G. Rusk, *A Statistical History of the American Electorate* (Washington, DC: Congressional Quarterly Press, 2001), 54.

[4]As cited in Gerald M. Pomper, *Elections in America: Control and Influence in Democratic Politics* (New York: Longman, 1980), 20.

[5]Pomper, *Elections in America*, 20.

[6]David Brooks, "Fragile at the Core," *New York Times*, June 18, 2009.

them than the other candidates. But what happens when an election proves to be a virtual tie? Worse yet, what happens when a candidate who receives fewer votes than his opponent is sent to office? As you know, this happened in 2000: Al Gore netted over half a million more votes than George W. Bush nationwide, but because of the nuances of the electoral college, Bush won. Some wondered whether the legitimacy of the federal government would suffer. Would the nation see increased instability? The question became moot with the terrorist attack of September 11, 2001, which quickly rallied Americans around their new president. Regardless of the election's outcome, support for the country during crisis helped solidify Bush's standing as America's leader. In other words, for most Americans, the issue was settled when the first jet slammed into one of the Twin Towers.

A similar possibility can arise when more than two candidates run for the same office. With only two candidates, the winner, by definition, has the support of a major-ity of voters. But when a third or fourth party candidate enters the fray, the winner, at least in the American system, often winds up with a plurality—but not a majority. A good example would be Bill Clinton's first election to the presidency in 1992. That year, Ross Perot captured some 19 percent of the vote, as noted earlier, and the con-test between Clinton and George H. W. Bush was rather close. In the end, Clinton netted just 43 percent of the popular vote. Given that election turnout (a measure of those who voted on Election Day divided by those who were legally allowed to vote in that election) was a bit over 50 percent, one can conclude that the most important political figure in the nation—perhaps the world—was brought to office with roughly 25 percent of the possible voters. Abraham Lincoln was elected with just 39.8 per-cent of the popular vote in 1860. Is it possible that this "minority election" affected Lincoln's legitimacy enough to play a role in the Civil War? Because third-party candidates have often joined presidential contests, and because the two major parties have been more or less balanced through the years, "plurality winners," as opposed to "majority winners," have occurred 16 times since 1824.[7] It is difficult to come to a conclusion about the effects of either electoral college–popular vote disagreement or plurality victories, but it is apparent that the American electoral system is stable enough despite them. There are two likely reasons for this: First, faith in elections runs so deep in the American psyche that eventual winners are seen as legitimate, regard-less of the potholes in the road. The aftermath of the 2000 election was not entirely placid, but very soon the public accepted the outcome of the election as rightful. Second, leaders in the American system are bound by a powerful political culture—a credo that dictates a code of conduct for defeated candidates. Ever since the election of 1800, when Thomas Jefferson and his followers defeated John Adams and his crew, defeated candidates have accepted election results regardless of how close or how many turned out to vote. Defeated candidates are gracious in the American system, from candidates for the White House to candidates for town councils.

Indeed, it must have been a bitter pill for John McCain to accept his loss in 2008, but he did so with grace and dignity. Box 2.1 is an excerpt from McCain's con-cession speech in 2008, in which he shows a great deal of respect for the legitimacy of the electoral process.

---

[7]Pomper, *Elections in America*, 132.

BOX 2.1   John McCain's Concession Speech

My friends, we have come to the end of a long journey. The American people have spoken, and they have spoken clearly. A little while ago, I had the honor of calling Sen. Barack Obama—to congratulate him on being elected the next president of the country that we both love.

In a contest as long and difficult as this campaign has been, his success alone commands my respect for his ability and perseverance. But that he managed to do so by inspiring the hopes of so many millions of Americans, who had once wrongly believed that they had little at stake or little influence in the election of an American president, is something I deeply admire and commend him for achieving.

This is an historic election, and I recognize the special significance it has for African-Americans and for the special pride that must be theirs tonight.

I've always believed that America offers opportunities to all who have the industry and will to seize it. Sen. Obama believes that, too. But we both recognize that though we have come a long way from the old injustices that once stained our nation's reputation and denied some Americans the full blessings of American citizenship, the memory of them still had the power to wound.

A century ago, President Theodore Roosevelt's invitation of Booker T. Washington to visit—to dine at the White House—was taken as an outrage in many quarters. America today is a world away from the cruel and prideful bigotry of that time. There is no better evidence of this than the election of an African-American to the presidency of the United States. Let there be no reason now for any American to fail to cherish their citizenship in this, the greatest nation on Earth. . . .

Sen. Obama and I have had and argued our differences, and he has prevailed. No doubt many of those differences remain. These are difficult times for our country, and I pledge to him tonight to do all in my power to help him lead us through the many challenges we face.

I urge all Americans who supported me to join me in not just congratulating him, but offering our next president our goodwill and earnest effort to find ways to come together, to find the necessary compromises, to bridge our differences and help restore our prosperity, defend our security in a dangerous world, and leave our children and grandchildren a stronger, better country than we inherited.

Whatever our differences, we are fellow Americans. And please believe me when I say no association has ever meant more to me than that.

It is natural tonight to feel some disappointment, but tomorrow we must move beyond it and work together to get our country moving again. We fought— we fought as hard as we could.

And though we fell short, the failure is mine, not yours.

I am so deeply grateful to all of you for the great honor of your support and for all you have done for me. I wish the outcome had been different, my friends. The road was a difficult one from the outset. But your support and friendship never wavered. I cannot adequately express how deeply indebted I am to you. . . .

I don't know what more we could have done to try to win this election. I'll leave that to others to determine. Every candidate makes mistakes, and I'm sure I made my share of them. But I won't spend a moment of the future regretting what might have been.

This campaign was and will remain the great honor of my life. And my heart is filled with nothing but gratitude for the experience and to the American people for giving me a fair hearing before deciding that Sen. Obama and my old friend Sen. Joe Biden should have the honor of leading us for the next four years.

I would not be an American worthy of the name, should I regret a fate that has allowed me the extraordinary privilege of serving this country for a half a century. Today, I was a candidate for the highest office in the country I love so much. And tonight, I remain her servant. That is blessing enough for anyone and I thank the people of Arizona for it.

Tonight—tonight, more than any night—I hold in my heart nothing but love for this country and for all its citizens, whether they supported me or Sen. Obama. I wish Godspeed to the man who was my former opponent and will be my president.

And I call on all Americans, as I have often in this campaign, to not despair of our present difficulties but to believe always in the promise and greatness of America, because nothing is inevitable here.

Americans never quit. We never surrender. We never hide from history. We make history. Thank you, and God bless you, and God bless America.

Source: MMIV CBS Broadcasting Inc. All rights reserved. Date accessed: July 2, 2007.
www.npr.org/templates/story/story.php?storyId=96631784

Americans find, then, that elections afford legitimacy and, as a result, a powerful dose of stability in their system. They may sometimes grumble in disappointment as one party or the other shifts in or out of power, but these transitions are rarely met with riots or rancor. Quite often, as was the case with the many Gore supporters, attention is turned quickly to the next election: "Okay, you've won this time, but we'll get you in the next election!" In fact, some would suggest American deference to election outcomes helps explain why alternative modes of political action—pathways that might be more effective in bringing about policy change—are used less often in the United States than in other political systems. More will be said of this "placebo effect" in a later section.

A Check on the Ruling Elite

Elections serve as a check on governmental leaders, pushing them to support policies that are popular with most voters. Upward of 25 percent of Americans were out of work during the Great Depression. It was the greatest economic crisis in America's history, and citizens were anxious for a dramatic change. Herbert Hoover and the Republicans believed that it was not appropriate for the federal government to provide assistance, and they rejected appeals for intervention. Hoover was sent to an early retirement in the election of 1932, as over 60 percent of all voters backed Franklin D. Roosevelt and his New Deal platform. Similarly, in 2006 and 2008, Americans came to the polls dissatisfied with the Iraq War, health care problems, and a widespread financial crisis. The Republicans, who had most recently controlled the Congress and the White House, felt the brunt of this dissatisfaction, and widespread Democratic victories occurred in both elections. As noted earlier, things turned in the other direction in the 2010 election.

   This is not to say that fear of losing the next election drives all politicians, under all circumstances, to heed the desires of voters. At times, a certain "independence" from public opinion is quite admirable. Early in 1948, Harry Truman issued an executive order ending racial discrimination in federal government employment and desegregating the armed forces. He made this move knowing that a majority of Americans would disagree and that his reelection might be in jeopardy. Coupled with other controversial moves, Truman saw his 75-percent approval rating plummet into the 40s.[8] Ironically, Americans often venerate leaders who have the courage to stand up in the face of public opinion and do the right thing. John F. Kennedy's Pulitzer Prize–winning book, *Profiles in Courage*, is an account of numerous politicians who did what was right and not simply what was popular. But this is not to say that the voters see things the same way. Harry Truman barely kept his job in 1948, netting a slim 49.6 percent of the vote, but many other "great" politicians have been sent packing for disregarding the interests of their constituents.

   Elections also help to control political elites by punishing corruption. Many in the earliest days of the American republic worried that elected officials would too easily succumb to greed, self-interest, and personal ambition—and that their system

Truman on the Whistle Stop Tour.   *Source:* Getty Images

[8]Robert Dallek, *Hail to the Chief: The Making and Unmaking of American Presidents* (New York: Hyperion, 1996), 25.

would afford few checks against such transgressions. Even the Federalists realized that greedy legislators might use the trappings of office and the policy arena to their private advantage. They believed that there was a natural tendency for people to be, or to become, corrupt.[9] Elections afford voters the opportunity to throw corrupt politicians from office—something we have seen numerous times.

There might even be a bit more at work here related to the very incentives that drive representatives. The framers argued that elections were a means of bestowing fame on a person—and that the love of fame would override self-interest. Alexander Hamilton argues, in "The Federalist No. 72," that even a lesser person, a person prone to vice and corruption, could be led to consider the public's welfare for his own "pride and vanity" or for the "marks of honor, of favor, of esteem" that come about through reelection.[10] Maybe fame and esteem, bestowed through elections, are more important to many than material gain acquired through greed.

These days, esteem is built through media exposure, but excessive media scrutiny might have its downsides. Admittedly, given the turn that the mass media has taken during the last few decades—its ever-greater focus on finding and disclosing candidate transgressions (discussed in detail in subsequent chapters)—the check that elections provide against corruption would seem even more potent. Yet some have suggested that heavy media scrutiny, often dealing with past transgressions and otherwise personal matters such as sexual escapades, has limited the number of citizens willing to become candidates. Conceivably, the filtering process has become too Draconian. This shrinking of the candidate pool, one might argue, does not serve the nation's long-term interest.

Civic Education

Democracy requires citizens to remain at least marginally aware of the issues of the day; if the public are not aware of policy options, or do not understand the alternatives, then governance will too easily fall to a small group of elites. A government would quickly turn from a government "by the people and for the people," to a government by and for elites.

To counter this, elections serve an educational role. In a relative sense, Americans pay only a limited amount of attention to public affairs—as noted earlier. In a 2008 poll conducted by the University of Michigan's National Election Study, respondents were asked how much attention they pay to government and politics. Only 26 percent noted that they followed things "most of the time" and 37 percent suggested "some of the time."[11] This poll was done during a very intense, very long presidential campaign. Moreover, given that such measures are prone to inflation (who among us is anxious to tell a pollster that we do not care about politics?), the picture is rather unflattering. Because many Americans are not interested in the goings-on of politics, levels of knowledge are low as well. Information about specific policies is even rarer.

---

[9]Michael J. Malbin, "Congress during the Convention and Ratification," in Kelly D. Patterson and Daniel M. Shea, eds., *Contemplating the People's Branch* (Upper Saddle River, NJ: 2000), 22.

[10]As cited in Malbin, "Congress during the Convention and Ratification," 22.

[11]American National Election Studies, "General Interest in Public Affairs 1960–2004." Accessed at: http://www.electionstudies.org/nesguide/toptable/tab6d_5.htm

What is most surprising about this is that levels of knowledge and interest are waning at precisely the same time that there are more and more media outlets devoted to politics. The Pew Research Center, in research conducted from 1989 to 2007, found that public knowledge of current affairs was changed little by news and information innovations (see Tables 2.2 and 2.3).

Things might be much worse if not for the frequency of elections, however. Many would balk at the notion that elections serve to educate citizens, given the growing number of 30-second television commercials and the craze for negative campaigning. Many studies suggest, nevertheless, that voters learn a good deal from elections even when campaigns are negative.[12] The time and energy put into convincing voters to

---

TABLE 2.2   Political Knowledge—Then and Now

Since the late 1980s, the emergence of 24-hour cable news as a dominant news source and the explosive growth of the Internet have led to major changes in the American public's news habits. But a new nationwide survey finds that the coaxial and digital revolutions and attendant changes in news audience behaviors have had little impact on how much Americans know about national and international affairs (Pew Research Center).

	1989 (%)	2007 (%)	Difference
Percent who could name . . .			
The current vice president	74	69	−5
Their state's governor	74	66	−8
The president of Russia*	47	36	−11
Percent who know . . .			
America has a trade deficit	81	68	−13
The party controlling the House	68	76	+8
The chief justice is conservative	30	37	+7
Percent who could identify . . .			
Tom Foley/Nancy Pelosi	14	49	+35
Richard Cheney/Robert Gates	13	21	+8
John Poindexter/Scooter Libby†	60	29	−31

*President of Russia trend from 1994.

†John Poindexter trend from April 1990 at the conclusion of his trial for involvement in the Iran-Contra affair while in the Reagan administration from 1985 to 1986.

Source: The Pew Research Center for the People and the Press.

Public Knowledge of Current Affairs Little Changes by News and Information Revolution: What Americans Know 1989–2007 (April 15, 2007).

Accessed at: http://people-press.org/report/319/public-knowledge-of-current-affairs-little-changed-by-news-and-information-revolutions

---

[12]See, for example, Stephen Ansolabehere and Shanto Iyengar, *Going Negative: How Political Advertisements Shrink and Polarize the Electorate* (New York: Free Press, 1997), Chapter 3.

TABLE 2.3 Political Knowledge Levels by News Source	High (%)	Moderate (%)	Low (%)
Nationwide	35	31	34
Among the regular audience of . . .			
Major newspaper websites	54	26	20
Daily Show/Colbert Report	54	25	21
NewsHour with Jim Lehrer	53	19	28
O'Reilly Factor	51	32	17
National Public Radio	51	27	22
Rush Limbaugh's radio show	50	29	21
News magazine	48	27	25
TV news websites	44	33	23
Daily newspaper	43	31	26
News from Google, Yahoo, etc.	41	35	24
CNN	41	30	29
Network evening news	38	33	29
Online news discussion blogs	37	26	37
Local TV news	35	33	32
Fox News Channel	35	30	35
Network morning shows	34	36	30

How to read this table:

Nationwide, 35 percent of Americans score in the high knowledge category (answering at least 15 of 23 questions correctly.) Among regular viewers of the *Daily Show* and *Colbert Report*, 54 percent scored in the high knowledge category.

Source: The Pew Research Center for the People and the Press.

Public Knowledge of Current Affairs Little Changed by News and Information Revolution: What Americans Know 1989–2007 (April 15, 2007).

Accessed at: http://people-press.org/report/319/public-knowledge-of-current-affairs-little-changed-by-news-and-information-revolutions

support one candidate over another yield a more informed citizenry. Elections serve as refresher courses on the conduct of government.

One experimental study found that the more campaign ads a citizen sees, the more informed that person is. This team of scholars writes, "The brevity of the advertising message may actually strengthen its informative value. The typical person's attention span for political information is notoriously short-lived . . . [and] the great majority of voters bypass or ignore information that entails more than minimal costs. . . . Campaign advertising meets the demand for both simplicity and access."[13] In the 2008 election, Barack Obama went as far as to buy 30 minutes of prime airtime

---

[13]Ibid., 60.

on several network television stations a week before the election to further connect with voters who are educated mostly through television ads. One week later, he went on to win the presidency in a campaign that emphasized not just television but new media outlets as well, which will be discussed in Chapter 11.

The "education function" is commonly cited in support of a vibrant party system, a topic taken up in Chapter 4. Political parties work to inform voters. By presenting information on issues, often in the form of a platform or legislative agenda, parties help voters make informed choices. One might hope that voters would always stay attuned to issues of the day, and some do, but many others simply bone up during election periods.

A Socialization Mechanism—A Way to Fulfill One's "Civic Duty"

As noted in the introduction, "socialization" refers to the process by which new members of society are introduced to social norms and ideologies, including the customs and beliefs of political systems. It is how a nation's values are passed from one generation to the next. A core element of American political culture is civic participation. It is expected that each citizen will occasionally leave his or her private world to become involved in the conduct of the state. Although one may not immediately recognize it, this idea lies at the heart of a limited government. Elections serve to introduce many Americans to their role as citizens. "Civic duty" is an amorphous term, but it does imply, at the very least, helping to choose who will run the government. By providing citizens this basic opportunity, it is hoped that additional acts of civic participation will follow. Many presume that elections serve to prime the pump of civic life in a democracy.

A Safety Valve

Finally, Americans take it for granted that changes of control over the government are always peaceful. They move from one administration to another, and from control by one party to the other, without violence, without lobbing sandbags into the windows of the White House or stationing sentries at the entrance of the Capitol. Defeated candidates and their supporters may not like the outcome, but accept the "will of the voters" peacefully. For voters, elections become the safety valve for discontent; rather than picking up a gun or a machete, Americans seek to win the next election.

This was not at all a settled matter during the early days of the American republic. Elections at the state and local level occasionally spilled over into violence. When the electorate was organized into opposing camps (the first political parties) for the heated rematch between Thomas Jefferson and John Adams in 1800, many worried that the only outcome would be violence. George Washington's "fatherly charisma" had created stability and calm in the previous contests, even as the nation was undergoing rapid transformation and developing a national identity. But in the 1800 contest, Washington was absent. In the end, the electorate selected Jefferson for the presidency and handed the legislature to his like-minded colleagues, thus switching control of government to a new party. To historian William Nisbet Chambers, the election of

1800 marked a high point in the nation's history—and perhaps even in the development of governments. He writes:

> It was the first such grand, democratic, peaceful transfer of power in modern politics. It was an example of a procedure which many old as well as many new nations have yet to experience, which many defeated factions or parties have found it difficult or intolerable to accept, but one which 1801 did much to "fix" on the American scene.[14]

Primary elections, which will be discussed in depth in Chapter 6, also serve as safety valves; they allow citizens a voice in choosing which candidates will run to represent them in a general election. Without primaries, violent conflicts might occur over which candidates should represent each party. Parties would have a difficult time ensuring support for their candidates, as dissatisfied members of the party who had no role in choosing a candidate would feel little reason to stay loyal. Primary elections maintain peace and encourage loyalty within both major political parties.

THE LIMITS OF ELECTIONS

It is fair to say that some people are a bit less optimistic about the role elections play in a democratic system.[15] Sure, Americans have come to rely on elections—elections have become a big part of American civic religion—but does that mean they are good for the nation? Americans also love fast food, but it's certainly not healthy or nourishing. Perhaps elections have serious limitations, but Americans' penchant for them is so great that to openly suggest shortcomings would be akin to trampling on the flag. Surely no red-blooded American can speak ill of the election process!

Elections as a Civic Placebo

When one carefully explores the many avenues for changing the course of government—for modifying the outcome of the policy process—elections emerge as a rather ineffectual choice. As noted earlier, elections do not ensure any redirection in policy; they merely guarantee the possibility that the people running parts of the government may change. Furthermore, many aspects of government are beyond the immediate reach of elected officials, and even when they are not, dramatic change is difficult. Some have even begun to speculate that the distrust many Americans feel toward government is due to the frustration over the election/policy disjuncture: "He told us that he would change things if he won the election. Well, he won the election, so why haven't things changed?"

---

[14]William Nisbet Chambers, *Political Parties in a New Nation: The American Experience, 1776–1809* (New York: Oxford University Press, 1963), 169.

[15]Howard L. Reiter, *Parties and Elections in Corporate America*, 2nd ed. (New York: Longman, 1993), 4–6.

An even bigger concern is that elections lead many citizens to believe that voting is their only chance to make a difference. They may be quite frustrated with the way things are going, but feel as though their only course of action is to vote or to help a candidate. This is called episodic participation, rather than ongoing involvement. Voting is enough, the conception goes, even when government seems way off track.

Perhaps if Americans did not hold elections in such high esteem, other modes of political participation that are more efficient might become more fashionable. American history has shown that significant change can occur when average citizens mobilize, lobby elites, take issues to the courts, or seek changes in their political culture. Writing of the civil rights movement during the 1960s, scholar Howard Reiter suggests, "From organizing voter-registration campaigns under threats of violence in the South to massive rallies in the North, the civil rights movement resorted to almost every form of political participation *besides* voting in order to overthrow the old system in the South."[16] By putting all eggs in only the elections basket, so to speak, the will of the people may actually be stifled.

A Poor Measure of Public Sentiment

It is widely held that elections drive officials down a particular policy course. This is the notion of an "electoral mandate," as outlined earlier. But that is not exactly what occurs. Instead, voters select a given candidate for any number of reasons, a particular policy choice being just one possibility. Each voter has a slightly different motivation or mix of motivations for choosing one candidate over another. Assuming that the results of an election mean a particular thing can prove problematic.

A good example might be the election of 1980, which matched incumbent President Jimmy Carter against Ronald Reagan. Reagan prevailed by a rather large margin, suggesting to many that the American electorate had shifted toward conservative ideas. The "Reagan revolution," as it was called, became the justification for aggressive changes. Reagan and his followers proclaimed a mandate and proceeded to make sweeping changes. Many Democrats, too, believed the election signified a "turn to the right" among the electorate and were quite willing to go along. The only problem, however, was that public opinion polls following the election suggested that much of Reagan's support came from voters displeased with Carter and much less from those interested in a dramatic policy shift. If anything, they were voting against Carter's failed economic policies. As noted by one presidential scholar,

> Studies show that there was not a clear turn to the right by voters in 1980. Reagan beat Carter by 10 percentage points; yet the election was no prospective issue vote or ideological mandate for Reagan. According to polls, the public was more liberal than Reagan on a number of issues. . . . There was no strong shift to the right.[17]

---

[16]Reiter, *Parties and Elections in Corporate America*, 7.

[17]Myron A. Levin, *Presidential Campaigns and Elections*, 2nd ed. (Itasca, IL: F. E. Peacock, 1995), 184. See also, Kathleen A. Frankovic, "Public Opinion," in Gerald Pomper, ed., *The Election of 1980* (Chatham, NJ: Chatham House, 1981), 97–102.

Moreover, Reagan benefited by the perception that he was strong, stately, a bit grandfatherly to some, and trustworthy. Voters simply liked Ronald Reagan—and disliked Carter. So, the translation of Reagan's landslide victory into a policy signal from the electorate was inaccurate and even counter to the notion that the will of the public should dictate public policy. In fairness, many Democratic victories have also been mistaken as an expression of a desire to radically change governmental policy.

Some might also point to the 2008 election. On the one hand, many, especially Democrats and supporters of Barack Obama, suggested the thumping of Republicans implied an interest in dramatic change. After all, Obama's campaign theme was "change we can believe in," and his party won the White House and control of both chambers in Congress. But within one year after the election, Obama's "change agenda" seemed stalled, if not collapsed. Republicans were winning governorships and special elections across the country and even Democrats seemed to be backing off from big policy adjustments. Perhaps the 2008 election simply reflected voter fatigue with George W. Bush, and not a desire for dramatic change.

The Atomization of Politics

Democracy, in its purest form, is a process that brings citizens together to resolve issues and disputes. This implies face-to-face deliberation—airing one's views and listening to the concerns of others. It is an interpersonal brainstorming process of give and take. Many college clubs and organizations operate in this fashion; issues are debated and resolved with a show of hands. Through discussion and extended deliberation, citizens become not only better informed about their own view on a particular matter, but also more sensitive to the opinions of others in the community. As noted by the philosopher John Stuart Mill, "He is called upon, when so engaged, to weigh interest not his own; to be guided in causes of conflicting claims, by another rule than his private partialities."[18]

Yet participating in political elections is, in many ways, an isolated, individualized act.[19] Citizens *discuss* candidates and platforms prior to the election with friends and family, but when it comes down to *behavior* (their vote), it is a private matter, done in the concealment of the polling booth. By turning elections into an individual act, private interests are more likely to supplant the public spirit. That is to say, very often the long-term stability of a system is predicated on citizens looking beyond their own short-term interest to the general welfare—something that elections may inhibit.

Constricting the Pool of Public Officials

A rarely heard argument against elections is that they limit the pool of candidates to only those willing to undergo the rigors of campaigning. Campaigning these

---

[18]John Stuart Mill, *Considerations on Representative Government* (New York: Liberal Arts Press, 1958), 114.

[19]Reiter, *Parties and Elections in Corporate America*, 4.

days requires a tremendous amount of time, huge sums of money, and often unsavory mudslinging and negative campaign commercials. Running for statewide positions, and to some extent congressional posts, has become a full-time job for a year or more prior to the election. A trend in the press coverage of candidates is to disclose ever-more intimate information. Who would want to go through this process? Many outstanding citizens, fully anxious to serve their community, state, or nation, will never do so because elections have become so difficult and personally invasive.

One of the best examples in the past few decades of this filtering effect is the case of Colin Powell, the former U.S. secretary of state. Many voters on both sides of the partisan fence would have relished the opportunity to vote for Colin Powell for president throughout the 1990s and again in 2000. In fact, polls for the 2000 election showed that Powell had twice as much early support as any other potential candidate.[20] Yet the voters never had the chance to vote for Powell because he refused to campaign for office. Apparently it was not a reluctance to serve, but rather a reluctance to undergo the campaign process. The following is an excerpt from an opinion piece in the *Philadelphia Inquirer* on Powell's decision not to run for the White House:

> Powell's decision last week to forgo the race has raised questions about whether the political process has become so uncivil, so demeaning and so grueling that it scares away some of the best and brightest. It is a national hiring system that almost always limits voters' choices to a handful of politicians—people who possess raw ambition and ego.[21]

Even more recent examples include former vice president Al Gore, former secretary of state Condoleezza Rice, New York City Mayor Michael Bloomberg, and Indiana Governor Mitch Daniels. Daniels was strongly encouraged to run for the presidency in 2012, but he decided against it because "What sane person would like to?"[22]

A Corrupt Process?

Finally, perhaps the greatest limitation of the election process might be its vulnerability to corruption. The heart of the election–democracy nexus is that citizens should have an equal opportunity to select leaders, and that one would do so based on the character of the candidates and the positions they take. Each candidate would stand on an equal footing—no candidate would have an unfair advantage—and the ultimate decision would be made by all of the citizens of the community. But what happens when some candidates have an advantage, such as more resources? What if laws limit

---

[20]One poll, sponsored by Hart and Teeter Research Companies, found that Powell was favored by 37 percent of respondents. The next closest potential candidate was Jack Kemp with 20 percent. See the Roper Center at University of Connecticut Public Opinion Online, December 11, 1996.

[21]Jodi Enda and Steven Thomma, "Powell's Decision Spotlights Trial by Fire," *Philadelphia Inquirer*, November 12, 1995, E01.

[22]Howard Kurtz, "2012's Cowards," *Newsweek*, May 29, 2011. Accessed at: www.newsweek.com/2011/05/29/2012-s-cowards.html on June 3, 2011.

which adults can vote and which cannot? Does it matter if a shrinking number of voters seem willing to make this decision? Should one care if most incumbent candidates—those already in office—have no serious opposition? What if legal barriers aid certain political parties and their candidates, while at the same time limit the potency of others? Does poor, biased, or limited media coverage of the campaigns corrupt the process?

Many of these topics and others will be discussed in the chapters to follow. The point here is that although elections offer a wonderful opportunity for government to respond to the will of the people in theory, the reality is often different. The real problem arises, some would suggest, when Americans hold so dearly to elections that they turn a blind eye to their practical limits.

Conclusion

If one were to ask what defines a "democratic system," most Americans might respond by suggesting the ability of average citizens to select governmental leaders. If we are allowed to select the personnel of government, then the system itself will respond to our needs and interests. In the American political system, "selecting leaders" has generally meant a reliance on elections. Indeed, historians and students of government would likely note that Americans' reliance on elections has contributed greatly to the nation's stability and to its democratic character. It is one of many elements of American body politic that has set the nation apart—and it has been a model for fledgling democracies across the globe. As Iraqis struggled to develop a democratic system after Saddam Hussein was toppled in 2003, for example, the focus quickly turned to the development of open and fair elections. Many Iraqis seemed to hang on to the idea that once elections were established, their road to recovery would be shorter and their oppression would finally ease. Like an oasis in the desert, many Iraqis saw elections as the first step to their recovery. Throughout history, the peoples of many other nations have felt much the same.

There is a great deal of wisdom to the idea that elections are a key element of democracy. But at the same time, although we might suggest that elections *can* serve democratic ends, there is no guarantee that the will of government will ultimately reflect the will of the people. In fact, one of the most destabilizing, discouraging developments for a public is to rely heavily on elections, only to find few changes in public policy. The theory and practice of elections often collide.

This chapter was designed to help the reader better understand both the potential and the limitations of elections. Rather than losing faith in the process, Americans seem, if anything, anxious to use elections more and more—and not just to decide the personnel of government but to also make direct policy changes (a process discussed in Chapter 10). But as we now know, placing too much faith in elections presents another set of challenges. Rather than "throwing the baby out with the bath water," perhaps the challenge in the years ahead will be to enact reforms so that what citizens expect from elections might better match what they actually get.

Critical Thinking

1. Harry Truman, a president now revered by many people from all parts of the political spectrum, barely won reelection in 1952 and left office after his second term with a very low approval rating. This was a result of Truman's decision to do what he felt was right, even if it was not popular with voters. When elected officials experience a conflict between what they feel is right and what the voters support, which should they choose?

2. It has been noted that some Americans have become skeptical of government. Some scholars believe that such discontent is a result of frustration over a separation between campaign promises and policies once in office. Will these feelings separate Americans from politics completely, or spur them to take a more hands-on role in government?

3. Barack Obama energized many young people to become involved in campaigns on a grassroots level during his 2008 run for the presidency. What needs to be done to ensure that these citizens stay involved in politics? Should we care if they become disconnected after their candidate wins?

4. Is the media too involved in candidates' lives and campaigns? What issues arise from this? Do you think the electoral process is too personal and grueling, or do you feel that a long, intimate process is necessary for voters to be informed? Would you ever change your vote based on a revelation made about a candidate's personal life?

On the Web

For voter resources and access to election research and data, visit the U.S. Election Assistance Commission's website at www.EAC.gov.

3

Legal Developments in American Elections

Throughout American history, numerous limitations were imposed on the participants of elections. It would seem rather ironic that Americans would define democracy, in part, through the election process, while at the same time their history underscores periods of broad disenfranchisement. Many groups of citizens were barred from the polling booth during much of American history. Americans cling to the notion, which Jefferson so forcefully articulated in the Declaration of Independence, that theirs is a limited government—meaning a system that springs from the will of the people—but many restrictions have been placed on who might be allowed a say in selecting public officials.

Fortunately, there has been a gradual but steady progression of legal changes that have expanded opportunities to participate in the elections. The system is much more open now than at any other point in American history. Yet another irony is that while the legal framework has changed to broaden participation, a shrinking number of Americans seem willing to participate. This issue will be taken up in subsequent chapters. In this chapter, we will discuss many of the institutional and legal changes that have reshaped the election process in the United States.

VOTING AND ELECTIONS IN THE CONSTITUTION

As already mentioned, the framers of the Constitution wanted to preserve the democratic ideals espoused during the American Revolution, but also to create a secure political system. Under the Articles of Confederation, widespread elections, mostly at the state legislative level, had created a turbulent process—at least in the minds of men gathered at the Constitutional Convention. As one delegate suggested, "The evils we experience flow from the excesses of democracy."[1] A number of mechanisms were used to accomplish the goal of creating a more stable system, including creating a limited electoral system. Elections would be used heavily at the state level, but for the national government, direct elections would be used to fill only one part of the government: the House of Representatives. The remaining part of Congress, the Senate, would be selected by the state legislatures, and, of course, the chief executive would be selected by an electoral college. As for the judiciary, citizens would have no direct role in filling these posts; judges were to be appointed by the executive and confirmed by the Senate.

The Electoral College

One of the most innovative and controversial aspects of American elections is the electoral college. It would be hard to overstate the importance of the electoral college in American politics. Occasionally, it shapes the "winner" of the election, as happened with George W. Bush in 2000, but in every presidential election, this complex mechanism shapes the election *process*, including party nominations, the selection of running mates, overall strategy, fund-raising, candidate events, distributing resources, media coverage, and much else. Depending on the state, citizens will experience presidential campaigns in vastly different ways because of the electoral college. Many argue that without this institution, elections would be much more democratic. Others suggest that given American structure of government, the electoral college is a necessary, albeit cumbersome, institution.

WHAT WERE THE FRAMERS THINKING?   The framers of American system believed that only men of the highest caliber and intellect should become president. They worried about politicians with "talents for low intrigue, and the little arts of popularity," as noted by Alexander Hamilton in "The Federalist No. 69." So they were hesitant to give average citizens a direct voice in selecting the president. Instead, they decided that a group of wise citizens should be assembled for the sole purpose of picking the president. This would be an "electoral college." But who, exactly, should make up this

---

[1]As quoted in James MacGregor Burns, *Cobblestone Leadership: Majority Rule, Minority Power* (Norman, OK: University of Oklahoma Press, 1990), 5.

group? One proposal, which had significant support at the Constitutional Convention, was to let Congress elect the president. Others suggested that this would blur the important separation between the branches. Also, many were concerned that average citizens should have *some* say in the process. The compromise was to allow each state to select its electors by whatever method that state deemed appropriate.

The electoral college was also a compromise that helped assuage a concern of delegates from small states. There were no political parties at the time, and it was assumed that each state would advance the candidacy of its "favorite son," meaning that each state's most popular politician would run for the presidency. If the selection of the president was based on popular vote, the largest states (the states with the most voters) would elect their favorite son every time.

So how does the electoral college solve this problem? The Constitution states that in order to become president, a candidate must receive a majority of electoral college votes. This does not mean the most votes (a plurality), but rather at least one-half of the overall number of electoral votes cast. If no candidate received at least 50 percent of the votes, the election is decided in the House of Representatives, where each state, regardless of its size, is given one vote. Because each state would advance a favorite son, and because there were no political parties, most assumed there would be few (if any) elections where a candidate netted a majority of electoral college votes. Most elections would therefore be decided in the House, where the small states would have the same say as the large states.

HOW THE ELECTORAL COLLEGE WORKS   As you probably know, the electoral college is a complex process. In brief, voters select electors to represent their state at a gathering that chooses the president. Figures 3.1 and 3.2 provide some details of the electoral college.

WHEN THINGS HAVE GONE WRONG   Originally, each elector was given full independence to name any person he saw fit and would cast two votes, naming two different people. The candidate who got the most votes would become president, and the runner-up would become vice president. During the first decade, only a handful of states allowed voters to pick electors; most were chosen by state legislatures. This method worked smoothly during the first two elections, when Washington was unanimously selected as president, but it began to unravel as soon as Washington announced that he would not accept a third term.

For one thing, political parties—which the framers had neither foreseen emerging nor wanted—burst onto the scene in the 1790s, leading to partisan electors rather than enlightened statesmen doing the choosing. Also, the original design was to have the top vote getter become president and the second-place finisher become vice president, but this proved completely unworkable as soon as competing political parties arose. In the 1796 election, this arrangement meant that John Adams got the presidency and his archrival, the leader of the opposing party, Thomas Jefferson, became vice president. For the next four years, each tried to outmaneuver the other.

Finally, the year 1800 brought an electoral rematch between Adams and Jefferson. This time, it seemed that Jefferson had come in first. But, in fact, Jefferson and his running mate, Aaron Burr, were tied: *All* of Jefferson's supporters in the electoral college had cast

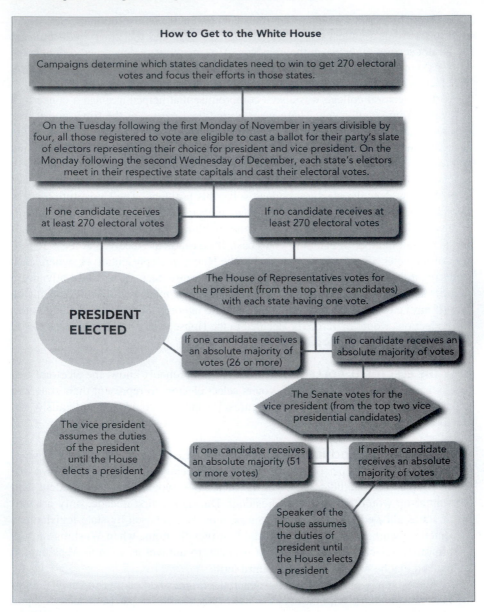

How to Get to the White House

Campaigns determine which states candidates need to win to get 270 electoral votes and focus their efforts in those states.

On the Tuesday following the first Monday of November in years divisible by four, all those registered to vote are eligible to cast a ballot for their party's slate of electors representing their choice for president and vice president. On the Monday following the second Wednesday of December, each state's electors meet in their respective state capitals and cast their electoral votes.

If one candidate receives at least 270 electoral votes

If no candidate receives at least 270 electoral votes

The House of Representatives votes for the president (from the top three candidates) with each state having one vote.

PRESIDENT ELECTED

If one candidate receives an absolute majority of votes (26 or more)

If no candidate receives an absolute majority of votes

The Senate votes for the vice president (from the top two vice presidential candidates)

The vice president assumes the duties of the president until the House elects a president

If one candidate receives an absolute majority (51 or more votes)

If neither candidate receives an absolute majority of votes

Speaker of the House assumes the duties of president until the House elects a president

FIGURE 3.1 How to Get to the White House

Source: Daniel M. Shea and Bryan Reece, 2008 Election Preview. Pearson Prentice Hall, 2008, Figure 4.1 (p. 47). Reprinted by permission of Pearson Education, Inc., Glenview, IL.

their second vote for Burr! The election had to be settled by the House of Representatives. Even though everyone knew that Jefferson was the "top of the ticket," Burr refused to back down, and it took dozens of votes in the House and much wrangling before Jefferson was finally named president and Burr had to settle for the vice presidency. As a result, the Twelfth Amendment was adopted, which says that in the electoral college, the electors must indicate who they are voting for as president and who they are voting for as vice president.

Step 1: The Electoral Formula

The number of electors for each state is determined by the following formula:

Number of U.S. senators from the state (always two)

+

Number of U.S. Representatives from the state

Step 2: Parties Nominate Electors

The political parties (or independent candidates) in each state submit to the state's chief election official a list of individuals pledged to their respective party's presidential candidate. The total number of nominated electors is equal in number to the state's allotted electoral vote.

Step 3: Parties Nominate Candidates

Parties hold national conventions to determine their party's nominations for president and vice president of the United States.

Step 4: Election Day

On the Tuesday following the first Monday of November in years evenly divisible by four, all those registered to vote are eligible to cast a ballot for their party slate of electors representing their choice for president and vice president.

Step 5: Casting Electoral Votes

On the Monday following the second Wednesday of December, each state's electors meet in their respective capitals and cast their electoral votes. One vote is cast for president and one for vice president. The electoral votes are then sealed and transmitted from each state to the president of the Senate. On the following January 6, the president of the Senate opens the seals and reads the votes before a joint session of Congress.

Step 6: Confirmation

The candidate for president receiving the majority of electoral votes is declared president of the United States. The vice presidential candidate with the absolute majority of electoral votes is declared vice president.

Step 7: Oath of Office

On January 20, the duly elected president and vice president are sworn into office and the president takes up residency at the White House.

FIGURE 3.2 How the Electoral College Works

There is yet another controversial part of the process: It is quite possible that the candidate who receives the most popular votes will not receive the most electoral votes. This can happen for two reasons. First, 48 of the 50 states use a winner-take-all model, also called the unit rule, under which the candidate who receives the most popular votes in that state gets all of that state's electoral votes. Second, the original scheme of allowing electors to use their own independent judgment was quickly replaced by partisan considerations. Today, partisan slates of electors compete against one another, meaning that if a Republican candidate wins that state, a Republican slate of electors is sent to the electoral college. The same is true for Democratic candidates.

These two changes—the unit rule and partisan slates of electors—make it *likely* that the most popular candidate (the highest vote getter) will become the president, but they do not *guarantee* it. In fact, the most popular candidate has been denied the presidency four times in American history:

- In 1824, five candidates were in the running, although one was felled by a stroke just before the election. (Despite being incapacitated, he finished in third place.) The second-place finisher was John Quincy Adams, who got 38,000 fewer popular votes than the top vote getter, Andrew Jackson. But no candidate won a majority of the electoral college. Adams was awarded the presidency when the election was thrown to the House of Representatives, which under the Constitution had to choose among the *three* top electoral college finishers. The fourth-place finisher, Speaker of the House Henry Clay, threw his support to Adams, who later named Clay as secretary of state. Jackson and his supporters howled that a "corrupt bargain" had deprived him of the White House, and Jackson ran again—this time successfully—in 1828.
- In 1876, nearly unanimous support from small states gave Republican Rutherford B. Hayes a one-vote margin in the electoral college, despite the fact that he lost the popular vote to Democrat Samuel J. Tilden by 264,000 votes. There were also credible complaints of crooked vote counting in certain disputed states. The election was decided only when a commission of senators, representatives, and a Supreme Court justice declared Hayes the winner.
- In 1888, Republican candidate Benjamin Harrison lost the popular vote by 95,713 votes to the incumbent Democratic president, Grover Cleveland, but Harrison won by an electoral college margin of 65 votes. In this instance, some say the electoral college worked the way it is designed to work by preventing a candidate from winning an election based on support from just one region of the country. The South overwhelmingly supported Cleveland, and he won by more than 425,000 votes in six Southern states. In the rest of the country, however, he lost by more than 300,000 votes. (Cleveland won a second term in a rematch election in 1892.)
- In 2000, Vice President Al Gore had over half a million more votes than George W. Bush (50,992,335 votes to Bush's 50,455,156). But after a recount controversy in Florida, and U.S. Supreme Court ruling in the case of *Bush v. Gore* (2000), Bush was awarded the state by 537 popular votes. Like most states, Florida has a winner-take-all rule, so the candidate who wins the state by popular vote gets all of the state's electoral votes. Thus, Bush became president with 271 electoral votes—the barest possible majority.

HOW THE ELECTORAL COLLEGE SHAPES CAMPAIGN ACTIVITIES   We can see that the mechanics of the electoral college can have a direct bearing on the outcome of elections. It can also have an impact on the way campaigns are conducted. For instance, the unit rule puts a premium on winning the right combination of states to net at least 270 (out of 538) electoral votes (see Figure 3.3). Because of the partisan predisposition of voters, the election outcome in many states often is never really in question (see Figure 3.4). For example, in these modern times, Republican candidates regularly win most Southern states by large margins—as John McCain did in the 2008 election. The Democrats, on the other hand, can count on West Coast states and most of the New England states. The number of "solidly Democratic" and "solidly Republican" states varies somewhat from year to year, but roughly speaking, there are about 35 to 40 in total. Conversely, only about 10 to 15 states have been "in play" during recent elections. In 2008, candidates fought it out in just 15 states.

So what, in theory, should be a national campaign for the presidency boils down to dramatic, intense efforts in about a dozen states. Campaign operatives

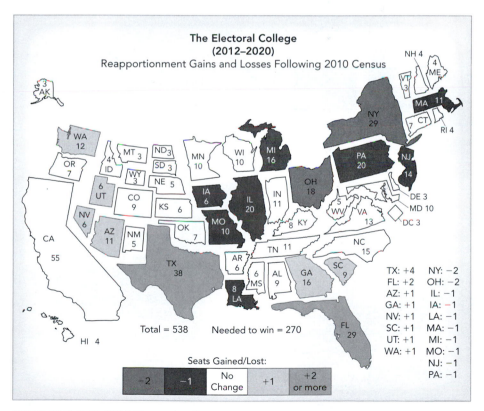

FIGURE 3.3 2012–2020 Electoral College Map

Source: Josh Putnam, 2011. "2012–2020 Electoral College Map," *Frontloading HQ.* Accessed at: http://frontloading.blogspot.com/p/2012-presidential-primary-calendar.html on June 9, 2011.

struggle to discern which states are solid and which are swing states, and to put together a winning combination. Will Colorado be in play this time? What about Ohio or Michigan? What about any of the states in the Southwest? How will different presidential and vice presidential candidates shape which states are in play?

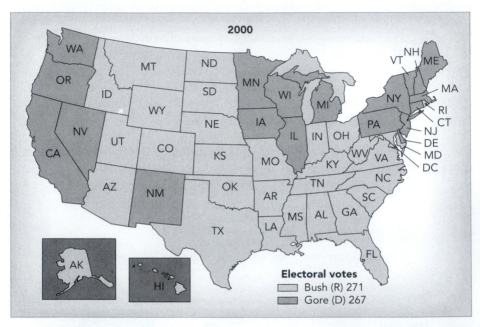

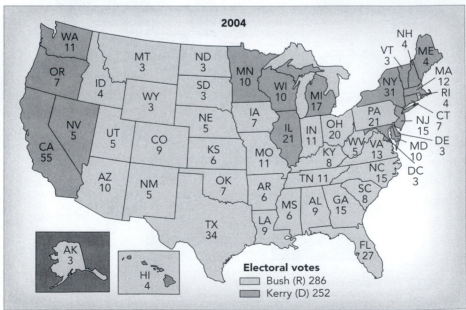

FIGURE 3.4 Electoral Votes for 2000, 2004, and 2008

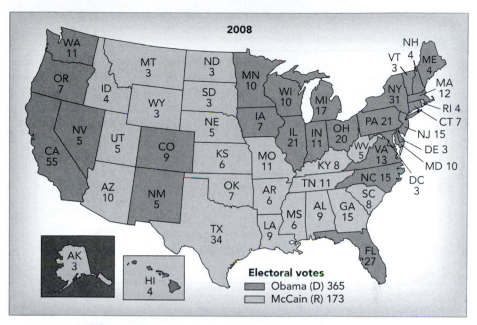

FIGURE 3.4 (continued)

Might a Republican from the Northeast put New Hampshire in play—or maybe even Maine? How about a Southern Democrat on the ticket—might he or she help create a swing state in that region, or is the entire region a lost cause for Democrats? Is it worth trying to create a swing state by expending tons of resources, or should the campaign simply work to win those states already in play? These calculations—and many, many others—shape the nature of any presidential campaign, and therefore the outcome of the election.

Moreover, residents living in swing states are bombarded with television ads, pamphlets, mailings, phone calls, rallies, media events, and so forth. In the states that are not in play, however, campaigns are relatively nonexistent. Table 3.1 takes a look the number of campaign visits made by Barack Obama and John McCain in the final two months of the 2008 presidential campaign. You will note that 57 percent of their campaign events were in just 4 states: Ohio, Florida, Pennsylvania, and Virginia, and nearly 90 percent were in just 10 states. In a different study, it was found that more than 99 percent of advertisement spending by the major party candidates from September 24 to November 4, 2008 took place in just 17 states. This means that in 33 states not a single ad was run in the last six weeks of the campaign.

Another unfortunate by-product of the unit rule is that voters in solid states feel as if their votes and efforts are irrelevant. Why should a Republican in New York or a Democrat in Wyoming, for example, bother to work for a candidate if the outcome of the election in their state seems a foregone conclusion? George Edwards, author of *Why the Electoral College Is Bad for America,* noted on NPR's *Morning Edition,* "It favors

TABLE 3.1	Campaign Events between September 5 and November 4, 2008			
Rank	State	Events	Percentage of total	Cumulative percentage
1	Ohio	62	20.7	20.7
2	Florida	46	15.3	36.0
3	Pennsylvania	40	13.3	49.3
4	Virginia	23	7.7	57.0
5	Missouri	21	7.0	64.0
6	Colorado	20	6.7	70.7
7	North Carolina	15	5.0	75.7
8	Nevada	12	4.0	79.7
9	New Hampshire	12	4.0	83.7
10	Michigan	10	3.3	87.0

Source: FairVote, "2008's Shrinking Battleground and Its Stark Impact on Campaign Activity," December 4, 2008.

some citizens over others depending solely on the state in which they cast their votes for president. So it's an institution that aggregates the popular vote in an inherently unjust manner and allows the candidate who is not preferred by the American public to win the election."[2]

THE 2008 ELECTION AND BEYOND   Given the outcome of the 2000 election, as well as other problems, many had expected a popular uprising to abolish the electoral college. Surely citizens would want to jettison this antiquated, undemocratic system. There was, indeed, a modest movement after that election, and it continues to simmer today. But in order to abolish the electoral college, the Constitution would have to be amended—a complex, difficult, time-consuming process. (Setting aside the Bill of Rights and the Civil War Amendments, the Constitution has been altered only 14 times in American history.) Surveys suggest that most Americans would like to have a direct vote for the presidency—to abolish the electoral college. At the same time, however, the prospect of passing a constitutional amendment seems limited (at least at present).

This does not mean that changes are unlikely. In 2007, a number of proposals emerged to transform the presidential election process. The state of Maryland, for example, passed a measure that could eventually create a more direct process of choosing the president without amending the Constitution. Specifically, in April of 2007, Maryland passed a law that would award the state's electoral votes to the winner of the national popular vote—so long as other states agree to do the same. The Constitution stipulates that each state can select electors as it sees fit, so if every state agrees to

---

[2]As stated on National Public Radio, *Morning Edition,* October 19, 2004. Accessed at: http://www.npr.org/templates/story/story.php?storyId=4115994

appoint electors who would vote for the winner of the national popular vote—no matter who wins the state—the national popular vote would decide the winner. This would be a way to nullify the electoral college without amending the Constitution.

Before long, other states agreed to make a similar move and the National Popular Vote Interstate Compact (NPVIC) was launched. By the fall of 2011, eight states and the District of Columbia had signed on to the plan. Several others have introduced legislation to join the compact. With California now in the group, the number of electoral votes totals 132—nearly 50 percent of those needed to win (270). All have agreed, nevertheless, that a change will not be made until states boasting at least 270 votes are included in the compact. In other words, they are about one-half the way there.

One of the most significant changes that would result from NPVIC would be the nationalization of presidential campaigns. Candidates would slug it out for votes throughout the nation, not just in particular states. Maryland State Senator Jamie Raskin, sponsor of the measure, said Maryland is largely ignored by presidential candidates during campaigns because they assume it is a solid Democratic state. His hope is that NPVIC plan will "kick off an insurrection among spectator states—the states that are completely bypassed and sidelined." Also, he argues, "going by the national popular vote will reawaken politics in every part of the country."

An even more controversial possibility is eliminating the winner-take-all provision state by state. In those states, electoral votes would be allotted to candidates at the congressional district level—as is currently done in Maine and Nebraska. Colorado made a move in this direction in 2004, as did California in 2008. Neither eventually passed the law, but the issue was again raised in Pennsylvania in the fall of 2011. The plan, backed by Governor Tom Corbett (R), would award the state's 20 electoral votes according to the winner of each congressional district.

What makes these plans so controversial is that many believed that they are politically motivated. Rather than being designed to enhance the value of voters in the state, many suggest they are bold attempts to undercut Democratic presidential candidates. For example, Democratic candidates have won Pennsylvania in every election since 1988, but the Republicans now control most of the state's congressional districts. All agree that if the proposal passes, Barack Obama would likely lose at least 10 electoral college votes in 2012 even if he were to win the state's overall vote. "This is all geared toward making sure a Democrat can never win another presidential election" said Pennsylvania Democratic state Senator Daylin Leach.[3] If every state had implemented a congressional district allocation plan in 2008, Barack Obama would have won 307 electoral votes instead of 365. It still would have been a victory, but it would have been much closer—even though the overall popular vote would have remained the same. Critics of these measures also argue that without other states making a similar change, the new process would make it more likely that whoever wins the national popular may not win the presidency. It would be the 2000 election all over again. It is a scheme, they argue, to manipulate the system. As noted by one commentator, "The

---

[3]ABCNews.Com, "Democrats and Republicans Clash Over Proposed Changes in Electoral College Rules," September 19, 2011. Accessed at: http://abcnews.go.com/blogs/politics/2011/09/proposed-changes-to-pennsylvania-electoral-votes-elicits-clashes/

prize for the audacious move would be enormous for Republicans: They would establish, arguably, a GOP lock on the presidency until the country's demographics and
political geography changed."[4]

Sponsors of the measure in Pennsylvania and elsewhere argue that it would be
a move to better reflect the wishes of voters. They also note that dividing some traditional Republican states, like Texas, could help Democratic candidates pick up a few
more electoral college votes. Yet, one has to wonder why a state that always goes for
Republican candidates—and is currently controlled by a Republican state legislature—
would make such a change? There are currently only two states that supported John
McCain in 2008 and are now controlled by a Democratic legislature: Arkansas and
West Virginia. McCain won every congressional district in Arkansas easily and West
Virginia is too small to make much of a difference.

Defenders of the electoral college argue that it adds to the popular support of winners.
In other words, somehow one feels that the victor has more legitimacy if the electoral
college vote is won by a landslide, even if that candidate has won the popular vote by only
a few percentage points. (In about one-half the presidential elections, the winner has actually netted less than 50 percent of the popular vote, given the closeness of elections and that
minor-party candidates often net a few percentage points of the vote.) The current system
helps promote the legitimacy of the winners, an important part of elections. The electoral
college also forces candidates to strive for wide geographical appeal, rather than concentrating all their efforts in a few large states. As noted by columnist George Will, "The system
aims not just for majority rule but rule by certain kinds of majorities. It encourages candidates to form coalitions of states with various political interests and cultures." Rural states
worry that they would fall by the wayside in the pursuit of the largest national vote. Others
worry that campaigns would focus almost exclusively on media and that the grassroots
efforts, that are essential to win particular states, would vanish. Finally, one has to wonder
how a nationwide recount would work.

State Control of Election Mechanics

One of the most curious and telling aspects of the Constitution is the delegation of election rules and qualifications to the states. Article I, Section 4 of the Constitution notes
that the "times, places, and manner of holding elections" is to be "prescribed in each
state by the legislature thereof." There are phrases and clauses that seem to ensure the
general right to vote, thus allowing Congress to act when necessary. But these passages
are vague. Most agree that the intent was to grant states a more or less free hand in
regulating the election process.

We might add that in order to help secure state ratification of the Constitution,
the Federalists offered to add a list of amendments designed to protect citizens from
acts by the government. This list became the first ten amendments, or the Bill of
Rights. None of these protections refer to voting. Given the wording and intent of the
original Constitution, and the absence of amendments related to a fundamental right to
vote, we can again infer that framers wanted the states to handle these sorts of issues.

---

[4]Jim Geraghty, "Could Pennsylvania Republicans End Obama's Hopes?" National Review Online,
September 14, 2011. Accessed at: http://www.nationalreview.com/campaign-spot/277178/could-
pennsylvania-republicans-end-obamas-reelection-hopes#

Historically, this leeway has allowed for the infringement of voting rights for many groups of voters, and continues to define who can vote in certain states. For example, in some states convicted felons cannot vote, but in others they can. Some states allow for same-day registration, but other states close registration 30 days from election.

Eligibility, Length of Terms, and Rotation

The Constitution is specific as to the eligibility of who can serve as an elected official in the federal government. Article I stipulates that to be allowed to serve in the House of Representatives, a person must be 25 years of age. It also stipulates that this person must have been a citizen of the United States for no less than seven years, and be a resident of the state from which he or she is elected. In the Senate, candidates must be at least 30 years old, a citizen for nine years, and an inhabitant of the state from which they are chosen "when elected."

The loose residency requirements for both chambers have led to a bit of controversy through the years. A fair number of House candidates have run for office in districts where they do not live, especially after reapportionment, but for the most part, they have been unsuccessful. At the Senate level, the success rate is likely a bit higher, because these contests attract national political celebrities, who find that their popularity extends beyond a particular state boundary. Two cases jump to mind: In 1964, Robert Kennedy, former attorney general and brother of the slain president, was interested in running for the Senate. His brother Ted was already in the Senate of Massachusetts, his home state. But New York had a race that year. Kennedy moved his official address to Manhattan and won. Similarly, Hillary Rodham Clinton, First Lady at the time, was

Hillary Clinton Running for office in New York.   *Source:* AFP Photo/Timothy A. Clary

recruited by the New York Democrats to run for the Senate. The Clintons purchased a home in Westchester County, and the voters sent her to Washington. In both instances, and in similar contests, the candidate was dubbed by many a carpetbagger. The term was coined after the Civil War to describe a nonresident who seeks to represent a locality for political or personal gain. In 2010, Ohio Congressman Dennis Kucinich, realizing that redistricting would likely put his reelection in jeopardy, sent out a call to liberal activists across the nation to find him a district where he could win in 2012.[5] He was unabashed in his desire to find a new "home."

With regard to length of terms, the House is set at two years, and the Senate, six. These durations cause little debate these days, but at the Constitutional Convention, a great deal of time was spent on the topic. Elections express the will of the people, so frequent elections would seem logical. In "The Federalist No. 52," Madison notes:

> As it is essential to liberty that the government in general should have a common interest with the people, so it is particularly essential that [the House] should have an immediate dependency on, and an intimate sympathy with, the people. Frequent elections are unquestionably the only policy by which dependency and sympathy can be effectually secured.[6]

There was the possibility that elections could be held every year, but most agreed that practical issues, such as travel time between the capital and one's home district, would make this option difficult. In the Senate, the six-year terms were a bit more contentious. Most of the framers believed that a slower, more deliberative body was necessary to check the passionate, turbulent House of Representatives. Longer terms would insulate senators from the passions of the public—allowing them to "enlarge and refine" the public will—and, of course, no policy could move forward without the consent of the Senate.[7] The longer terms were clearly designed to slow down the democratic process.

Coupled with this long term of office is rotation. The Constitution stipulates that just one-third of the Senate be elected every two years and that the two seats of a state must be elected in different years. This was done to buffer the Senate from the public, as only one-third of the chamber can be removed at one time. Today, few average Americans question this system, but its chilling effect on popular movements might give them pause.

CONSTITUTIONAL AMENDMENTS

This is not to say that the original place of elections holds sway today. For one thing, there have been a series of amendments that have opened the election process to more and more citizens, while at the same time placing elections even closer to the core of the American political psyche.

---

[5]Alex Isenstadt, "Redistricting Imperils Dennis Kucinich," *Politico*, January 12, 2011. Accessed at: http://www.politico.com/news/stories/0111/47457.html on June 3, 2011.

[6]Alexander Hamilton, James Madison, and John Jay, *The Federalist Papers,* with introduction by Clinton Rossiter (New York: Signet, 1961), 327.

[7]Ibid., 82

The Civil War Amendments

The first constitutional changes to broaden the scope of the electorate were the Fourteenth and Fifteenth amendments. These amendments, plus the Thirteenth Amendment banning slavery, were passed soon after the Civil War and are commonly referred to as the Reconstruction or Civil War Amendments. They represent the desire of the Northerners to both punish the South and confirm the rights of citizenship for black Americans (then known as Negroes). These amendments represent the first attempt to write a broader level of suffrage into the Constitution.

The Fourteenth Amendment deals with voting rights indirectly. The first clause guarantees citizenship and the rights of citizenship to all persons born or naturalized in the United States.[8] While in modern times it might be assumed that this includes voting rights, it should be remembered that at the time female citizens were denied voting rights. Thus in its second clause, the Fourteenth Amendment is an incentive for states to grant their minority citizens the right to vote, essentially basing representation in both Congress and the electoral college on not just the population of a state, but also on the percentage of its male citizens over 21 who could vote. If states refused to give African-Americans the vote, they would receive fewer Congressional seats and electoral college votes.[9]

The authors of the Fourteenth Amendment clearly hoped this clause would force states to broaden the franchise, but they were soon proved wrong. While the Southern states were forced by the Federal Reconstruction Acts to give the vote to African-Americans,[10] several Northern states refused to do the same. Indeed, after 11 referendums on the matter in eight Northern states, only two approved black suffrage.[11] Seeking to guarantee the vote for African-Americans, and to gain an electoral advantage from a wave of presumably Republican-voting blacks, the Republican Congress passed the Fifteenth Amendment. The amendment stated that "race, color, or previous condition of servitude" could not be used to deny a person the right to vote. Representing the first clear broadening of suffrage in the Constitution, this amendment helped move America closer to the democratic ideal called for in the Declaration of Independence.[12]

Poll Tax and the Twenty-Fourth Amendment

The Twenty-Fourth Amendment to the Constitution outlawed the poll tax in 1962. Previously, the poll tax had been one of the major barriers to African-American voting. By 1962, when the amendment was proposed, the tax was used in only five states, and generally amounted to only a dollar or two. The U.S. Commission on Civil Rights had found that the use of this tax was not generally discriminatory.[13]

---

[8]Alan P. Grimes, *Democracy and the Amendments to the Constitution* (Lexington: Lexington Books, 1978), 43.
[9]Ibid., 44, 45.
[10]Ibid., 51.
[11]Ibid., 53. Iowa and Minnesota approved African-American suffrage, while Wisconsin, Connecticut, Kansas, Ohio, Michigan, New York, Missouri, and the Nebraska Territory rejected it.
[12]Ibid., 58.
[13]Ibid.,131–132.

BOX 3.1   Civil War Amendments

Please consult the Constitution for the exact wording of the Thirteenth, Fourteenth, and Fifteenth amendments.

Amendment	Why It Is Important
Thirteenth— Prohibition of Slavery	This is the first of the three Civil War Amendments. Slavery is prohibited under all circumstances. Involuntary servitude is also prohibited unless it is a punishment for a convicted crime.
Fourteenth— Citizenship, Due Process, and Equal Protection of the Law	**Section 1.** This section defines the meaning of U.S. citizenship and protection of these citizenship rights. It also establishes the Equal Protection Clause, meaning that each state must guarantee fundamental rights and liberties to all of its citizens. It extended the provisions of the Fifth Amendment of due process and protection of life, liberty, and property and made these applicable to the states. The Due Process Clause had been especially important for the expansion of civil rights and liberties as the Supreme Court interpreted it in a flexible manner to recognize new rights (e.g., privacy, right of choice for abortion) and to apply the Bill of Rights against the states.
	Section 2. This section changed the Three-Fifths Clause of the original Constitution. At the time of ratification of this amendment, all male citizens, 21 or older, were used to calculate representation in the House of Representatives, If a state denied the right to vote to any male 21 or older, the number of denied citizens would be deducted from the overall state total to determine representation.
	This was the first time that gender was entered into the Constitution. It was not until 50 years later (in 1920, with the Nineteenth Amendment) that women were granted the right to vote.
	Section 3. This section disqualifies from federal office or elector for president or vice president anyone who reveled or participated in an insurrection (the Confederate Army after the Civil War) against the Constitution. This was specifically directed against citizens of Southern states. Congress by a two-thirds vote could override this provision.
	Sections 4, 5. Section 4 covers the Civil War debts; Section 5 grants to Congress the very specific authority to create legislation that will implement and enforce the provisions of the Fourteenth Amendment. Unlike the Bill of Rights, which is intended to protect individuals by limiting the power of the federal government including Congress, Section 5 intends to empower Congress to create laws that will protect individuals from actions by states that violate their rights.
	Although the Thirteenth and Fourteenth amendments were designed to end slavery, and provide citizenship, due process, and equal protection rights for freed slaves and their offspring, they were interpreted very narrowly until the 1960s. Civil rights activists had to use the courts to force legal, political, and social change to allow all individuals, regardless of color or race, to enjoy full civil rights.
Fifteenth— The Right to Vote	**Sections 1, 2.** This final Civil War amendment states that voting rights could not be denied by any states on account of race, color, or previous servitude. It did not mention gender. Accordingly, only male citizens 21 or over were guaranteed the right to vote by this amendment. Some states sought to defeat the intent of the amendment by adopting additional restrictions to voting right (such as poll taxes, whites-only primaries, and literacy tests) in order to block the participation of African-American voters.

Nevertheless, the poll tax had symbolic value and aroused heated emotions among many liberals. While its effect on the size of the electorate may have been negligible, especially since the poll tax was still allowed in state and local elections, the amendment struck down one of the last symbols of American democracy's elitist and racist past.

Women's Suffrage and the Nineteenth Amendment

The Nineteenth Amendment was the product of a long grassroots movement. We can date the beginning of organized agitation for the vote from 1848, when the feminist "Declaration of Sentiments" was issued. This document, ratified by the first women's rights convention at Seneca Falls, New York, was modeled on the Declaration of Independence. Throughout the second half of the 19th century, the feminist movement gained steam, propelled by women's experience fighting for abolition of slavery and broad-based public education. Frontier life helped fuel the movement for women's voting rights as women were considered equal to their husbands in that rugged area. The first state to grant women the right to vote was Wyoming in 1890, followed by Utah and Idaho in 1896. Conversely, urbanization also helped the feminist movement, as education, lower birthrates, and the need for many women to work outside the home combined to break down traditional gender roles.[14]

Thus, the passage of the Nineteenth Amendment was one of the greatest accomplishments of the Progressive Movement. Pressure for the Nineteenth Amendment came mainly from the western states, and opposition was mainly from the South and from eastern conservatives who feared that women would support further progressive causes, such as child labor restrictions.[15] The Nineteenth Amendment nevertheless represents a monumental achievement, and the largest enlargement of the American electorate in a single act.

The Twenty-Sixth Amendment

The Twenty-Sixth Amendment, giving 18-year-olds the right to vote, was the last amendment to extend the franchise. It was the product of the massive social movements of the 1960s and the baby boom of the post–World War II period. By the late 1960s, a growing proportion of Americans were in their late teens. These college-aged men and women had proved not only that they could be active in politics, but that they could be effective in promoting change.[16] The fact that young men who were not able to vote in elections were going off to die in the Vietnam War was likely another part of the movement. The slogan "old enough to fight, old enough to vote" was heard often during the late 1960s and early 1970s.[17]

---

[14]George Anastaplo, *The Amendments to the Constitution: A Commentary* (Baltimore: Johns Hopkins University Press, 1995), 131.

[15]Alan P. Grimes, *Democracy and the Amendments to the Constitution* (Lexington: Lexington Books, 1978), p. 4–95.

[16]Ibid., 131.

[17]Ibid., 146.

Women Suffragettes standing outside of their headquarters in Cleveland, Ohio in 1912.
Source: akg-Images/Newscom

Initially, Congress attempted to lower the voting age through the Voting Rights Act of 1970. The Supreme Court partially thwarted this attempt by ruling that although Congress could lower the voting age in federal elections, it had no jurisdiction over state or local elections. Thus a curious situation emerged, where 18-year-olds would be allowed to vote for president but not for governor or city council officials. To remedy this, Congress passed the Twenty-Sixth Amendment, on July 1, 1971, giving citizens 18 and older the right to vote in all elections. The amendment passed with little objection and was ratified in three-and-a-half months.[18]

CHANGES DURING THE PROGRESSIVE PERIOD

Political parties had spread to the local organization level by the 1830s and became extremely powerful by the end of the 19th century—a topic discussed in detail in Chapter 6. These strong local organizations were dubbed party "machines." They controlled public policy because they controlled the election process. In response to this corruption, a cry for reform grew louder and louder, culminating in a series of changes collectively called the Progressive Era election reforms.

One of the most significant of these changes was the use of the direct primary. Prior to this, party leaders would simply handpick their candidates, often the ones most likely to follow the party bosses' every wish. One of the most flamboyant party

---

[18]Ibid., 142–147.

leaders of the day, Boss Tweed of New York City, once commented, "I don't care who does the electin', so long as I do the nominatin'." If you could not run as a major party's candidate, chance of winning the election was slim at best. The solution was simple: Mandate that each party nominate its candidates by vote among all party members, not just the party leaders. From about 1904 to 1914, the direct primary craze swept the nation, and today nearly all local, state, and federal candidates are nominated through a direct primary process.

The direct primary is where the average members of a party, often dubbed "the rank and file," vote for candidates to run in the general election for their party. The winner becomes the party's nominee and faces the other party's nominee in the general election. The first municipality to use the direct primary was Crawford County Pennsylvania in 1846. Few communities did the same until the entire state of Wisconsin did so in 1904, due in no small measure to the state's progressive champion, Robert M. LaFollette. LaFollette gained a national reputation as a reformer, and soon one state after another followed his advice and adopted the direct primary as the means of nominating candidates.

Today, primaries are used to nominate local, state, and federal candidates. However, over the years, the precise means of conducting these primaries has become quite varied, a topic discussed in detail in Chapter 6. For now it is enough to note that there are two broad types:

- Closed primaries, used in about one half of the states, restrict the nomination process to enrolled members of the party. For example, in primary elections in New York, only registered Democrats can vote in a contest for Democratic contenders, and likewise for Republicans.
- The other approach is open primaries. Here voters can cast their ballot for candidates in either party. In Texas, for instance, you need not be a registered Democrat to vote in the Democratic primary (again, the same is true for Republicans). In general, the shift has been toward opening the system to allow more and more citizens access to the primary process—as opposed to only the rank and file of the party.

As will be discussed in Chapter 6, a few states have even tried a system known as a blanket primary, where voters are allowed to participate in primaries for both parties at the same time. Here a voter might vote in the Democratic primary for governor, the Republican primary for Senate, and perhaps even a Green Party primary for House of Representatives. Both Republican and Democratic Party committees have balked at this process and have taken the issue to the federal courts.

Another set of progressive reforms was designed to clean up the general election process, namely the all-too-common practice of fraudulent voting. Party bosses, for example, might pay people to travel around the city to vote in numerous polling places. To this day, party operatives can be heard reminding supporters on Election Day, only half jokingly, to "vote early and vote often." Residency and registration were the solution. Residency laws stipulate that a person can vote only where he or she has resided for a prescribed period of time. The length of time varies from state to state, but the 1970 Voting Rights Act established a maximum of 30 days. In recent elections, states, such as Maine, Minnesota, New Hampshire, Oregon, Wisconsin, and

Washington, allowed residents to register up to and on Election Day, but in most others, there was once again a stipulated pre-Election Day cutoff.

Again, the idea behind residency and registration was to reduce corruption. In recent years, however, these laws have become controversial. Some have even suggested that they are the foremost reason why many Americans do not show up on Election Day. In a provocative book entitled *Why Americans Still Don't Vote: And Why Politicians Want It That Way*, scholars Frances Fox Piven and Richard Cloward argue that these laws have always been about keeping certain types of voters out of the process.[19] These measures were not about corruption but about control. Perhaps trying to find a middle ground, Congress passed legislation in 1993 requiring states to allow citizens to register to vote at numerous public offices, such as a motor vehicle office. The so-called Motor-Voter bill also stipulates that states must permit mail-in registration. Election data since the adoption of the motor-voter bill suggest it had a negligible impact on the number of Americans coming to the polls. As Figure 3.5 suggests, about one quarter of the citizens not registered to vote offer causes related to deadlines and being unfamiliar with the process.

But the issue of registration remains controversial. In the wake of the 2010 elections, several states made moves to eliminate same-day registration. The argument,

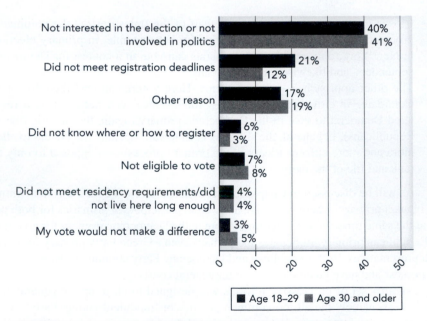

FIGURE 3.5 Main Reason Why People Were Not Registered, 2008
Source: The Center for Information & Research on Civic Learning and Engagement, "Main Reason Why People Were Not Registered, 2008. Accessed at: www.civicyouth.org/ on June 5, 2011.

[19]Frances Fox Piven and Richard A. Cloward, *Why Americans Still Don't Vote: And Why Politicians Want It That Way* (Boston: Beacon Press, 2000)

once again, is that corruption in elections can be limited by mandating that citizens register well in advance of elections.

Yet another progressive measure was the Seventeenth Amendment, providing for the direct election of U.S. senators, ratified in 1913. Prior to this, senators were selected by state legislatures, which were often controlled by the party machines. Stripping this privilege from the bosses and giving it to average citizens was seen as an important democratic move.

STATUTORY CHANGES OVER TIME

The Constitution is not the only source of law that has defined who shall participate in elections in America and who shall not. Numerous federal and state statutes, or laws, have been used to limit and broaden the process.

Restrictive State Laws

There were many state-level limitations on voting in the early days of the republic. There were religious qualifications in some states for roughly a decade prior to the ratification of the Constitution, as well as property ownership and tax-paying requirements. The property-owning requirements were generally phased out by the 1820s, and none of the states entering after that time had property requirements for voting. Tax-paying requirements were not fully phased out until the Twenty-Fifth Amendment outlawed the poll tax, discussed earlier. However, the tax-paying requirements were generally so broadly written that any citizen who paid any tax was allowed to vote.[20] The notable exception to this was the South's Jim Crow–era poll taxes.

Southern states used their power to regulate elections in the 1890s to keep African-Americans from the polls. Collectively called Jim Crow laws, these laws were employed by Southerners to impose a variety of restrictions—literacy tests, poll taxes, complicated registration requirements, residency requirements, and the infamous grandfather clause (which exempted a voter from the complicated requirements if his grandfather had voted before 1860). Using these restrictions, Southern states managed to disenfranchise most blacks and poor whites who would threaten the dominance of the conservative wing of the Democratic Party. Many other insidious tricks were used, such as locating a community's polling place in a remote area or near the site of recent black lynchings. Outright intimidation and threats of violence were commonplace.

A favorite exclusionary tool was the white primary. The Democratic Party dominated the South after the 1870s, so the winner of the Democratic nomination contest was the de facto winner of the election. Southern election laws held political parties to be "private organizations" with the right to decide their own membership, and state parties took advantage of that by excluding blacks from their primaries. Thus, while blacks might enjoy the right to vote in the general election, as stipulated in the Fifteenth Amendment, they could not vote in the only election that counted for

---

[20]Alexander Keyssar, *The Right to Vote: The Contested History of Democracy in the United States* (New York: Basic Books, 2000).

them—the Democratic primary.[21] This practice remained in effect until the Supreme Court decision in *Smith v. Allwright* (1944)[22] in which the Court said that primaries were part of the electoral system and therefore the exclusion of blacks from this process violated the Fifteenth Amendment.

Voting Rights Act of 1965

Americans felt especially proud of their accomplishments during WWII. They were an "exceptional" nation, the beacon of democracy for struggling peoples around the world. This was hypocritical considering the treatment of African-Americans in the South. By the 1950s, a growing number of federal measures were passed to better secure basic rights. The Civil Rights Act of 1957 created a Civil Rights Commission with the power to investigate voting rights violations and to suggest changes.[23] The most significant change came with the 1965 Voting Rights Act. This act stated that in any congressional district in which fewer than 50 percent of adults went to the polls, a five-year "emergency state" would be triggered. Affected districts could change their election regulations only with the approval of the civil rights division of the Justice Department, and the emergency could only be ended by appeal to a federal court with evidence that no discriminatory devices had been used in the previous five years. In addition, the Justice Department could send election examiners into the states to register voters and observe elections. Although the 1965 Voting Rights Act did not end discrimination, it became the most important tool protecting the right to vote.[24] Election data certainly reflect the act's importance: Black voter registration in 11 Southern states in 1960 was a meager 29.7 percent. By the end of the decade, this figure had more than doubled, to 63.4 percent.[25]

A number of the provisions in the Voting Rights Act called for periodic renewal, which Congress has done several times—most recently in 2006. Generally speaking, these measures garner broad bi-partisan support, but in 2006, a group of 80 legislators supported an amendment to strip the requirements for translators or multilingual ballots for U.S. citizens who do not speak English. This effort was unsuccessful, but many suspect that as the debate over immigration heats up the issue of mandatory multilingual ballots will resurface.

Help America Vote Act

The Help America Vote Act (HAVA) was signed into law in 2002 by President George W. Bush as a result of problems in the 2000 presidential election. Its goals were to update the voting systems by replacing punch cards with computerized systems, to create a commission to manage federal elections (called the Election Assistance Commission [EAC]), and to establish federal election standards for states.

---

[21]Ibid., 111.

[22]321 U.S. 649 (1944).

[23]L. Sandy Maisel, *Parties and Elections in America: The Electoral Process,* 3rd ed., (Lanham, MD: Rowman & Littlefield, 1995), 95.

[24]Keyssar, *The Right to Vote*, 264–265.

[25]Maisel, *Parties and Elections in America*, 97.

In the 2004 presidential election, HAVA withstood the test, proving to increase voter turnout and decrease fraud. The U.S. Election Assistance Commission reported to Congress on the 2004 election, finding the following:

- *National Election Data:* With 47 states and territories reporting, there was an 8-percent increase in registered voters in the United States, totaling about 13 million new voters.
- *Provisional Voting:* Over 1 million provisional votes were counted in the November 2004 elections. Seventeen states used provisional voting for the first time, and 1.5 million people cast a provisional ballot, of which more than 1 million (68 percent) were counted.
- *Funding for States to Meet HAVA Requirements:* More than $2.2 billion was distributed to 46 states and territories to enhance the election process and to help states meet HAVA requirements.
- *New Voting Equipment:* Since 2000, at least 25 percent of the nation's voters were using new voting equipment, with another 30 percent using new equipment by 2006.
- *Statewide Voter Registration Databases:* At least nine states had developed and used a statewide voter registration database to help increase access to the process and reduce opportunities for fraud.
- *Poll Workers:* An increase in the number of trained poll workers served across the country on Election Day. In the EAC survey, 12 states reported a full complement of poll workers in 2004.[26]

THE CONTROVERSY OVER VOTER ID LAWS

Also in the wake of the 2010 election, five states (Wisconsin, Texas, Tennessee, South Carolina, and Kansas) have instituted new laws requiring voters to bring state-approved identification cards (such as a driver's license) to voting booth. Indiana already had a similar law on the books, and nearly one dozen other states have made comparable moves in previous years. Supporters of these measures argue that IDs are required for many public events, so it simply makes sense that they should be required for voting. These laws will limit corruption and add legitimacy to the process, they argue. Shortly after South Carolina moved to require voter ID cards for all voters, the governor of the state, Republican Nikki Haley, commented, "We continue to improve the levels of South Carolina in terms of integrity, accountability, and transparency. I have heard from people out of state how impressed they are that we took it upon ourselves to say, 'We are going to make sure we maintain the integrity of our voters.'"[27]

Those who oppose voter ID measures argue that upwards of 10 percent of citizens currently do not have state-recognized ID cards, and that by requiring to show IDs at the polls will disenfranchise groups of voters. They suggest voter fraud is a tiny issue—certainly less significant than low voter turnout. Moreover, opponents

---

[26]U.S. Election Assistance Commission. "EAC Reports to Congress on Election Reform Process in 2004" (February 9, 2005). Accessed at: http://www.eac.gov/eac_reports_to_congress_on_election_reform_progress_in_2004/

[27]Yvonne Wenger, "Debate Rages Over South Carolina's Voter ID Law," *Postandcourier.com*, May 19, 2011. Accessed at: www.postandcourier.com/news/2011/may/19/debate-rages-over-south-carolinas-voter-id-law/

argue that the real intent of the laws is not to limit voter fraud, but to keep a particular type of voter from the polls. They point to studies that suggest citizens without state-issued ID cards are disproportionately poor and minority; likely Democratic voters. "A number of state legislatures have taken up these bills and I think that it's a growing concern nationally that the effect is going to be the suppression of the vote," said Victoria Middleton, executive director for the South Carolina American Civil Liberties Union.[28]

We know that the legislature and governor in every state that has mandated voter ID laws after the 2010 election are controlled by Republicans. We also know this may not be the last word on the issue. The 1965 Voting Rights Act empowers the Department of Justice to review all election-law changes, especially states with a history of discriminatory voting practices. For example, South Carolina's law is slated to be reviewed. Also, because these measures are quite controversial, congressional action may be forthcoming, particularly if the Democrats take control of both chambers in the near future.

REDISTRICTING

The Great Compromise at the Constitutional Convention stipulated that the Congress be divided into two houses, one with an identical number of officials from each state (the Senate) and the other based on the population of each state (the House of Representatives). To know the number of citizens in each state, the Constitution stipulates that a census be conducted every ten years and that the apportionment of seats to each state be dependent upon the findings of this count. This chore of creating precise districts has been left to the states—and is the source of considerable controversy.

Some states in the earliest days of the republic simply made at-large districts. If they were granted three seats in the House, then they would simply elect three members from the entire state. There are no districts per se, but one state. Most states, however, chose to divide their state into the number of congressional districts equal to the seats they had in the legislature; a state granted five seats in the House would have five congressional districts.

The idea of changing legislative districts in response to population shifts stems from the American idea of geographic representation. The representatives should be directly responsible to a group of people living in a specific geographic location.

The tricky and controversial part of the process came when the exact lines or boundaries for the districts were to be drawn, and redrawn every ten years based on a state's overall population and population shifts within the state. This process of redrawing the boundaries of legislative districts is called redistricting or reapportionment. (This process also takes place for state legislative districts.) State legislatures have been given this responsibility. Given that these bodies have nearly always been partisan (controlled by a majority of members from one party), few would be surprised to hear that the process has been rife with bias.

---

[28]Kevin Dolak, "State Voter ID Laws Draw National Scrutiny," *ABCNews.Com*, September 8, 2011. Accessed at: http://abcnews.go.com/blogs/politics/2011/09/state-voter-id-laws-draw-national-scrutiny-2/

The practice of drawing districts for political advantage is called gerrymander-ing, named after founding father Elbridge Gerry who, as governor of Massachusetts, drew an odd-shaped district in order to elect a political ally.[29] An observer com-mented that the new district looked like a salamander (as noted in Figure 3.6), and another responded by saying it was not a salamander, but rather a "gerrymander." The idea is to create districts that will support candidates of the majority party—regardless of its shape. This has been done in a number of ways, but mostly through either "packing" or "cracking." Packing is where the opposition is lumped into one area. For instance, if the state has five districts, the idea would be to make one of these districts overwhelmingly filled with supporters of the other party. The party in power—the one drawing the lines—would give up one seat, but the other four districts would be shaped to nearly guarantee their victory. Cracking is when the opposition is broken into pieces so that it does not have a majority in any district.

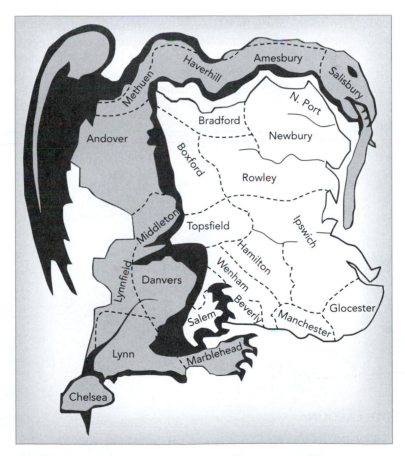

FIGURE 3.6 Gerrymandering Map from 1812

[29]Gary W. Cox and Jonathan N. Katz, *Elbridge Gerry's Salamander* (Cambridge: Cambridge University Press, 2002), 3.

As one might have guessed, the redistricting process was also used to minimize the electoral weight of African-Americans and other minority groups. A state might boast, for example, a 20-percent black population, but through cracking, it is likely that these voters would never be able to elect an African-American legislator without the help of white voters.

For the most part, the issue of reapportionment has been tricky for the courts. On a number of occasions, courts refused to dive into the controversy, arguing that the issue was a "political question," and therefore not justifiable.[30] Additionally, the complexity of the reapportionment process makes judicial intervention difficult.

Amendments to the Voting Rights Act of 1965 passed in 1982 approached the racial gerrymandering issue from an entirely different angle. The idea was to use census data to help construct districts that would better ensure the election of minority legislators. Following the 1990 census, 24 minority-majority districts were created, 15 with a majority of African-American voters and 9 with a majority of Hispanic-American voters. The scheme seemed to work, given that in each of these districts a minority legislator was chosen by the voters. Nevertheless, two issues jumped to the fore: First, the resulting districts were often exceptionally odd shaped. A perfect example was North Carolina's 12th Congressional District, which included an 85-mile strip of Interstate 85 connecting black communities in Durham and Charlotte (see Figure 3.7). Second, the overt consideration of race in drawing such highly

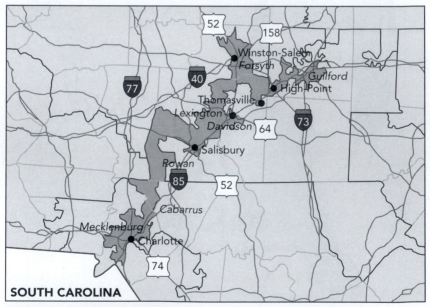

FIGURE 3.7 North Carolina's 12th Congressional District After the 1990 Census.
Source: Nationalatlas.gov

---

[30]Maisel, *Parties and Elections in America,* 207.

irregular districts was challenged in the courts as an affront to equal protection clause of the Fourteenth Amendment. And although the courts have tended to stay out of redistricting disputes, this time they joined the fray. In a series of cases, the Supreme Court remained a bit vague, but seemed somewhat supportive of plans that bolster the chances for minority representation. It has suggested reluctance to allow highly irregular shaped districts (*Shaw v. Reno*, 1993) and to approve schemes that use race as the principal criteria for drawing lines (*Miller v. Johnson*, 1995).

The Number of Residents per District

Related to the contentious issue of drawing district lines is the issue of the number of residents per district. Oddly enough, the Constitution is silent on this matter, so for most of American history, many states did not seek to ensure parity between districts. For example, we might imagine a state with two urban areas, perhaps at opposite corners of the state, and one agricultural region in the middle. If that state were allotted three representatives, we could imagine a district for each of the cities and one for the rural area—regardless of the exact population distribution. The residents in these areas more likely have similar interests, which would be reflected by the legislator. At the state legislative level, county lines were often used as district boundaries. On the other hand, Americans believe that each vote should have the same weight in the political process—that all men and women are equal in the process—and mal-proportioned districts violate this goal. (Interestingly, few seem anxious to challenge the legitimacy of the U.S. Senate, where states like Vermont and California, with dramatically different populations, boast the same number of seats.)

The issue came to a head in a suit brought by a group of Tennessee residents who claimed that the state had denied them their equal protection under the law by refusing to draw state legislative districts of equal size. The Court had previously found similar cases to be beyond its jurisdiction, but a new and more liberal court decided that the Tennessee districts were so malapportioned that they constituted a violation of the constitutional rights of the plaintiffs.[31] The case *Baker v. Carr* (1961) established the "one person, one vote" principle, and while it applied only to state house districts, the Court extended this logic to the upper chamber of state legislatures in *Reynolds v. Sims* and to U.S. Representatives' districts in *Wesberry v. Sanders*, both in 1964.[32]

These decisions sparked a revolution in the way legislative districts were drawn. In the post-*Baker* world, geographic concerns took a back seat to equal population in all districts. These cases also mandated that redistricting happen every ten years regardless of any changes in the number of legislators, since the new census meant the old districts almost certainly did not have equal population. Perhaps most important, *Baker v. Carr* inserted the courts in the redistricting process, thereby leaving any plan open to a court challenge. Along with the mandate under the 1965 Voting Rights Act to protect against racial discrimination, *Baker v. Carr* has made redistricting a tedious process of moving district lines block by block until the

---

[31]Cox and Katz, *Elbridge Gerry's Salamander*, 12.
[32]Ibid., 13.

population was correct, while constantly under the threat that a court would find the entire scheme unconstitutional.[33]

Reapportionment

Finally, the redistricting process has been contentious because the allotment of seats per state shifts with each new census—a process known as reapportionment. As noted in Figure 3.8, the ratio of residents to House member was set at 1 to 30,000 in 1800, leading to 65 House members in the first session of Congress. So as the population grew, so too did the number of representatives. The size of the House jumped from 141 in 1800, to 240 in 1830. By 1910, the House had grown to 435 members, which seemed large enough, so a cap was enacted. Since that time the ratio has gotten smaller and smaller; today, there are roughly 700,000 residents for each House district.

This in itself has become controversial, but bigger still is the allocation of these 435 seats. The fastest growing states net seats after each census, and states that are growing at a slower speed (Only Michigan seems to be shrinking in population) lose seats. After the 2010 census, for example, eight states gained at least one additional House seat: Arizona, Florida, Georgia, Nevada, South Carolina, Texas, Utah, and Washington. Texas gained an additional four seats. Ohio lost two seats, and Illinois, Iowa, Louisiana, Massachusetts, Michigan, Missouri, New Jersey, New York, and Pennsylvania each lost one seat.[34] Losing seats in the national legislature can be devastating for a state, as it results in loss of federal funds. Also, when states lose seats, it often forces some of the states' existing representatives—the incumbents—to

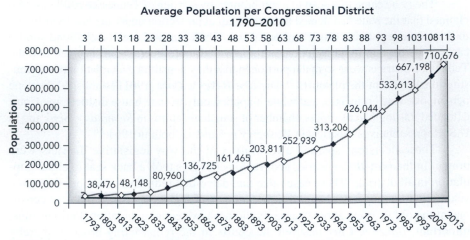

FIGURE 3.8 **Average Population by Congressional District over Time**
Source: Thirty Thousand. Accessed at: www.thirty-thousand.org/pages/QHA-03.htm 2010 Census Data. Accessed at: http://2010.census.gov/2010census/data/

---

[33]Ibid., 25–28.
[34]U.S. Census 2010, "Apportionment Data." Accessed at: http://2010.census.gov/ 2010census/data/appor-tionment-data-text.php

run against one another. There is nothing an incumbent hates more than to run against another incumbent for reelection.

The Texas Redistricting Battle

The contentious nature of redistricting is evident after every census—and in most state legislatures. In 2003, the situation came to a head over a plan to create new congressional district lines in Texas. In a somewhat unprecedented move, Texas Congressman and House Majority Leader Tom DeLay inserted himself into the process. The outcome of his efforts and meetings with state legislative leaders, also Republican, was a redistricting plan that many Democrats saw as overwhelmingly partisan. According to Democrats, the scheme would make at least 22 of the state's 32 congressional districts Republican—up from their then-current 15 seats. Moreover, they argued that the plan would deprive millions of minorities' voting rights. Republicans responded by arguing that previous redistricting plans had guaranteed the Democrats an artificial advantage, and that their plan better matched demographic shifts throughout the state.

To stop the state legislature from adopting the plan, many Democrats in both the House and Senate refused to even come to vote on the measure—thereby denying the Republicans a quorum. Fearing that the governor, also a Republican, would send state troopers to bring them to the legislature and force a vote, 53 Democrats left the state and took up residence in an Ardmore, Oklahoma, hotel in May of 2003. Without a quorum, the plan stalled. But by midsummer, two of the Democrats broke ranks to provide the Republicans a quorum. Immediately after the measure was signed into law, the Democrats filed suit in federal court arguing that the district plan violated the Voting Rights Act of 1965 in that it diluted the voting strength of minorities. The court disagreed, however, siding with the Republicans. While the court agreed that politics played a big role in the process, it felt the new lines did not create illegal racial discrimination.[35]

Some states are moving toward using impartial third parties to draw district lines. Iowa has taken this trend the farthest, using a complex computer program administered by a non-partisan commission to draw geographically compact and equal districts. These districts can then be voted up or down by the state legislature, but not amended. This process has spared Iowa from court challenges and has made its politics more competitive. For example, in the 2002 election, three out of five of Iowa's U.S. House races were considered competitive, compared to one out of ten for the rest of the nation.[36] One may doubt if districting by computer was the intent in *Baker v. Carr*, but it seems to be the logical result of the strict "one person, one vote" doctrine.

ADDITIONAL STATE-LEVEL REGULATIONS

Much of this chapter has discussed the structure of federal elections, but it should be noted that the vast majority of elections take place at the state and municipal levels. We seem to give presidential and congressional elections more of our attention, but

---

[35]See, for example, Ralph Blumenthal, "G.O.P. Is Victorious in Remapping." *New York Times,* January 7, 2004, Section A. 12.

[36]Adam Clymer. "Why Iowa Has So Many Hot Seats." *New York Times,* October 27, 2002.

an astute observer of American politics will realize that the real action is elsewhere. This brief section explores a few more state and local electoral factors. Many election laws and regulations are quite similar to those found at the federal level, but there are additional distinct provisions.

Forty-nine states have a bicameral legislature, with a Senate and a House (often dubbed the assembly or general assembly). Nebraska has a one-house, nonpartisan legislature. Most states follow the national model and hold elections for state house posts every two years. There is considerable variance when it comes to the Senate; some have two-year terms, and a good many others have four-year terms. About one-half the states with four-year terms use a rotation process where half of the Senate is up for reelection every two years. As far as the length of terms for governors goes, all 50 states use four years. With few exceptions (Louisiana, Mississippi, and New Jersey), state legislative and gubernatorial elections are held during even-numbered years.

As noted earlier, residency requirements for voters are set at the state level, but are capped by federal statute at no more than 30 days prior to an election. In an effort to attract more voters on Election Day, the trend has been to shorten the period. Today, nine states allow voters to register to vote on Election Day, as noted in Figure 3.9.

Campaign finance regulations greatly vary from state to state. In roughly 17 states, including Alabama, Illinois, and Nebraska, any amount can be given to state office candidates; there are no campaign finance laws. In the other 33 states, a citizen, group, or political party is restricted in the total amount it can give, with the average being about $500. As for total expenditure limits, about a dozen states have established voluntary caps on the amount a state-office candidate can spend. A handful of states now provide public funding for state posts. Quite often those states that provide some public monies for campaigns also cap the amount those candidates can spend. The trend seems to be greater restrictions on both contributions and expenditures.

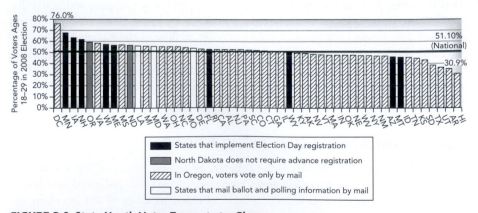

FIGURE 3.9 State Youth Voter Turnout at a Glance
Source: Kei Kawashima-Ginberg, Amanda Nover, and Emily Hoban Kirby, "State Election Law Reform and Youth Voter Turnout," The Center for Information & Research on Civic Learning and Engagement, July 2009. Accessed at: www.civicyouth.org/PopUps/FactSheets/ State_law_and_youth_turnout_Final.pdf on June 5, 2011.

Maine and Vermont, for example, recently passed drastic campaign reform measures designed to reduce corruption (or the appearance of corruption) in the electoral process.

Conclusion

While the framers of American system believed in the democratic process, their understanding of the best mechanism for turning the will of the citizenry into public policy was unclear. Elections had been tried at the state and local levels, but they were often rowdy, turbulent events. Most of these men believed that elections had the potential to push public officials into policy choices that were popular, not in the nation's long-term interest. Elections could reflect the will of the people, but perhaps the process should be indirect, less immediate. This would create more stability in the system. In defending the electoral college, Alexander Hamilton offered a look of what the framers thought of direct elections: "[A]n intermediate body of electors will be much less apt to convulse the community with any extraordinary or violent movements."[37] Simply stated, he felt that direct elections have the potential to churn the citizenry into acts of violence.

This ambivalence was reflected in the Constitution, where there was only one part of the national government dependent on direct elections: the House of Representative. As America began to mature, however, faith in the electoral process thrived. After the Corrupt Deal of 1824, average Americans began to see elections as *the* tool to popular control. Election fever swept across the nation by the middle of the 19th century, a period historians have called the age of Jacksonian Democracy. (Andrew Jackson defeated John Quincy Adams in 1828 due, in large measure, to a dramatic expansion of voter turnout.)

Elections did not become a means of empowerment for *all* Americans, of course, until very late in the 20th century. Baring women, African-Americans, Native Americans, newly arrived immigrants, and some other groups of citizens from the voting booth ensured the dominance of wealthy white men. With cries for broader suffrage, change occurred. One constitutional amendment after another expanded the pool of Americans able to participate in the system. Those wishing to limit the process retreated to state and local barriers, such as Jim Crow laws used to keep blacks from the election process, but here too the tide for voting rights was overwhelming. Today, there are few barriers to voting for citizens 18 years of age or older, with the notable exception of convicted felons in most states.

Along with the many institutional adjustments, the *process* of conducting elections has dramatically changed as well. Early Americans would scarcely recognize the conduct of contemporary campaigns. One scholar has gone so far as to suggest that "it can be argued that the contemporary election process represents one of significant transformations in our nation's history."[38] The structure, laws, and institutions tell an important part of the story, but there is much more to explore—as you will soon read.

---

[37]Ibid., 412.

[38]Daniel M. Shea, *Campaign Craft: The Strategy, Tactics, and Art of Political Campaign Management* (Westport, CT: Praeger, 1996), 3–4.

Critical Thinking

1. Many Americans would like to jettison the electoral college. But are there ways to make the electoral college more representative? How would recounts be conducted in very close elections if the unit rule were eliminated? Also, are there ways to nullify the electoral college without amending the Constitution?
2. How have expanded voting rights affected the democratic process?
3. Some have suggested lowering the voting age to 16, or perhaps giving younger Americans some sort of "voting learner's permit." Would this be a good idea?
4. In the past, gerrymandering was used to quell the voice of minorities. Currently, it has been suggested as a way to give racial minorities power. How would this work? Do you agree with this sort of approach to enhance the representation of minorities in Congress?

On the Web

To explore how the winner-take-all system allows each state to alter the electoral college count, visit www.270towin.com, where you can use an interactive electoral map to view past election results or create your own simulation.

4

The Evolution of Political Parties

One of the great ironies of American politics is that the forces that many of the constitutional framers feared the most have proven to be the instruments that have made elections work—and many believe have made the American democratic process endure through the ages. Political parties burst on the scene in the late 1790s and forever changed the way elections are conducted and the way the American system of government operates. Many shun the very idea of "partisan politics," but few scholars, pundits, or politicians could imagine a democratic system where parties are not an integral part of the system. Parties are the black sheep of American politics—shunned, but still very much a part of the family. As noted by a team of scholars, political parties are "institutions Americans love to hate."[1]

---

[1]John K. White and Daniel M. Shea, *New Party Politics: From Jefferson and Hamilton to the Information Age* (New York: Bedford/St. Martin's 2000), 14.

WHAT IS A POLITICAL PARTY?

There is no single definition of "political parties" that satisfies everyone. In fact, two scholars or students of politics might define "parties" in different ways. The principal difference seems to be what we might expect from parties—the goals of party activity. One definition, often called the pragmatic party model, suggests that parties are organizations that sponsor candidates for political office under the organization's name with the hopes of controlling the apparatus of government. The ends are control of government, which has often meant the perquisites of control (e.g., patronage jobs, government contracts). On the other side of the spectrum is the responsible party model. Here "parties" implies organizations that run candidates to shape the outcome of government—to redirect public policy. Rational parties work to win elections to control government, while responsible parties work hard during elections in order to shape public policy. The former is instrumental; the latter, ideological. Which of the two better fits American political parties? This is a hotly debated issue and there is no clear answer. What is clear, however, is that there are three characteristics that distinguish political parties from other organizations such as interest groups, unions, trade associations, and political action committees.[2] Those differences are as follows:

- Political parties run candidates under their own labels. Many groups work hard to win elections. The National Rifle Association (NRA) and the American Federation of Labor—Congress of Industrial Organizations (AFL-CIO), for example, help particular candidates in every election. But such organizations do not nominate candidates to run under their labels. Only political parties do this.
- Political parties have a broad range of concerns, dubbed a platform. They are umbrella organizations that develop positions on an array of policy questions. Most interest groups limit their efforts to a narrow range of topics. The NRA, for instance, is concerned with regulations on guns, and the Environmental Defense League is primarily concerned with issues related to pollution and the protection of ecosystems.
- Ever since the Progressive Period—roughly the turn of the 20th century—political parties have been subject to numerous state and local laws. They are "quasi-public" institutions. Interest groups, on the other hand, are purely private and free of government regulations. Indeed, the extent to which parties are also private organizations has been recently debated in the federal courts.

Party Functions

Just as there is disagreement over the precise definition of "party," so too there is dispute over party functions. Following is a list that most agree upon. It contains numerous overt functions—activities that the public can see and clearly measure—and it also boasts many latent functions—theoretical activities one hopes that parties provide. The extent to which a function is manifest or latent has changed over time.

---

[2]The following list is culled, in large measure, from White and Shea, *New Party Politics*, 19.

Organizing the Election Process   Creating a system of elections to pick governmental leaders is much easier said than done. One could imagine dozens, perhaps even hundreds, of citizens vying for a single office, thus leaving voters confused and discouraged. How would one study the positions, personalities, and qualifications of each candidate? Parties serve important organizing functions as they trim the pool of office-seekers to party nominees, and they also establish a platform of issues for their candidates. Both of these functions help organize the process for voters.

Providing a Voting Shortcut   Psychologists tell us that humans are cognitive misers: We wish to make rational decisions with the least amount of information necessary. Parties help in this regard, given that voters need not know everything or even very much about a candidate, other than his or her party affiliation, to cast an informed, rational vote. If, for example, a voter prefers Republican policies and an election pits a Republican against a Democrat, then the voter can make an informed choice with no other additional information. Without party labels, the voter would have to study each candidate's positions in detail. Forced to undertake such a chore, many voters would simply sit on the sidelines.

Recruiting Candidates   Anxious to win elections, parties often recruit good, qualified citizens to run for office. By doing so, parties ensure that voters are given solid choices and that the winner is qualified to govern.

Providing a Screening Mechanism   On the other hand, parties often screen unqualified, perhaps even corrupt, would-be candidates. Receiving a party nomination is a critical step in winning a post in government. Parties deny endorsements to weak office-seekers, not wishing to be tarnished by their shortcomings. (Unfortunately, most would agree that this screening mechanism is far from perfect!)

Helping Candidates   Parties help candidates put their best foot forward to voters. In the past, assistance was primarily labor; party workers would spread the word about their party's candidates. More recently, parties provide numerous high-technology campaign services, such as polling, computerized targeting, radio and television productions, and direct mail. Of course, fund-raising has also become a huge part of how parties lend a hand.

Organizing a Complex Government   One can be struck by the complexity of the American government. There are three branches of the federal government, two houses in one of those branches, a massive bureaucracy, and a state/local sphere with an equally intricate system. This complexity was, by design, part of the checks and balances envisioned by the framers, but the outcome has been what some have called constitutional obstruction—the many ways the Constitution makes swift action difficult. Parties help bring the many pieces of the American system into united action. For example, throughout American history, political parties have helped bridge the gap between executives (presidents, governors, or mayors) and the legislature, and to bring bicameral legislatures into united action. Strong parties are no guarantee of overcoming constitutional obstruction, as we have seen throughout American history, but one can only imagine how much worse things would be without them.

Aggregating Interests   In their efforts to win elections, parties try to build coalitions of groups. Just as the American government is complex, so too is American society. Parties want to win elections, and citizen groups want a say in the policy process. The outcome of this mutually beneficial relationship is that individual and group interests are melded into a broad philosophy of governing. While many would find this hard to believe, political parties can often help to transform special interests into the public interest.

Educating Citizens   When each party moves to build support for its candidates, the by-product is voter education. Voters not only know more about the candidates because of party activities, but know more about government policies and the workings of the American system as well.

Providing an Accountability Mechanism   Because the American political system is so complex, it is difficult for voters to make accountability judgments. Whom should Americans blame if the economy turns sour or medical costs skyrocket? Who should get credit if crime rates fall or inflation stays in check? A growing inclination is to give the president credit or blame, but this is often an oversimplification. More likely, and indeed more accurately, voters have used parties to forge these assessments. If the party in power has done a good job, its candidates are voted back into office at all levels. If things have gotten worse, the other party is given a chance. This process works best when one party controls all parts of the government, called unified party control. Divided party control is when each party controls at least one part of the government. During most of American history, control has been unified, but during the past 30 years divided system has been the norm. Much more will be said on this issue later.

Performing Social Functions   Although less today than in the past, parties provide many Americans with civic/social opportunities. Party-sponsored potluck dinners, ice cream socials, and barbecues have been a common feature in many communities throughout the United States. These political events bring people out of their homes into the public realm—they help turn individuals into citizens.

Promoting Civic Participation   Either as part of their mission to build a fuller democratic system or simply in an effort to win the election at hand, parties promote political participation. This has included the cultivation of candidates, donors, volunteers, and of course voters on Election Day through get-out-the-vote efforts. Many studies have found that communities with strong political parties have higher levels of voting and political participation.[3]

THE COMPONENTS OF POLITICAL PARTIES

One of the most confusing aspects of political parties is precisely what the term implies. By the 1950s, political scientists developed what is called the tripartite view of parties. As suggested in Figure 4.1, political parties boast three interrelated elements: party-in-government (PIG), party-in-the-electorate (PIE), and party-as-organization (PO). Indeed, "PIG-PIE-PO"

---

[3]See, for example, Frendreis, John P., James L. Gibson, and Laura L. Vertz, "Electoral Relevance of Local Party Organizations," *American Political Science Review*, 1990, 84: 225–235.

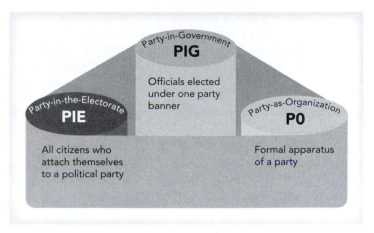

FIGURE 4.1 The Three Interrelated Elements of Political Parties

became the mantra of an entire generation of party scholars. This is often referred to as the "tripod" model of political parties in the United States.

Party-in-government refers to officials elected under a particular party banner. All the Republicans in the House of Representatives, for example, make up one piece of the GOP (Grand Old Party) PIG. They call themselves the House Republican Conference. If they have a majority in the chamber, their leader is the Speaker of the House; if not, he or she is the minority leader. Other segments of the Republican PIG include the Republicans in the Senate and the president when he (or she) is a member of the GOP. There are also sub-branches of the national PIG, such as governors, state-level elected officials, municipal officials, and so on. There is also a "Republican Governors Association." The Democrats in the House of Representatives call themselves the House Democratic Caucus. This structure extends all the way down to municipal government. For example, all of the Democrats in the Buffalo City Council consider themselves more or less part of the same group.

Although all the elected members of a party consider themselves, broadly speaking, part of the same "team," official structures are office-specific. For instance, there is an actual Senate Democratic Caucus and a House Democratic Caucus—they meet, debate, plan strategy, and vote—but there is no "Congressional Democratic Caucus."

The American system is rather unique in that PIG structures are weak. In many other democracies, there is an expectation that elected officials will vote with their parties on most matters. Dissenters, or those who vote with the opposition party on issues, are rare. At times, there is a great deal of pressure designed to force officials to "stay in line." In the American system, however, party leaders *hope* that members vote with the party, but the tradition is that elected officials can stray without serious repercussion. To be sure, most *voters* in America look down upon "party politics" and applaud their elected official's "independence." One should keep in mind that the single-best predictor of how a legislator will vote on any given bill is his or her party affiliation. Most elected officials vote with their parties most of the time, but in the American political system, a degree of autonomy is both expected and accepted.

There are many ways to measure the extent to which legislators stick with their parties, and the most common is called party unity scores. This is the percentage of votes on legislation in which a majority of Republicans oppose a majority of Democrats, for example. It is a measure that can be used to describe the partisan nature of any legislative body, including Congress, state legislatures, county legislatures, and city councils. Regarding Congress, party unity scores have shifted over time. A low point was the middle decades of the 20th century when the Democrats controlled Congress, but their caucus was made up of an awkward mix of northeastern liberals and Southern conservatives—the latter being dubbed boll weevils. The two wings of the Democratic Party disagreed passionately on many issues, especially civil rights legislation, leading unit scores to drop into the 30-percent range. By the 1990s, the Republican Party in the South had become significant, making it a more comfortable home for conservative politicians. Today, most federal legislators from the South are Republicans, and party unity scores are much higher, as noted in Figure 4.2.

Party-in-the-electorate refers to those who attach themselves to a particular party. When an average citizen says that he or she is a "Democrat," a "Republican," a "Green," or a "Libertarian," that person is acknowledging membership in a PIE.[4]

PIE is an ambiguous concept and the source of much scholarly debate. Some suggest that one's attitude, or his or her party identification (ID), is enough to consider him or her partisan. Party ID is the deep-seated feeling that a particular party best represents one's interests and outlook toward government and society. For example, if a citizen suggests to a pollster that he or she thinks of himself as a "strong Republican," this person would be considered part of the PIE. Most assessments of PIE in America rely upon such attitudinal measures—the most common is a 7-point scale where "strong Democrat" and "strong Republican" are at the ends of the scale, and true "independents" are at the "4" mark. Using such a measure, social scientists estimate that about 70 percent of Americans consider themselves partisan. As Figure 4.3 suggests, this percentage has dropped a good bit since the 1950s. Figure 4.4 takes a look at party identification using a three point scale— Democratic, Republican, and Independent. Here about 60 percent consider themselves partisan.

Other social scientists suggest that one's *behavior* is more important than his or her attitude when it comes to determining partisanship. If a person votes for Democrats most of the time, then perhaps this person should be tagged a "Democrat" regardless of what he or she might tell a pollster. Straight-ticket voters are those who support candidates of the same party in each election, and in one election after another. Voters who switch back and forth between the parties on Election Day, or from one election to the next, are called split-ticket voters. They might vote for the Republican gubernatorial candidate, the Democratic candidate for the House of Representatives, and the Green Party candidate for mayor. Voting behavior of this sort would suggest that the citizen is a non-partisan, or what we often call an independent. (Contrary to what many believe, as of yet there is no official "independent party.") As noted in Figure 4.5, the number of split-ticket voters has also grown, although there has been a slight decline in recent elections. This is another indicator that the number of hardcore partisans in the electorate is shrinking.

---

[4]White and Shea, *New Party Politics*, 20.

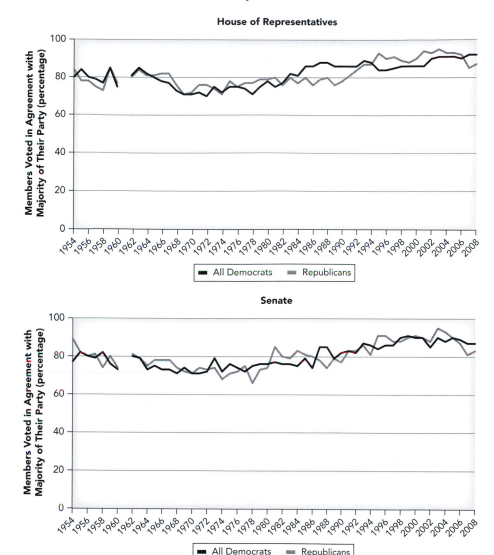

FIGURE 4.2 Party Unity in Congressional Voting
Source: http://www.brookings.edu/governance/govwatch/party_unity/party_unity_house
.aspx Reprinted by permission of Gallup, Inc.

For those who consider themselves true partisans, the impact of this alle-
giance on their vote choice is significant. Those who see themselves as a "strong
Republican" or a "strong Democrat" nearly always vote with their party on Election
Day. Conversely, very few strong partisans "defect," and when they do so, it is usu-
ally caused by a powerful short-term force, such as a war or the state the economy.
Generally they return to their parties in the next election.

Another possibility to measure PIE would be to rely on official voter registration lists. Is the voter enrolled at his or her local board of elections with a particular

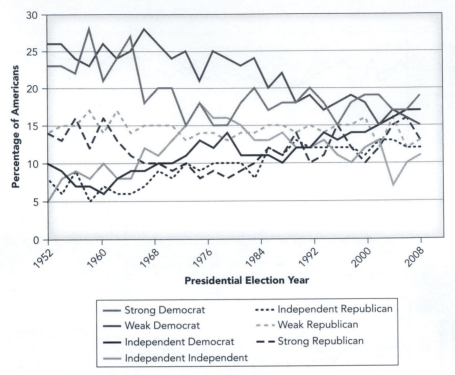

Presidential Election Year

—— Strong Democrat	···· Independent Republican
—— Weak Democrat	— - Weak Republican
—— Independent Democrat	— — Strong Republican
—— Independent Independent	

FIGURE 4.3 Seven-Point Partisanship Scale 1952–2008

Question Text: "Generally speaking, do you usually think of yourself as a Republican, a Democrat, an independent, or other?" (If Republican or Democrat) "Would you call yourself a strong (Republican/Democrat) or a not very strong (Republican/Democrat)?" (If independent or Other [1966 and later: OR NO PREFERENCE]) "Do you think of yourself as closer to the Republican or Democratic Party?" Party Identification Seven-Point Scale 1952–2008.

Source: The American National Election Studies. Accessed at: http://www.electionstudies.org/ nesguide/toptable/tab2a_1.htm

Note: (a) In 1966, "don't know" was combined with apolitical; in all other years, "don't know" is excluded as missing data. (b) The American National Election Studies did not conduct a time series study in 1996.

party? Party enrollment, a legalistic approach to measuring PIE, makes some sense, except that many register with a party when they become voting age, only to change their attitudes and voting habits over time. Some might head off to their local board of elections to change their registration, but most would probably not.

Another possibility is that true membership in PIE comes from an active involvement with a party. There are two possibilities here: voting in primary elections and helping parties undertake activities. Primaries are elections that allow citizens to select party nominees. Each of the candidates on a primary election ballot is vying for the party's nomination, the privilege of representing the party in the general election in November. There are many ways to conduct primary elections, which are discussed in the Chapter 6, but the point here is that it is still another concrete way of deciding who is a member of a party. Not surprisingly, the

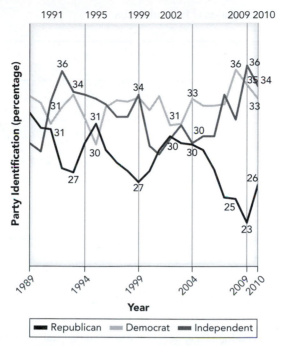

FIGURE 4.4 Party Identification Using 3-Point Scale

Source: From *Trends in Political Values and Core Attitudes: 1987–2009, Independents Take Center Stage in Obama Era* (Washington, DC: Pew Research Center for the People and the Press, May 21, 2009), p. 12. Accessed at: http://people-press.org/reports/pdf/517.pdf. Reprinted with permission. 2010 update from http://people-press.org/reports/questionnaires/645.pdf

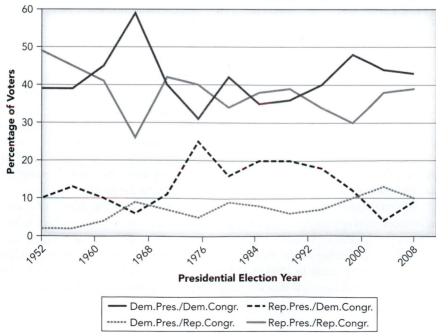

FIGURE 4.5 Split-Ticket Voting Presidential/Congressional 1952–2008

Source: The American National Election Studies. Accessed at: http://www.electionstudies.org/nesguide/toptable/tab9b_2.htm

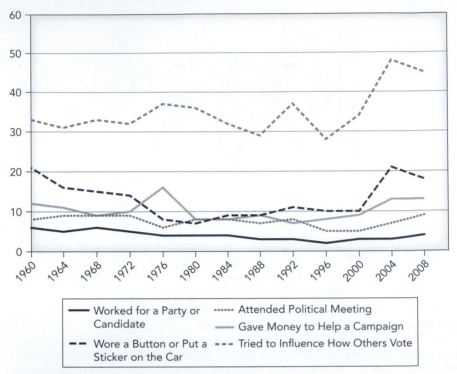

FIGURE 4.6 Campaign Participation, 1960–2008

Source: The American National Election Studies. "Political Involvement and Participation in Politics: Campaign Participation." Tables 6.B.1–6.B.5. Accessed at: www.electionstudies .org/nesguide/gd-index.htm#9

number of citizens participating in primary elections has also shrunk over the years. In 2008, for example, a year characterized by a long, hard-fought presidential nomination contest, less than 20 percent of the electorate came to the polls to pick party nominees.

The second way citizens can be active with a party is by helping it undertake activities. This would be the most rigorous way of deciding which citizens are in a PIE, as only about 5 percent of Americans either give money or help parties undertake grassroots functions. Figure 4.6 shows two measures of direct party involvement over time: attending party functions and contributing money to the party.

We might also choose to measure the concept of PIE as the degree of connection between average citizens and the parties. Data indicate that a shrinking number of Americans appear anxious to build an emotional connection to a political party. For example, according to the Pew Research Center, the number of independents increased from 32 percent in 2008 to 34 percent in 2010, as noted in Figure 4.4.[5] One explanation of this change is that the parties have somehow angered voters, and the

[5]The Pew Research Center for the People and the Press, "Trends in Political Values and Core Attitudes: 1987–2009" (May 21, 2009). Accessed at: http://people-press.org/reports/pdf/517.pdf

withdrawal is some sort of backlash. More likely is that a growing number of new voters are simply indifferent to parties. Political independence, once thought of as a sign of apathy and ignorance, has become a virtue.

Party-as-organization refers to the formal apparatus of the party, including party headquarters, offices, and leaders. It is the official bureaucracy of the party, and it is found in the form of "committees" in every state and in nearly every community in the nation. If one goes to the Internet and looks up "Republican Party" or "Democratic Party," a local number and address can be found in most instances.

POs exist at each of the layers of the American political system. At the national level, there are the Democratic National Committee and the Republican National Committee. Each state has both a Republican Party and a Democratic Party. There is an Indiana Democratic Party, a New York State Democratic Committee, an Arizona Democratic Party, a Republican Party of Texas, and a California Republican Party, for instance. Much the same can be found at the county and municipal levels; there is a Crawford County Republican Committee in Western Pennsylvania and a Farmington Democratic Town Committee in Massachusetts. At the very bottom of the structure, one occasionally finds ward or precinct organizations. The Chicago Democratic Committee is comprised of a mass of different precinct organizations.

Many casual observers of party politics believe that a formal hierarchy exists between the layers—that the national parties control the state parties and that the state organizations dictate orders to the county/municipal committees. This is not the case. A somewhat unique aspect of the American parties is that, while there is a good bit of interaction between layers of the system, most of it centering on the sharing of resources, few commands or orders are thrust upon lower-level committees. For the most part, party organizations at all levels of the system operate as semi-autonomous units. The same is true with regard to horizontal linkages; county organizations in a state might touch base occasionally, but for the most part they go it alone.

Party activities and functions are conducted by the party organizations through activists—sometimes called party hacks. In most cases, these are volunteers, giving their time and efforts because they believe in the party's mission (its approach to government). Some see their efforts helping at some point in the future with perhaps a job or a chance to run for office, or they simply enjoy the social aspects of involvement. National parties—and a growing number of state party committees—use a mix of volunteers and paid staffers. Some of the larger county and city committees do much the same, but most at the municipal level are purely amateur (nonpaid).

Throughout much of American history, some party organizations took on a rather distinctive, aggressive form. These units, called party machines, were especially strong in larger cities around the turn of the 20th century, such as in New York City, Boston, Chicago, Philadelphia, and Kansas City. The leader of a machine was referred to as "the boss." Party machines carried a double-edge sword: On the one hand, their strong desire to win elections to control patronage jobs, city contracts, and regulations, coupled with an efficient, military-like organization, had the effect of bringing otherwise disenfranchised citizens into the process. This was particularly important for newly arrived immigrants, of which there was a flood in the second half of the 19th century. In exchange for their help on Election Day, party bosses and their machines provided them a social safety net. If someone needed a job, if some citizens were evicted from their apartments and needed another place to live, if someone needed a loan to pay for a funeral, or if some cash was needed to post bond for a "confused" son, the machine would often lend a hand. In exchange for this help, voters would support the party's slate of candidates on Election Day. To many—including many of the residents of these cities—machines created a demo-cratic accountability mechanism: If the machine failed to take care of the citizens of the community, that party was simply voted out of office and a new group was given a chance.

On the other hand, a great deal of corruption was thrown into the mix of machine politics. Election fraud was rampant. One of the last of the big city bosses, Richard Daley of Chicago would proclaim to his workers on Election Day, with only a veneer of levity, that they should "vote early and vote often."[6] As the machines controlled the reins of government, they also rigged the workings of the government to suit their political needs and to line their own pockets. For example, in many cities, public employees were required to kick back a portion of their pay to the machine—generally about 2 or 3 percent. The humanitarian efforts of the party machines extended only to supporters and to those who were able to vote. Many minority groups, namely African-Americans, did not benefit from machine assistance because these groups were of no use to party machines, given that most could not vote.

For these reasons and others, a series of reforms were ushered in at the end of the 19th century, collectively called the Progressive Movement, as discussed in Chapter 2. This movement was successful in bringing about big changes in the workings of party machines: The civil service robbed machines of patronage (jobs to hand out to loyal sup-porters), the secret ballot removed the machines' control of people's votes on Election Day, and the direct primary stripped their ability to control nominations. Local party organizations survived these changes, but machines faced overwhelming challenges and slowly faded from the American scene.

Unlike the decline with regard to individual partisanship, the fate of party organizations at the dawn of the 21st century is muddled. State and national party organizations seem to be doing well; they have benefited from a massive influx of campaign contributions and have more equipment and staff and better facilities than at any other point in American history. But the picture is much different at the local level. Local party organizations, what two scholars call the "mom and pop shops of the party system,"[7] are finding it difficult to survive. This is true mostly because they rely on volunteers. As individuals seem less interested in partisan politics, they are even less interested in putting in a few hours at the party headquarters. Whereas a few decades ago many local committees were vibrant, dynamic organizations, today this would be the exception. America has entered a "baseless" party system— an era where parties are strong at the national and state level, but decrepit at the community level.[8]

---

[6]Ibid., 50.
[7]Ibid., Chapter 7.
[8]Ibid., Conclusion.

Has the Tripod Outlived Its Usefulness?

Fifty years ago, when the tripod view of parties was introduced, it seemed to make perfect sense. There was a tight connection between each of the components. Party organizations were responsible for picking nominees, and selected candidates ran in the general election with their party's help. Once in office, these elected officials paid close attention to the wishes of the local parties, or else risked abandonment in the next election. Through all this work at the local level, party organizations helped to build a strong attachment among average citizens to the parties. It was a tight, complete package. But today, the picture is more complicated. Local party organizations are withering at the same time state and national units are thriving. Fewer voters consider themselves partisan than in the past, but elected officials seem quite interested in talking about their independence while back home, while sticking to the party line when at the capital. Given these changes, many have begun to question the usefulness of the tripod. Perhaps it is an outdated concept. This issue will be debated for some time to come, but for our concerns, it is important to recognize that "political party" has different components in the United States and that the relationship between these parts is dynamic.

THE HISTORY OF PARTIES IN AMERICA

As with nearly every aspect of the American political system, the nature of the party system has changed over time. Following is a review of four periods in American history. Two points will emerge from this exploration: First, from nearly the beginning, political parties have been the centerpiece of the American electoral process. Second, the story of parties in the United States continues to unfold; what they look like, what functions they serve, and how they fit in the electoral pathway today will likely be much different in the years ahead.

Phase I: The Arrival of Parties in America (1792 to 1800)

James Madison warned his fellow Americans about the dangers of party-like organizations, which he called "factions," in "The Federalist No. 10." "The friend of popular government," wrote Madison, "never finds himself so much alarmed for their character and fate as when he contemplates their propensity for this dangerous vice."[9] A few years later, George Washington suggested much the same. In his famous "farewell address," Washington proclaimed: "Let me . . . warn you in the most solemn manner against the baneful effects of the spirit of party . . . It is truly [Americans'] worst enemy."[10] Many other statesmen and early political thinkers drew a similar word of caution: Political parties were the bane of democratic systems.

What drove these apprehensions? Prior to this period, political systems that allowed average citizens the opportunity to speak out and organize invariably

---

[9]Alexander Hamilton, James Madison, and John Jay, *The Federalist Papers*, with introduction by Clinton Rossiter (New York: Signet, 1961), 77.

[10]As cited in Paul M. Angle, *In These Words* (New York: Rand McNally, 1954), 140–141.

degenerated into rival groups, each vying for their own interests. Consideration of the "whole" came second to consideration of the "self." This was particularly likely in early America, given that a national identity—and indeed a "national" citizenship—would not develop until much later. (Many have suggested that this national identity was forged by the Civil War.) The freedom to speak one's mind and to come together with like-minded citizens made it even more likely that factions or parties would emerge.

The framers of the American political system were students of the Enlightenment—a 17th-century European intellectual movement that stressed the importance of human intellect and reason in answering all questions. They put a premium on discussion, debate, and deliberation in sorting out issues. Concerning public policy, the framers believed that with due time and careful deliberation, the just or correct answer would emerge, but a system wrapped in party politics would likely lead to prolonged dispute and in the end stalemate. In short, they believed that parties were antithetical to reason and careful deliberation.

Even so, within a decade after the adoption of the Constitution, parties burst on the American political scene. Wishing to fill his cabinet with the best and the brightest of the day, George Washington selected Thomas Jefferson for secretary of state and Alexander Hamilton as Treasury secretary. Both men were distinguished and intelligent, and each had impressive Revolutionary War credentials (deemed important for the legitimacy of the new government). The problem, nevertheless, was that Hamilton and Jefferson passionately disagreed about the future of the nation. Jefferson believed that America's hope lay in small, agriculture-based communities. He had faith in ordinary citizens, particularly the farmer: "Those who labor in the earth are the chosen people of God, if ever He had a chosen people."[11] He also distrusted a strong national government. Hamilton, on the other hand, believed that the future of the nation lay in the development of vibrant urban centers, based on a strong manufacturing sector. He was a capitalist through and through and believed that a strong central government was the best mechanism to ensure long-term economic growth. Unlike Jefferson, Hamilton was suspicious of average citizens and believed that it would be best for elites to run the government.

The two men got along in Washington's cabinet for a while, but it was just a matter of time until their divergent philosophies would spill over into heated debate. The spark was a plan that Hamilton put forward to kick-start the nation's economy. Among other things, Hamilton called for the full payment of wartime debt—called full assumption. To finance the Revolutionary War, the national government was lent money by foreign nations and states. Wealthy individuals had bought war bonds because they believed in the revolt against King George III and assumed that if they were lucky the government would pay back some of the money at a later time. Few expected to be paid back in full. Hamilton argued that by helping those who had lent a hand during the Revolution, confidence in the new national government would build, and nearly $80 million would be put in the hands of those likely to invest in American commerce.

---

[11]As cited in White and Shea, *New Party Politics*, 28.

A second component of Hamilton's plan was a heavy national investment in infrastructure improvements—for instance, in roads, bridges, ports, and canals. He believed that doing so would increase the flow of goods and services, thus leading to a general rise in living standards. But, of course, this too would require a great deal of national government resources.[12]

To pay for these two projects, Hamilton proposed a tax on distilled spirits—which became known as the Whiskey Tax. This was not a sales tax, but rather an excise tax, meaning a levy on the production of the product. This was a heavy tax as well—eight cents per gallon. Given that a gallon of liquor cost about 32 cents in those days, this tax represented a 25-percent jump.[13] More controversial was that most whiskey producers were farmers in the South and West, so to many, the plan reeked of northeastern industrial elites placing the burden of "economic development" on the backs of the working poor.

Opposition to Hamilton's plans grew, with the leading critic being none other than Thomas Jefferson. Hamilton and Jefferson squared off on a daily basis, leading Washington to comment that the two went at it "like two cocks"[14] in a pen during cabinet meetings. Soon the battle extended beyond Washington's inner circle to the halls of Congress and to newspapers across the nation. Lines were being drawn, sides were being taken, and the public was slowly becoming "partisan."

Hamilton's plans passed through Congress. In a surprise move, Jefferson actually endorsed the plan in exchange for Hamilton's support in moving the nation's capital from New York to a small piece of land on the Potomac River in Virginia. But the controversy surrounding the plan continued to simmer in the hinterlands. In 1794, shortly after the plan's approval, a group of farmers in western Pennsylvania refused to pay the tax. Federal troops were sent to collect but they were met with armed resistance. This event, called the Whiskey Rebellion, was one of the first tests of the rule of national law in the states. Washington decided to confront the farmers head-on. In September of 1794, Washington issued a proclamation ordering the militia to assemble and march against the insurgents:

> Every form of conciliation not inconsistent with the being of Government, has been adopted without effect . . . [and] Government is set at defiance, the contest being whether a small portion of the United States shall dictate to the whole union, and at the expense of those, who desire peace, indulge a desperate ambition; Now therefore I, George Washington, . . . deploring that the American name should be sullied by the outrages of citizens on their own Government; . . . but resolved . . . to reduce the refractory to a due subordination to the law; Do Hereby declare . . . that a force . . . adequate to the exigency, is already in motion to the scene of disaffection; . . . And I do, moreover, exhort all individuals, officers, and bodies of men, to

---

[12]White and Shea, *New Party Politics*, 37–38.

[13]Ibid.

[14]Profiles of U.S. Presidents. "George Washington—First Term." Accessed at: http://people-press.org/reports/pdf/517.pdf

contemplate with abhorrence the measures leading directly or indirectly to those crimes, which produce this resort to military coercion.[15]

Over 150 prisoners were taken by federal troops, but all were later pardoned by Washington.

A second issue that helped solidify the partisans behind Jefferson and Hamilton was the French Revolution in 1793. Many, including Jefferson, thought the American government owed the French revolutionaries its support. It was, after all, a struggle for self-rule and the expulsion of aristocracy—precisely what had transpired on American soil a few years earlier. Indeed, Thomas Paine, the great revolutionary pamphleteer, was so inspired by these events that he moved to France to help the revolutionary forces. But to Hamilton and his colleagues, the French Revolution signaled the emergence of anarchy and mob rule. When the violence spread into a war with Britain, Hamilton argued that America should support England. Washington sought to keep America out of the conflict, to remain neutral. He sent James Monroe to Paris and John Jay to London to negotiate neutrality treaties. But when Jay returned with an agreement that clearly supported Britain, a firestorm erupted. The debate over the Jay Treaty pitted Jefferson and his followers, who opposed it, against Hamilton and his group, who favored its ratification.[16]

It is hard to overstate the extent to which these issues—Hamilton's economic policies and the Jay Treaty—stirred public emotions. These were huge issues and there seemed little room for compromise, especially on the Jay Treaty. By the election of 1796, Jefferson had bolted from Washington's cabinet and thrown his hat into the ring for the presidency. Washington had decided to retire, leaving the position open to Vice President John Adams, who sided with Hamilton on policy matters. Adams edged out Jefferson on Election Day. A glitch in the Constitution outlining the electoral college noted that the second place candidate would become vice president, meaning that Jefferson was obligated to serve as the second-in-charge—an awkward arrangement, to be sure. (This provision was changed in 1804 with the passage of the Twelfth Amendment, mandating that presidential and vice presidential candidates run as a team.)

Animosity between the two groups got even worse during Adams's administration when, in an effort to stifle criticism of his policies, Adams pushed through Congress the Alien and Sedition Acts in 1798. These laws made it a crime to denounce the federal government, made it more difficult to become a naturalized citizen, and made it much easier for the federal government to deport outspoken, critical aliens.[17] To Jefferson and his colleagues, it was an all-too-clear bit of evidence that Adams, Hamilton, and the rest of their followers had abandoned the cause of the Revolution.

The response was to organize at the community level for the next election in 1800. In other words, the plan was to create party organizations to rally support for Jefferson and his party, now called the Democratic-Republicans. (Oddly, this was the

---

[15]National Endowment for the Humanities Endowment, "Washington and the Whiskey Rebellion." Retrieved February 2003 from http://edsitement.neh.fed.us/view_lesson_plan.asp?ID=311

[16]White and Shea, *New Party Politics*, 37–39.

[17]Jay M. Shafritz, *The Dorsey Dictionary of American Government and Politics* (Chicago: Dorsey, 1988), 17.

beginning of today's Democratic Party.) Adams and Hamilton responded by creating the Federalist Party, and by also organizing at the local level. (One should not confuse the Federalist Party with the supporters of the Constitution in 1789, the Federalists.) One prominent scholar of American history dubbed this period the "great consolidation"; the period when parties finally emerged in America.[18]

Jefferson won the election of 1800 narrowly, and his Republican colleagues stormed into the majority of both houses in Congress. Jefferson proclaimed his success the "second revolution." The direction of public policy changed, and those who had been convicted under the Alien and Sedition Acts were pardoned. The election of 1800 also proved that parties could face each other in heated debate, but then let voters decide. The election marked the first time that one group replaced another group in control of government peacefully. Not only were parties not dangerous, as many speculated, but they seemed to exemplify precisely what citizens might want in a democratic system: a mechanism for airing differences of opinion regarding the proper course of government and then mobilizing support behind sets of candidates.

Finally, the election of 1800 galvanized the idea of legitimate opposition. This is the belief that in a democratic society the public is well served by organized opposition to the group in power. It is yet another check in the American system. As noted by one scholar, "The principle of uncontested elections never was accepted in the United States . . . The Republic was born as a result of political opposition, and with minor deviations from this principle, it was an orientation that was persistently maintained and exercised in the period up to 1800."[19]

Phase II: The Heyday Period (1828 to 1900)

The dispute over political parties was settled with the election of 1800. Even James Madison, who had written about the bane of "factions" in *The Federalist Papers*, embraced parties in his later years.[20] Ironically, while there now seemed little to fear from political parties, the nation moved into a period of one-party politics, often referred to as the Era of Good Feelings. Jefferson was anxious to mend fences and to calm anxieties. The Federalists faded from the scene; from 1804 to 1820, the Republicans won between 53 and 92 percent of the electoral college votes, and between 53 and 92 percent of the seats in Congress.[21]

The tranquility was shattered with the alleged Corrupt Deal of 1824. The Federalists had disappeared in Congress, but within the Republican ranks, blocks of legislators had developed. By 1824, five Republican candidates threw their hats into the ring for president: Henry Clay, Speaker of the House; John C. Calhoun, secretary of war; John Quincy Adams, son of John Adams and former secretary of state; William Crawford, former Treasury secretary; and Andrew Jackson, hero of the Battle of New Orleans during the War of 1812. On Election Day, Jackson carried more votes

---

[18]William Nisbet Chambers, *Political Parties in a New Nation: The American Experience: 1776–1809* (New York: Oxford University Press, 1963), Ch. 5.

[19]Samuel J. Eldersveld, *Political Parties in American Society* (New York: Basic Books, 1982), 27.

[20]E. E. Schattschneider, Party *Government* (New York: Rinehart, 1942), 1.

[21]White and Shea, *New Party Politics*, 41.

than either of the other candidates, but did not receive a majority of electoral college votes. The election was turned over to the House of Representatives, pursuant to the Constitution, where most observers expected Jackson to carry the day given that he had won more votes and electors than either of the other candidates. But some believe a deal was made between second-place candidate John Quincy Adams and Henry Clay, who had come in fourth: Clay would use his powers as Speaker of the House to throw the election in Adam's favor if he would make Clay secretary of state—often considered the second-most important position in the federal government. Adams became president and shortly thereafter kept his promise to Clay.

The backlash from the deal spread across America, manifesting itself in two ways. First, the Democratic-Republicans were torn apart, leading to the creation of the Whig Party. Its leaders were Adams, Clay, and Calhoun. Their platform centered on states' rights, individual freedom, and lower taxes. The remaining Democratic-Republicans shortened their name to the Democratic Party—and their leaders were Jackson and New York politician Martin Van Buren. Second, Jackson, with Van Buren's advice, used local parties to rally opposition to Adams.

It was a rebirth of party politics, this time located at the community level. Party operatives spread the word that unless average citizens became involved, elite deals of this sort would be common. It was a call to the average citizen to stand up and exert his role in the political process. This emphasis on individual involvement ushered in a new era in electoral politics, what historians have called Jacksonian Democracy. This was a move toward egalitarian politics and social life. Politics *was* for the average person—not just the economic and social elite. Not surprisingly, Jackson won his rematch against Adams in 1828, and the percentage of the adult male population participating in 1828 was nearly four times higher than in 1824.[22]

The rage for electoral politics spread across the nation. Realizing the potential of average citizens to change the course of government, coupled with aggressive local party organizations that pushed, prodded, and pulled every male citizen into the process, individuals became political. Participation in elections reached record levels. Almost every aspect of social life centered on party politics and elections. Writing of the late 1830s, historian Joel Silbey notes, "For most Americans, politics was not a separate sphere divorced from their socioeconomic and personal concerns. Rather, politics was woven into the fabric of the society at all levels."[23] The reflections of European observers, such as Alexis de Tocqueville, Charles Dickens, and many others, suggested the same—as did levels of turnout during most of the 19th century, which often approached 85 percent. In brief, the 62-year period stretching from the 1820s to the 1890s can be dubbed the heyday of local party politics and popular electoral participation.

---

[22]George C. Edwards, III, and Stephen J. Wayne, *Presidential Leadership: Politics and Policy Making* (New York: St. Martin's, 1999), 61.

[23]Joel H. Silby "Beyond Realignment and Realignment Theory: American Political Eras, 1789–1989." In Byron Shafer, ed. *The End of Realignment? Interpreting American Electoral Eras* (Madison, WI: University of Wisconsin Press, 1991), 11.

The Civil War Disruption

Although local party politics was cemented in American political and social life, the lines of cleavage between the parties shifted during the midpoint of the 19th century. The most significant disruption was caused by the issue of slavery. It is fair to say that both the Whigs and the Democrats were anxious to avoid the slavery question. Competition between the two was fierce and neither party wanted to alienate their Southern or northeastern supporters. It was better to dodge the question altogether. "Northern abolitionists were often uncomfortably seated next to slave holders in presidential cabinets and in the halls of Congress."[24] But as new states were admitted to the Union, the slave question was thrust to the fore and the delicate balance was tested. Should these new states be free or should they be allowed slavery? The halls of Congress erupted in controversy. In 1846, the Wilmot Proviso, which prohibited slavery in areas acquired during the Mexican–American war, was introduced in Congress. It passed the House, where members from Free States held a majority, but failed in the Senate due to the Southern bloc. Both parties were split into factions. The Whigs were broken into the conscience Whigs, who opposed slavery, and the cotton Whigs who did not. The Democrats were divided along similar lines. The Kansas–Nebraska Bill was an attempt at finding a compromise: New states would decide for themselves whether or not to allow slavery—a concept dubbed popular sovereignty. But instead of satisfying each side, the measure added fuel to the fire. By 1854, a group of abolitionists from both of major parties met in Ripon, Wisconsin, to create a new political party: the Republican Party. One participant observed, "We came into the little meeting held in a schoolhouse Whigs, Free Soilers, and Democrats. We came out of it Republicans."[25]

For the next few elections, several political parties battled it out. Things came to a head in the election of 1860. Abraham Lincoln, the Republican nominee, was able to secure an electoral college victory by receiving a majority of votes in the more populous Northern states. He lost all of the mid-coast states and every Southern state. His nationwide popular vote total fell well short of a majority. This seemed to be the final straw for Southern states, and many soon seceded from the Union—leading to the Civil War. The election also restructured the party system. By 1864, the system had once again settled into two camps: the Republican Party, essentially the party of the North, and the Democratic Party, the party of the South and Midwest.

Phase III: The Party Decline Era (1900 to 1980)

The Industrial Revolution was an important phase in America's economic development, but it was also a dark era in American history. Economic prosperity for the owners and operators of factories came at the expense of workers. Colossal fortunes were being made by some, but most citizens found themselves working long hours in unsafe, unsanitary factories or sweatshops for minuscule wages. By the 1880s, a growing number of Americans—mainly middle class—set to work cleaning up the

---

[24]White and Shea, *New Party Politics*, 45.
[25]Ibid., 46.

political and economic system. This movement became known as the Progressive Movement, as noted earlier.

With regard to cleaning up corrupt politics, a number of changes were made: To strip political machines of their ability to use patronage jobs to fortify their hold on government, the merit system (also called the civil service system) was developed. To reduce the likelihood of pressure at polling places, the Australian ballot (or "secret ballot") was instituted. And to reduce the chance that party bosses would simply hand-pick nominees who would tow the party line, the direct primary was established. In this system, average members of the party—the rank and file—would cast a secret ballot on primary Election Day to pick the party's nominee. All told, these and many other reforms greatly reduced the potency of party machines.

Another blow to party bosses was disclosure of corruption in the popular press. "Muckraker" was a name given to investigative journalists who uncovered both political and economic misdeeds. "Newspapers, magazines, and books exposed evidence of abuse—from entire police departments in partnership with gangsters, to churches owning whole blocks of foul-smelling slums, to an entire U.S. Senate 'on the take.'"[26]

The effect of these new laws and the flurry of media coverage were devastating for party machines. The reins of government were slipping from machine hands, and the public's affinity for party politics was shaken. The Progressive Era marked a sea change in the place of party organizations in American politics. Party machines were still important institutions, especially for candidates who needed party volunteers to reach out to voters, but their heyday had come to a close.

THE RISE OF CANDIDATE-CENTERED POLITICS.   Public attitudes about political parties had grown especially sour by the late 1960s. This was a turbulent period in American history, and for many Americans, parties were "part of the problem." The number of Americans considering themselves partisan took a nose dive, and it seemed that America was headed toward a partyless age. David Broder's 1971 book *The Party's Over* seemed to capture the mood of the times.

On top of this—and perhaps partly fueling this change—candidates came to realize that parties were no longer necessary or even desirable. Historically, party workers were needed to bring the candidates' messages to the voters, but by the 1960s, television, radio, and direct mail could reach more voters in one single day than party operatives could contact in weeks. Party assistance also came with a price tag: dictates from the party boss and the perception that the candidate was a "pawn" of the party leaders. It became advantageous to run your own show and be seen as "independent minded." On top of all this, new-style campaign consultants (discussed later) burst on the scene in the 1960s. These operatives could be hired, and their allegiance would be solely to the candidate.

This phase in party history, referred to as the candidate-centered era, seemed to reverberate throughout the political system. As candidates pitched themselves as independent, voters saw little reason to hold to any notion of partisanship. Party

---

[26]Ibid., 66.

organizations lost even more sway, and as more citizens became "independent," voting cues were lost, leading to lower election turnout. Once in office, elected officials saw little reason to stick to the caucus, leading to less policy coherence and a less-efficient legislative process. Moreover, because of these changes, divided government has been the norm since 1968, rather than the exception. In 1968, voters selected a Republican president (Richard Nixon) and kept a Democratic Congress. Since then—over 40 years—America has had unified government for just 7 years. The precise ramification of this is a contentious topic in political science—with some suggesting significant problems and others being a bit more sanguine. At the very least, divided government represents a new, significant development in American politics—due in large measure to the rise of candidate-centered politics.

Phase IV: Organizational Resurgence

Candidate-centered politics changed the American political landscape, and many had come to believe that parties were fading from the scene. But if anything is true about political parties, it is that they are adaptive creatures, anxious to adjust when confronted with adverse conditions. National party operatives, at first mostly at the Republican National Committee, realized that they were quickly becoming irrelevant and that changes needed to be made. Instead of sharpening their relations with voters, however, the parties chose to expand their services to candidates. Parties became service-oriented, meaning that they chose to broaden activities to include a host of high-technology services to candidates. They developed, for example, computerized direct mail operations, in-house television and radio production studios, and sophisticated polling operations. This also meant hiring new professionals—their own new-style campaign consultants—and greatly expanding their facilities.

Without raising huge sums of money, the service-oriented approach would fail. So, beginning in the 1980s, both parties implemented massive fund-raising operations. Table 4.1 charts the rise in national party funds from the early 1960s to 2010. Even when adjusted for inflation, the pace of growth is staggering.

There have been significant ramifications of this change. For one, the parties seemed back on their feet, once again central players in elections. Books like *The Party Goes On*,[27] *The Party's Just Begun*,[28] and *The Parties Respond*[29] each told a tale of adaption and rebirth. One team of scholars suggested "the phoenix has risen from the ashes."[30] Even a quick tour of either party's national headquarters today would suggest parties are doing quite well—surely players in the electoral pathway of politics.

---

[27]Xandra Kayden and Eddie Mahe Jr., *The Party Goes On: The Persistence of the Two-Party System in the United States* (New York: Basic Books, 1985).

[28]Larry J. Sabato, *The Party's Just Begun: Shaping Political Parties for America's Future* (Glenview, IL: Scott, Foresman, 1988).

[29]L. Sandy Maisel, ed., *The Parties Respond: Changes in the American Party System* (Boulder, CO: Westview, 1990).

[30]Kayden and Mahe, *The Party Goes On*, 3.

TABLE 4.1	Party Finances		
Political Party	Election Cycle	Amount Spent ($)	Difference from Previous Year ($)
Democrat	2000	510,680,670	
	2002	459,331,677	−51,348,993
	2004	710,416,993	251,085,316
	2006	606,366,662	−104,050,331
	2008	956,049,411	349,682,749
	2010	736,953,436	−219,095,975
Republican	2000	679,776,825	
	2002	685,951,827	6,175,002
	2004	875,704,006	189,752,179
	2006	723,583,118	−152,120,888
	2008	792,186,627	68,603,509
	2010	618,304,450	−173,882,177

Source: Open Secrets. Political Parties page.
Accessed at: http://www.opensecrets.org/parties/index.php

On the other hand, there have been negative reverberations. Sophisticated services require ever more resources, and in an effort to get around campaign finance laws (discussed in Chapter 9), new loopholes were being discovered each year, leading to cynicism among voters. At precisely the same time that party organizations are regaining their footing, party identification has declined, and although the national parties have done well during this period, the revitalization has not stretched to the local, grassroots level. Finally, while many candidates appreciate the help they get, the parties have realized that they can get more mileage out of targeting their efforts to only a handful of races. Those candidates selected as part of this group are, of course, pleased, but those not chosen for help become bitter. In short, the revitalization of the national party committees has been significant, but it has also transformed the nature of the party system.

Conclusion

More will be said of party politics in America in Chapters 5 and 6. Here we have reviewed a few key definitions, such as what distinguishes parties from other organizations, and how we might think of the various components of parties. Moreover, we have charted the history of parties in America, dividing this material into periods.

At the dawn of the American experiment, most had assumed that any organization designed to capture control of government would be adverse to the interests of the whole. James Madison suggested as much in *The Federalist Papers*, and George Washington was explicit in his warnings about parties in his farewell address. But what these great men—and many others—failed to recognize is that parties or, at the very least, similar electoral organizations are inevitable in any free society. Whether they emerge in response to a desire to change public policy or simply to grab control of the reins of office is unclear. What seems elementary, nevertheless, is that they will emerge. Moreover, the services they can provide enhance the democratic process. Parties can educate voters, aggregate interests, afford a check on the ruling elite, mobilize opposition and, in short, turn private citizens into public beings. There is more to party politics than mere "partisan wrangling."

There is not a modern democracy that does not boast political parties. Indeed, some time ago, a prominent political scientist went so far as to suggest, "It should be flatly stated that political parties created democracy and that modern democracy is unthinkable save in terms of political parties."[31] While some might suggest this a bit of an overstatement, few would dispute that parties have been and will continue be an integral part of the election process for years to come. What these structures look like and what they seek to accomplish in the 21st century is, however, anyone's guess.

Critical Thinking

1. Name some key functions of political parties. Is democracy well served by these structures or are they a hindrance? Do parties help empower average citizens?
2. What is the tripartite view of political parties? Has this model become outdated? If so, why?
3. How did parties become such an important part of American politics, especially given the many fears of the framers of the American system?
4. Do you think America would be better off if politicians shunned party labels—would non-partisan legislature better represent the wishes of Americans?
5. It has been said that individual party identification is a rational cognitive shortcut. What do you think this implies?

On the Web

If you are interested in viewing the platforms of the two major political parties, check out www .democrats.org, or www.gop.com. For third-party information, see the "On the Web" section following Chapter 5.

---

[31]Schattschneider, *Party Government*, 1.

CHAPTER
5

Minor Parties in the United States

The previous chapter (Chapter 4) began our discussion of party politics. For most Americans, parties come in two brands: Democratic and Republican. The two-party model simply makes sense to many Americans. It is an aspect of the American electoral system that seems deeply rooted in the American psyche. As will be seen later, one of the reasons why the two-party model appears fixed is simply the power of momentum; America has a two-party system because it seems like it has always had a two-party system. At the same time, however, a shrinking number of Americans appear excited about the two major parties. A dramatic shake-up does not seem on the immediate horizon, but polling data point to changing attitudes toward minor parties, as noted in Table 5.1.

If Americans seem to want more choices, why do minor parties languish in the American political setting? Has there ever been a period in American history when minor parties played a significant role in the electoral process? Do not most other democratic

| TABLE 5.1 | Support for a Viable Third Party 1944–2010 |

	Roper	Gallup	USORC	CNN/USA Today	Rasmussen	Gallup
Date of poll	8/44	9/68	11/81	10/94	5/07	9/10
Usually satisfied, two parties are adequate	78%	67%	53%	40%	23%	35%
Like to see a strong new party	14%	27%	43%	53%	58%	58%
Other/don't know/no opinion	8%	6%	4%	4%	19%	7%
Sample size (N)	5,131	1,500	1,005	1,007	1,000	1,021

Source: Christian Collet, "Third Parties and Two-Party System." *Public Opinion Quarterly*, Vol. 60 (1996): 431–449.

Jeffrey Jones, "Americans Renew Call for Third Party." *Gallup.com*, September 2010. Accessed at: www.gallup.com/poll/143051/americans-renew-call-third-party.aspx

political systems rely upon a multi-party model? If so, why is America unique? This chapter confronts what one might call the "minor party paradox": You will soon read that while there may be support for a multi-party system in the United States, the persistence of a two-party model is quite likely. The chapter begins with the many barriers to minor party success and moves to a brief history of minor parties in American elections. The chapter ends with speculation regarding the future of minor parties.

BARRIERS TO MINOR PARTY SUCCESS

The barriers to minor party success in the United States can be divided into two categories: institutional and attitudinal, as noted in Figure 5.1.

Institutional Barriers

Institutional barriers refer to legal components created by statute, court decision, or the Constitution. The most significant of these is the single-member district, first-past-the-post system used in legislative elections. In the American model, legislative

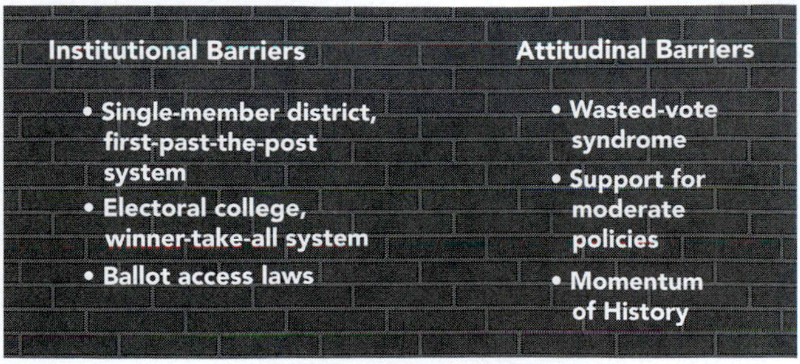

Institutional Barriers	Attitudinal Barriers
• Single-member district, first-past-the-post system	• Wasted-vote syndrome
• Electoral college, winner-take-all system	• Support for moderate policies
• Ballot access laws	• Momentum of History

FIGURE 5.1 Existing Barriers to Minor-Party Success

districts boast only one legislator—one elected official—and this person is sent to office by simply receiving more votes than any other candidate. This process alone propels a two-party model, and here is how: One might imagine, for instance, that in the first election, candidates from three parties vie for the office. One candidate nets 45 percent of the vote and the others about 27 percent each. Because the first candidate received more votes than the others, and because only one person can represent the district, the person who got 45 percent is sent to Washington (or to the state capital). The defeated parties get nothing for their efforts. This process might continue for a few elections, but eventually, operatives of the two defeated parties will consider joining forces—if they are not too ideologically far apart. After all, their combined strength is greater than the other party's, so by working together they can win. A party might be ideologically pure and refuse to merge with another, but eventually losing gets old and the inclination to join forces with the party closest to its ideology becomes irresistible. This is called Duverger's law after the famous French sociologist Maurice Duverger who wrote about this in the 1950s. In many European systems, legislative districts are multi-member and proportional (proportional representation). This means that if a party receives 30 percent of a district's vote and the district sends three legislators to parliament, the party gets one seat. So in that system, the party gets a prize for its efforts, but in the American model, it would get nothing.

An example in contemporary politics would be the Green Party of North America. This left-leaning, environmentally centered party has been plugging along in American politics for some time with little success at the ballot box. It might continue to slog through elections and build its grassroots organizations, but political groups need occasional successes to retain members. In the 2000 presidential election, the Greens nominated consumer rights activist Ralph Nader as their candidate. Nader netted less than 3 percent of the popular vote, which is bad enough, but the real rub was that Nader's support seems to have tipped the scales in favor of the Republican, George W. Bush. Because Al Gore, the Democrat, lost by only a fraction of votes in several states, and by a fraction of electoral college votes overall, it is entirely possible that he would have become president if Nader had withdrawn from the contest. Although Nader did so unintentionally, writes Harvard professor Barry C. Burden, he "nonetheless played a pivotal role in determining who would become president following the 2000 election."[1] To put it another way, many suggest that support for Nader helped elect the Republican—the candidate farthest away from the beliefs of the Greens. To be fair, many Greens argue that Gore lost the election for reasons other than their support for Nader.

The third-party vote share has exceeded the winning candidate's margin of victory in several elections in the last century. While analysts disagree on the precise effects of these so-called election spoilers, it is hardly beyond reason to suggest that they, too, played roles in shaping election outcomes. Figure 5.2 compares winning margins of victory and third-party vote shares from 1900 to 2008; during that period, third parties' vote shares exceeded the winner's margin of victory eight times.

---

[1] Barry C. Burden, "Ralph Nader's Campaign Strategy in the 2000 U.S. Presidential Election," *American Political Research*, Vol. 33 (2005), 672–699.

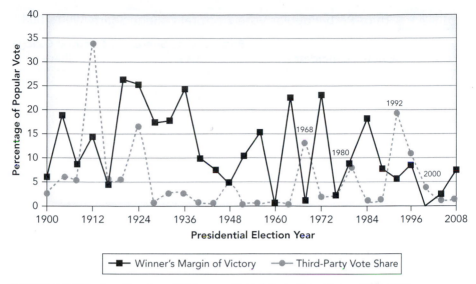

FIGURE 5.2 Winning Margins of Victory and Third-Party Vote Shares 1900–2008

Note: Third-party vote share is the total percentage of the popular vote that all third-party candidates received. Winner's margin of victory is the percentage difference between the two highest vote getters.

Source: Compiled by the author.

Another institutional barrier is the Electoral College, where 48 states have decided to allocate their electoral votes as a bloc—a "winner-take-all" system (as noted in Chapter 3). This is often referred to as the unit rule. (Two states that do not follow this system are Maine and Nebraska, which allocate electors at the congressional district level, with the winner of the statewide contest receiving an extra two electors.) In order to have a chance at winning the presidency, a candidate has to win states outright; nothing is gained by running a strong second. A perfect example here would be Ross Perot in 1992 receiving 19 percent of the popular vote, but not a single electoral college vote because he did not win any state or any congressional district in Maine or Nebraska. "Like the single-member district system, the winner-take-all feature of the electoral college means that third parties have little chance of winning any state's electoral votes, let alone carry a sufficient number of states to elect a president."[2] As seen in Table 5.2, third-party candidates won electoral college votes only four times in the 20th century: in 1912 (Theodore Roosevelt), 1924 (Robert La Follette Sr.), 1948 (Strom Thurmond), and 1968 (George Wallace).

A third powerful institutional barrier to minor party success is the public funding of presidential elections. Ever since the early 1970s, candidates for the presidency can receive federal funds for both their primary and general election campaigns, as noted

---

[2]John F. Bibby and L. Sandy Maisel, *Two Parties or More? The American Party System,* 2nd ed. (Boulder, CO: Westview, 2003), 62.

| TABLE 5.2 | Third-Party Popular Vote/Electoral College Share 1900–2008 |

Year	Notable Candidates	Popular Vote Share (%)	Electoral College Share
1900		2.84	0
1904	Eugene Debs	6.00	0
1908	Eugene Debs	5.39	0
1912	Theodore Roosevelt	35.00	88
1916		4.65	0
1920	Eugene Debs	5.53	0
1924	Robert La Follette Sr.	17.14	13
1932		2.95	0
1936		2.65	0
1948	J. Strom Thurmond, Henry Wallace	5.38	39
1968	George Wallace	13.86	46
1980	John B. Anderson	8.23	0
1992	H. Ross Perot	19.55	0
1996	H. Ross Perot	10.05	0
2000	Ralph Nader	3.754	0
2004	Ralph Nader	1.00	0
2008	Ralph Nader	1.53	0

Note: Popular vote share (%) is the total percentage received by all third-party candidates.

Source: Dave Leip's Atlas of U.S. Presidential Election, "Election Result."

Accessed at: http://uselectionatlas.org/

Electoral College Vote Data: FairVote, "Third Parties Earn Votes."
Accessed at: http://archive.fairvote.org/?page=1030

in Table 5.3, but not every candidate gets the same amount. Major-party candidates, defined as those whose party received at least 25 percent of the popular vote in the previous election, are entitled to "full funding" (roughly $84 million in 2008). Candidates from minor parties receive a much smaller amount and must cross a 5-percent threshold to receive any money whatsoever. This creates a powerful self-fulfilling prophecy: Without the money, minor-party candidates languish and generally fail to cross the 5-percent threshold, which, of course, bars them from getting federal funds for their next effort. It is very rare that minor parties receive federal funds. This has occurred only three times since the public financing system took effect in 1976: John Anderson, 1980; Ross Perot, 1996; and Pat Buchanan, 2000.[3]

While less recognized, the direct primary system has a powerful impact on maintaining the two-party model. It has been said that primary elections create a safety

[3]Federal Election Commission, "Public Funds in Presidential Campaigns: 1976–2008." Accessed at: http://www.fec.gov/press/press2009/20090608Pres/4_PublicFundsPresCmpgns.pdf

TABLE 5.3 Presidential Public Funding

	1976 ($)	1980 ($)	1984 ($)	1988 ($)	1992 ($)	1996 ($)	2000 ($)	2004 ($)	2008 ($)
Primary Matching Funds Paid to Candidate									
Republicans	9,745,917	20,760,484	10,100,000	35,495,823	15,858,507	43,996,632	26,961,585	0	17,528,025
Democrats	15,203,584	10,671,171	26,225,655	31,114,979	24,628,595	14,036,889	29,366,518	27,441,957	2,598,653
Other parties	0	0	193,734	938,798	2,366,482	504,830	5,933,266	891,968	881,494
General Election Grants									
Republicans	21,820,000	29,440,000	40,400,000	46,100,000	55,240,000	61,820,000	67,560,000	74,620,000	84,103,800
Democrats	21,820,000	29,440,000	40,400,000	46,100,000	55,240,000	61,820,000	67,560,000	74,620,000	
Other parties		4,242,304				29,055,400	12,613,452		
Parties Convention Grants									
Republicans	1,963,800	4,416,000	8,080,000	9,220,000	11,048,000	12,364,000	13,512,000	14,924,000	16,820,625
Democrats	2,185,829	4,416,000	8,080,000	9,220,000	11,048,000	12,364,000	13,512,000	14,924,000	16,820,625
Other parties							2,522,690		
Total public funding payouts	72,739,130	103,385,959	133,479,399	178,189,600	175,429,584	235,961,751	239,541,511	207,421,925	138,753,222

Source: Federal Election Commission, "Presidential Public Funding Fact Sheet: 1976–2008."

Accessed at: www.fec.gov/press/bkgnd/Pres_Fund/Pres_Public_Funding.pdf. As explained earlier, other parties have difficulties being competitive as they are severely limited when it comes to public funding. This is an institutional barrier against minor parties.

Note: Barack Obama declined federal funds for his general election campaign in 2008.

valve for the major parties. When a major-party voter gets upset with one candidate, he or she can vent frustration in the primary by supporting someone quite different, but within the same party. Without primaries, upset voters would look elsewhere—to minor-party candidates. As noted by a team of scholars, primaries are a "uniquely American institution" that "channel dissent into the two major parties."[4]

Finally, the two-party system is maintained by myriad state ballot access laws. States have an interest in limiting the number of candidates on a general election ballot. Would we really want to choose between 40 or 50, or perhaps even 100 candidates? Probably not. But what should be the restrictions on ballot access? Beginning at the turn of the 20th century, states devised schemes to limit the number of candidates and at the same time make things easier for the major parties. (After all, the regulations were being written by members of the two major parties!) Generally speaking, parties whose candidates receive 25 percent in the previous election are automatically provided a place on the ballot. Other parties have to gather a great number of petition signatures to be allowed a spot on the ballot. In Pennsylvania, for example, minor-party presidential candidates must collect nearly 24,000 signatures in a 14-week period to be placed on the November ballot.[5] This is a time-consuming, difficult, and expensive chore minor parties have to undertake that the major parties do not.

Table 5.4 lists the number of petition signatures required to list a third-party or independent candidate on the presidential ballot for each of the 50 states. While a few

TABLE 5.4	**Ballot Access for Third Parties**		
Presidential Petition Requirements			
State	**1992**	**1996**	**2008**
Alabama	5,000	5,000	5,000
Alaska	2,035	1,968	3,145
Arizona	14,072	14,798	(est) 21,500
Arkansas	0	0	1,000
California	134,781	147,238	158,372
Colorado	5,000	5,000	5,000
Connecticut	14,620	7,500	7,500
Delaware	reg 144	(est) reg 170	5,800
District of Columbia	3,072	(est) 3,500	3,900
Florida	60,312	65,596	104,338
Georgia	26,955	(est) 31,000	42,489
Hawaii	3,545	3,728	4,291
Idaho	4,090	4,822	5,985

(continued)

[4]Ibid.
[5]Ibid., 70.

State	1992	1996	2008
Illinois	25,000	25,000	25,000
Indiana	29,890	30,700	32,742
Iowa	1,000	1,000	1,500
Kansas	5,000	5,000	5,000
Kentucky	5,000	5,000	5,000
Louisiana	0	0	0
Maine	4,000	4,000	4,000
Maryland	10,000	10,000	(est) 32,500
Massachusetts	10,000	10,000	10,000
Michigan	25,646	31,112	30,000
Minnesota	2,000	2,000	2,000
Mississippi	0	0	1,000
Missouri	20,860	10,000	10,000
Montana	9,531	9,473	5,000
Nebraska	2,500	2,500	2,500
Nevada	9,392	3,770	5,746
New Hampshire	3,000	3,000	3,000
New Jersey	800	800	800
New Mexico	2,069	2,292	16,764
New York	15,000	15,000	15,000
North Carolina	43,601	51,904	69,734
North Dakota	4,000	4,000	4,000
Ohio	5,000	5,000	5,000
Oklahoma	35,132	41,711	43,913
Oregon	36,092	14,352	18,368
Pennsylvania	37,216	(est) 32,000	(est) 24,000
Rhode Island	1,000	1,000	1,000
South Carolina	10,000	10,000	10,000
South Dakota	2,568	3,113	3,356
Tennessee	25	25	25[*]
Texas	38,900	43,913	74,108
Utah	300	300	1,000
Vermont	0	0	1,000
Virginia	13,920	(est) 16,000	1,000
Washington	200	200	1,000
West Virginia	6,346	6,837	15,118

(continued)

TABLE 5.4	Ballot Access for Third Parties (*continued*)		
State	**1992**	**1996**	**2008**
Wisconsin	2,000	2,000	2,000
Wyoming	8,000	8,000	3,868
Total signatures	698,614	701,322	(est) 854,362

Source: For 2008 data: Libertarian Party, "Ballot Access Update '08."
Accessed at: www.lp.org/ballot-access.

For 1992 and 1996 data: Direct Democracy, "Ballot Access News."

Accessed at: www.directdemocracy.com/index.php?option=content&task=view&id=172 on July 15, 2009.

Note: (a) The chart here shows the number of signatures for a third-party or independent candidate to get on the ballot for president. When a state has several methods, the easier method is represented in this table.

(b) All numbers represent signatures on a petition, except for Delaware, where it is the number of party members.

*Each of the 11 elector candidates must get 25 signatures, for a total of 275.

states have relaxed their signature requirements for presidential ballot access, the number of signatures required for nationwide access increased between 1992 and 2008. Figure 5.3, on the other hand, displays the total number of signatures required to place third-party candidates on the ballot for every congressional district as a percentage of the population; this number, clearly, has decreased markedly since the mid-20th century.

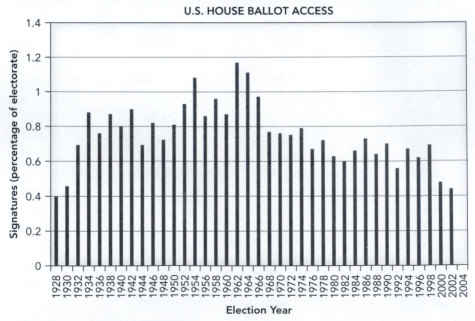

FIGURE 5.3 House Ballot Access

Source: Ballot Access News, Vol. 17, No. 7 (October 1, 2001).
Accessed at: www.ballot-access.org/2001/1001.html

Attitudinal Barriers

Laws and the Constitution are not the only hurdles to minor parties' success in America. The momentum of history is a powerful force. There has never been a prolonged period of time when the United States has had a multi-party model. Minor parties seem odd—the exception rather than the rule. It is more than simply a logical tautology to suggest that America has a two-party model because it has always had a two-party model. Much related, a powerful element in American political culture is the acceptance of compromise and incremental change. Americans do not expect dramatic changes in public policy, and there is evidence to suggest that they appreciate slow change and middle-of-the-road policies. Both components make support for alternative parties, often thought more "radical," less likely.

Perhaps the greatest attitudinal hurdle is the "wasted-vote syndrome." Americans seem anxious to have their vote count—to help actually make a difference in selecting who will serve in office. Because minor-party candidates usually stand little real chance of victory—or so the voters are told by the media—most Americans are reluctant to "waste" their vote in support of a minor party on Election Day. It is revealing that support for minor-party candidates often peaks several weeks before the election; as the election approaches, voters abandon the minor-party candidate, hoping to add their voice to the contest between the viable candidates. This would also explain why so many Americans will tell pollsters that they want more parties in the process, but at the same time, minor-party candidates suffer on Election Day. There is much to frustrate minor-party candidates and activists, but wasted-vote syndrome, which has been seen as recently as 2008, must surely top their list. In a Zogby International survey conducted on March 14, 2008, independent candidate Ralph Nader polled at 6 percent; ultimately, he would go on to win only 0.56 percent of the popular vote on Election Day, less than one-tenth of his earlier showing.[6]

Are there generational issues at play? Interestingly, a 2004 study conducted by the American Association of Retired Persons found that 54 percent of baby boomers feel that a strong third party is needed.[7] Yet, most age groups seem to respond consistently when asked about their partisan inclinations, according to American National Election Studies.[8] At times of political discontent, when many people are unhappy with the political situation, every age group sees a rise in the number of voters supporting independent candidates. Since the 1970s, almost every generation has entered politics with many independents, but has gradually become more inclined toward one of the major parties. This can be explained by many of the barriers discussed earlier. As people become less idealistic and more realistic, they do not want to waste their vote on someone who is not likely to win an election.

---

[6]Zogby International, "Zogby Poll: McCain Bests Both Obama, Clinton in 3-Way General Election Tests" (March 15, 2008). Accessed at: http://www.zogby.com/news/readnews.cfm?ID=1467

[7]"New Political Survey of Older Americans Finds Boomers Want Third Party, Seniors Focus on Candidate's Personal Qualities," *Senior Journal* (July 20, 2004). Accessed at: http://seniorjournal.com/NEWS/Politics/2004/4-07-20Survey.htm

[8]American National Election Studies, "Party Identification 3-Point Scale 1952–2004: Percent among Demographic Groups Who Responded 'Independent.'" Accessed at: http://www.electionstudies.org/nesguide/2ndtable/t2a_2_3.htm

In summary, minor parties confront a hostile environment in the American setting. There are numerous laws and regulations that limit their chances for success, as well as deep-seated attitudinal factors that make matters worse. Democracies across the globe flourish with multi-party systems, but the chances of one arising in the United States are slim—but perhaps improving. If voter support for additional choices remains high, it is conceivable that significant changes might occur. In the short term, however, the pathway of American electoral politics will be paved by two-party brick layers.

THIRD PARTIES IN AMERICAN HISTORY

Though minor parties have slim chances for victory, they do play a role in the system. Minor parties have sprouted up throughout American history and have changed the political landscape. This section takes a brief look at several of the more significant third parties.

The Anti-Masons

Due in large measure to the Corrupt Deal (mentioned in Chapter 3), by the late 1820s there was a widespread reaction against elite politics. This mood translated into, among other things, a potent minor party movement and the development of the Anti-Masons. In nearly every community in the United States at the time, there was a Masonic Lodge, or Freemason organization. These lodges were secretive clubs, boasting members from the social, economic, legal, and political elite of the local area. Many prominent politicians were Freemasons, including George Washington, Henry Clay, and Andrew Jackson. Members were bound to secrecy concerning the goings-on of the group, which included many rituals. In 1826, the backlash against these secretive, elite groups led to the creation of a political party, the Anti-Masonic Party.

By the 1830s, the Anti-Masons had organizations throughout the nation, but especially in New York and throughout New England. Their candidate in the 1832 presidential race, William Wirt, netted 8 percent of the popular vote and seven electoral college votes (all from Vermont). Their efforts at the state level were even more successful, however; they won gubernatorial contests in Vermont and Pennsylvania and numerous state legislative posts in New England. By the end of the 1830s, the party began to fade, due in large measure to the popularity of Democrat Andrew Jackson, who endorsed many of the Anti-Mason policies. Among other things, the most lasting impact of the party came from its use of conventions to nominate presidential candidates.

The Free Soil Party

A number of abolitionist groups burst onto the scene in the years leading up to the Civil War. The most significant of these was the Free Soil Party, founded in 1848. That year, nearly 20,000 delegates converged at the party's nominating convention in Buffalo, New York. They nominated former president Martin Van Buren as their candidate and set off to spread the word. On Election Day, they garnered just 10 percent of the popular vote, nearly all from Northern states. This did not translate into a single electoral college vote. But in the next presidential election, a new party, the Republicans, captured the support of many abolitionist voters, and the Free Soil Party faded into the history books.

The American (Know Nothing) Party

Slavery was not the only major issue in the pre–Civil War days. Another burning concern, especially for urban blue-collar workers, was the influx of immigrants (mostly Irish Catholic). Jobs were scarce, and these newly arrived Americans were desperate enough to work for pennies. The American Party emerged as an openly bigoted group aimed at limiting the role of immigrants in economic and political life. Among other things, the party called for a 20-year residency requirement to earn the right to vote, and wanted to bar immigrants from ever holding public office. Members deflected questions about their party with the set phrase, "I know nothing about it," and "Know-Nothing" became the popular name for the party.

What is even more surprising than the mean-spiritedness of this party is the level of success it achieved. In 1854, the American Party won scores of congressional and state legislative seats, mostly in the Northeast. In Massachusetts, for example, it won 347 of 350 state house seats, all of the state senate and congressional contests, and even the governorship.[9] A similar level of success was seen in New York, Rhode Island, New Hampshire, and Connecticut.[10] In the 1856 presidential election, the American Party netted a whopping 21 percent of the popular vote and eight electoral college votes. Four years later, the party was split over the slavery issue and soon disappeared from the national scene. The brief life of the Know Nothing Party is clearly one of the darker tales of American electoral history.[11]

The Populist Party

Within a few decades after the Civil War, an agricultural depression gripped the nation. Farmers in the upper Midwest were especially hard hit. This depression was occurring at nearly the same time as the Industrial Revolution. Business owners, dubbed robber barons, were making fortunes in the bourgeoning cities, often at the expense of the working class. Hardships and growing concerns about staggering inequities in wealth distribution led to the formation of several economic-based political parties, most notably the Populist Party.

The Populists, sometimes referred to as the People's Party, emerged in 1891. Their platform called for, among other things, the public regulation of railroads (given that commodities were shipped back East on railroads), the free coinage of silver (as a means to increase the amount of money in circulation), and the implementation of a graduated income tax. They nominated James Weaver as their presidential candidate in 1892, and he went on to capture 8 percent of the popular vote and 22 electoral

---

[9]"The American Party (The Know-Nothing Party) Comes to Power in Massachusetts in 1955," The Massachusetts Historical Society. Accessed at: http://www.masshist.org/objects/2005january.cfm

[10]John K. White and Daniel M. Shea, *New Party Politics: From Jefferson and Hamilton to the Information Age* (Boston: Bedford/St. Martin's, 2000), 283.

[11]Ibid.

votes, nearly all from Midwestern states. After that election, the party's strength grew. By 1896, the party's leaders realized, however, that their chance of picking up a good many congressional seats was small, and their hopes for capturing the White House just as distant. They opted to merge with the Democrats by endorsing William Jennings Bryan. After all, Bryan had endorsed much of the Populist agenda, and by working together, the chances of victory in November were good.

The strategy did not work, however, as Bryan was defeated by Republican William McKinley. The Populist Party quickly faded from the political scene. Many of its proposals, however, were picked up by both the Democrats and the Republicans and were eventually adopted into law. Commenting on the role of parties like the Populists, political scientist Clinton Rossiter noted, "One of the persistent qualities of the American two-party system is the way in which one of the major parties moves almost instinctively to absorb (and thus be somewhat reshaped by) the most challenging third party of the time."[12]

The Progressives

On three occasions, a "progressive party" had an impact on the American political process. The first time was in the early part of the 20th century. The Progressive Movement had captured public attention and numerous reforms were undertaken. But there was no party-based movement until Theodore Roosevelt was denied his own party's nomination in 1912. Four years earlier, Roosevelt, then the sitting president, decided to step aside and champion the nomination of his friend and secretary of war, William Howard Taft. Taft was nominated by the Republicans and was sent to the White House. But Roosevelt became disappointed in Taft's failure to push the progressive agenda. He told his fellow Republicans that a mistake had been made and that he should receive the nomination in 1912. But party members were quite reluctant to deny a president renomination, so despite Roosevelt's objections, they handed the nomination to Taft again. Roosevelt and a group of his supporters stormed out of the GOP (Grand Old Party) nominating convention and started a new party—the Progressive Party. Roosevelt was chosen as the party's nominee. Declaring himself ready for the challenge, Roosevelt likened himself to a bull moose. The party quickly picked up the nickname of the Bull Moose Party.

Republican voters divided their support between Roosevelt and Taft. Roosevelt picked up 27.4 percent of the popular vote (88 electoral college votes) and Taft 23.1 percent of the vote (8 electoral votes.) Democrat Woodrow Wilson netted 42 percent of the vote and a whopping 435 electoral votes (due in large measure to the unit rule). Roosevelt's candidacy had, in effect, given the election to the Democrat. The Bull Moose Party faded from the scene because of the loss, and Wilson picked up many of the progressive causes.

By the 1920s, progressive issues had once again captured the public's attention, and the party experienced a bit of a resurrection. In 1924, the party held a presidential nominating convention and emerged with Robert La Follette Sr., a firebrand reformer from Wisconsin, as its nominee. La Follette was a tireless campaigner and a splendid

---

[12]Clinton Rossiter, *Political Parties in America* (Ithaca, NY: Cornell University Press, 1997), 73.

orator, but on Election Day, he netted just 16 percent of the popular vote. The only state that he won was his own. Once again, the Progressive Party faded.

Finally, in 1948, the Progressive Party was again dusted off for a run at the presidency. That year, a group of liberal Democrats came into conflict with their party's leader, President Harry Truman, and his "get tough" policy with the Soviet Union. Former Democratic vice president Henry Wallace was picked as the Progressive Party's candidate. His platform included, among other things, anti-lynching laws, scrapping the electoral college, and a system of national health care insurance. Wallace drew large crowds and seemed to have a message that resonated with many Democratic voters. Yet on Election Day, he drew only 2 percent of the popular vote—but nearly gave the election to the Republican, Thomas Dewey. The race between Truman and Dewey was extremely close in three states—New York, Maryland, and Michigan—and went to Dewey by a whisker. But for Wallace, Truman would have won these states and the electoral college count rather handily. The same scenario played out in California, but there, Truman was able to edge out Dewey and win reelection despite Wallace's efforts. The Progressive Party disappeared, this time, it would seem, for good.

Segregation-Based Parties

Halfway through the 20th century, two parties emerged in the South focused on the civil rights movement and the desire to maintain the status quo of racial segregation. The first, in 1948, was the States' Rights Party, also known as the Dixiecrats. Their nominee for the presidency was J. Strom Thurmond, then governor of South Carolina. He netted just 2.5 percent of the overall vote, but was able to win five Southern states for an electoral college total of 38. The party folded after the election. Thurmond switched his affiliation to Republican Party and went on to serve for four decades in the U.S. Senate.

Most assumed that the stir over the Dixiecrat Party was long gone, but in the fall of 2002, it returned to the front page. At Thurmond's retirement celebration, the sitting majority leader of the Senate, Republican Trent Lott of Mississippi, commented:

> I want to say this about my state. When Strom Thurmond ran for president, we voted for him. We're proud of it. If the rest of the country had followed our lead, we wouldn't have had all these problems over all these years, either.[13]

Given that Thurmond's candidacy was based on maintaining segregationist policies, Lott's comments seemed insensitive to most and quite outrageous to many. In the end, Lott was forced to resign his post as majority leader of the Senate.

Another segregationist party emerged in the 1968 election, the American Independent Party. George Wallace, then governor of Alabama, had flirted with a run for the White House as a Democrat four years earlier but realized that the chances of wresting the nomination from Lyndon Johnson were slim. In 1968, he again saw the

---

[13]Jay Rosen, "The Legend of Trent Lott and the Weblogs," Press Think: Ghost of Democracy in the Media Machine (March 15, 2004). Accessed at: http://journalism.nyu.edu/pubzone/weblogs/pressthink/2004/03/15/lott_case.html

BOX 5.1   Lott's Dixiecrat Comments

"EDITORIAL: Lott's Words Carry Heavy Weight"
December 13, 2002

A poor choice of words. Over and over again. "I want to say this about my state: When Strom Thurmond ran for president, we voted for him. We're proud of it. And if the rest of the country had followed our lead, we wouldn't have had all these problems over all these years, either."

Those were the poor choice of words by incoming Senate Majority Leader Trent Lott, R-Miss., while at Thurmond's 100th birthday and retirement celebration earlier this month, according to the *Washington Post*. In response to those words, people present at the reception gasped or remained silent and political and civil rights leaders called for Lott's removal.

What's more interesting about his comment is that it's not the first time he's endorsed Thurmond's 1948 race for president. Thurmond ran on the Dixiecrat ticket, which stood for segregation, and carried the states of Mississippi, Alabama, Louisiana, and South Carolina. One of the more controversial phrases the aging senator is known for is, "All the laws of Washington and all the bayonets of the Army cannot force the Negro into our homes, our schools, our churches."

In 1980, Lott and Thurmond spoke at a rally for then-presidential candidate Ronald Reagan in Mississippi. After Thurmond made his speech, Lott followed up by saying, "You know, if we had elected this man 30 years ago, we wouldn't be in the mess we are today," according to CNN. Also in the late '90s, it was learned that Lott had made speeches at the Council of Conservative Citizens, which is the group formed in the shadow of segregationist white Citizens' Councils of the 1960s. In one of those speeches, Lott said, "The people in this room stand for the right principles and the right philosophy. Let's take it in the right direction, and our children will be the beneficiaries."

It's these phrases that makes one wonder—who is this man and what decade is he from?

No Republican has called for his removal, but some of the senator's allies are cringing from his comments, saying his two recent apologies have not been clear.

Ken Conner, Family Research Council president, said the Republican Party has had trouble attracting black voters because of Lott's remarks. Conner said Lott's comments continue to reinforce the racist stereotype of Republicans. Even President Bush delivered a speech on Thursday saying any indication that segregation was acceptable is "offensive, and is wrong."

It's unfortunate that the GOP is plagued by comments like these. Maybe Lott will learn his lesson and realize that today's problems have nothing to do with the outcome of the 1948 presidential election. It makes us wonder why a powerful political leader is still dwelling on the glory days of a segregationist South and not on the problems—like the economy or homeland security—that plague our country today.

Source: "Editorial: Lott's Words Carry Heavy Weight," *Iowa State Daily* (December 13, 2002).
Accessed at: www.iowastatedaily.com/opinion/article_65e9ca27-b246-53f5-993e-7e35e4b94e84.html

chances of a Democratic nomination as far-fetched, so he decided to organize a new party, calling it the American Independent Party. Wallace's proclamation of "segregation today, segregation tomorrow, segregation forever,"[14] made several years earlier, became the rallying point of his presidential bid. He also stressed a "law and order" platform. On Election Day, Wallace won nearly 10 million votes, some 13.5 percent, and 46 electoral college votes (all of which came from the Deep South). Wallace fell short of winning the election, but he did shape the outcome of the contest: By taking Southern states out of the Democratic base, Wallace ensured the election of Republican Richard Nixon. The South could no longer be taken for granted by the Democrats, and in fact, the 1968 election marked the end of Democratic presidential dominance in the region.

The American Independence Party dissolved after the election. Wallace threw his hat into the ring again in 1972, but this time as a Democratic candidate. Shortly after entering the race, however, he was shot by a would-be assassin and paralyzed from the waist down. Wallace withdrew from the race and spent the rest of his life in a wheelchair. Before his death, in 1998, Wallace accepted integration and noted the profound injustices of his earlier segregationist policies.

John B. Anderson and the 1980 Election

The 1980 presidential election saw a higher-than-average share of the vote go to third-party and independent candidates—8.3 percent, the most since Wallace's 1968 run. Concerned and angry about the country's direction, many voters rejected Jimmy Carter, whom they saw as ineffective. John B. Anderson, a moderate Republican congressman from Illinois, had initially sought the Republican nomination and had polled well in early primaries. But after Reagan secured the nomination, Anderson organized an independent bid for the presidency. Anderson courted voters disillusioned with Carter who were yet unwilling to embrace Reagan's conservatism; Anderson mainly appealed to moderate "Rockefeller Republicans" and independents in the Northeast, West, and his home state of Illinois. Although he polled as high as 25 percent early in the contest,[15] Anderson—in keeping with the pattern followed by most third-party candidates—saw his numbers drop consistently until Election Day, when he took 6.6 percent of the total.[16] Interestingly, the 1980 election also saw the Libertarian Party, which stressed the importance of limiting the size of government, win its highest popular vote share in history, taking more than 1 percent, with almost 1 million popular votes;[17] the Libertarian candidate, Ed Clark, finished ahead of Anderson in Alaska.[18]

---

[14]Alabama Governor, Inaugural Addresses and Programs, SP194, Alabama Department of Archives and History.

[15]Mark Bisnow, *Diary of a Dark Horse: The 1980 Anderson Presidential Campaign* (Carbondale, IL: Southern Illinois University Press, 1983), 214.

[16]U.S. Election Atlas, "1980 Presidential General Election Results." Accessed at: http://uselectionatlas.org/RESULTS/national.php?year=1980&off=)&f=1

[17]Ibid.

[18]Paul R. Abramson et al., "Third-Party and Independent Candidates in American Politics: Wallace, Anderson, and Perot," *Political Science Quarterly*, Vol. 110 (1995), 349–367.

The Reform Party

The last significant third party in American politics was the Reform Party. In 1992, many Americans seemed unsure about the two major-party candidates, sitting President George H. W. Bush and Arkansas Governor Bill Clinton. Rumors began to spread of a third potential candidate, Texas billionaire H. Ross Perot. Excitement grew and Perot soon announced that he would enter the race if volunteers would secure his name on the ballot in all 50 states (see the previous ballot access discussion). This was soon done and Perot entered the fray. Although polls showed the Texan doing well, and in fact leading the pack at points throughout the early summer, Perot withdrew his candidacy by August. But in another surprise move he reentered the race in October. By then Perot's popularity had waned, and on Election Day, he netted 19 percent of the popular vote, which did not translate into a single electoral college vote. Most analysts agree that his running had little effect on the outcome of the race.

Perot's political star seemed to keep a bit of its luster after the election. Instead of fading from the scene, Perot decided to put his efforts into creating a viable third

---

BOX 5.2   A Quick Look at Political Ideology and Minor Party Politics

Political ideology is a consistent set of basic beliefs about the proper purpose and scope of government. Americans generally tend to fall into two camps: liberals and conservatives, although at various points in our history, many have been reluctant to identify themselves as either, and some have always identified with other ideologies. To a large extent, minor parties have emerged when individuals believe that the two major parties either do not adequately express their general view of government, or when a particular issue seems to cut across this ideological divide.

In general terms, liberals tend to support social and cultural change (especially in connection with issues of equality) and want an activist government that encourages change. Conservatives, by contrast, tend to favor traditional views on social, cultural, and economic matters and demand a more limited role for government in most spheres. Although there is some ideological variation within each party, today's Republican Party is, generally speaking, the party of conservatives, whereas most liberals tend to identify with the Democratic Party.

This neat division has not always been the case. Throughout much of American history southern Democrats were staunchly conservative, particularly with regards to what they believe to be states' rights mattes. Conservative southern Democrats were called "Boll Weevil," a term derived from a bug common on southern plantations. The term "Solid South" was also used to describe the overwhelming dominance of the Democratic Party in that region. This was a historic vestige of the Civil War and reconstruction. One should remember that Abraham Lincoln was a Republican, and the Republican Party controlled the national legislature in the war's aftermath—reconstruction. This resentment of Republicans lasted in the South for well over 100 years. But that did not mean these voters and politicians embraced a liberal ideology. The staunchest opponents of desegregation in the 1950s and 1960s, for example, were southern Democrats. The shift of conservative Democrats to the Republican ranks began in the 1960s, and most would mark the completion of that shift as 1994. That was the first election in American history where a majority of House and Senate members from the South were Democratic.

(continued)

Conversely, many Republicans, particularly from the Northeast, were liberal. They may have been somewhat conservative on fiscal matters, but many of these politicians and voters were clearly progressive on social issues. A good example would be New York Governor Nelson Rockefeller; a life-long Republican and a social progressive. This group was sometimes called "Gypsy Moths."

Although not nearly as popular as liberal and conservative ideology, a number of people today identify with populist and libertarian ideology. Populists believe that the government can be a positive agent to protect "common people" (which historically included farmers and workers) against the moneyed elite. Populists favor governmental action to promote equality but also support policies to uphold order. Libertarians support individual liberty in economic, personal, and social realms over government authority. Libertarians acknowledge that government must have some authority, but they believe that most governmental action must be severely regulated and limited.

There is also a common myth about ideology. Many Americans believe that liberals prefer more government involvement, while conservatives favor less government involvement. This more-less distinction holds true when looking at economic issues and spending on public goods that benefit many people. For instance, liberals favor government spending on environmental protection, education, public transportation, national parks, and social services. In these areas of public policy, conservatives want smaller governmental budgets and fewer governmental programs. However, when it comes to government involvement with respect to social issues, conservatives generally support more governmental intervention in the form of restrictions on abortion, pornography, and same-sex marriage, while liberals tend to prefer less government intervention in these same areas.

Today, the critical difference between liberals and conservatives concerns not so much the scope of governmental activity as the purpose of governmental actions. Generally speaking, conservatives approve of using governmental power to promote order, including social order, though there are exceptions to these generalizations. Conservatives typically favor firm police action, swift and severe punishments for criminals, and more laws regulating behavior, such as teen curfews. Such beliefs led many conservatives to support stringent anticommunist domestic and foreign policies in the 1940s and 1950s. Programs to fight domestic terrorism (such as the USA PATRIOT Act, which was initially bipartisan and very popular as an immediate reaction to the September 11, 2001) now gets more conservative than liberal support. Conservatives want to preserve traditional patterns of social relations, including the importance of the domestic role of women in family life and the significance of religion in daily life and school. Conservatives today do not oppose equality, but they tend not to view securing equality as a prime objective of governmental action.

In general, liberals tend to worry more than conservatives do about the civil liberties implications of the USA PATRIOT Act and government surveillance of potential terrorists. Liberals are less likely to approve the use of governmental power to maintain order but are more willing to use governmental power to promote equality. Thus they tend to support laws to ensure that homosexuals receive equal treatment in employment, housing, and education. They favor policies that encourage businesses to hire and promote women and minorities, and they want to raise the minimum wage and provide greater access to health care for all people.

Finally, it is important to note that what might seem like inconsistencies for scholars is a natural, logical ideology for an individual. A person might be conservative in some respects, but liberal in others. Politics, as in much in life, is in the eye of the beholder—or should we say the eye of the voter!

party—the Reform Party. Two issues lay at the heart of the Reform Party: cleaning up the electoral system (removing big money from the process) and reducing the federal deficit. Perot entered the 1996 presidential contest and, of course, received his own party's nomination. This time he netted only 8.4 percent of the vote—and again not a single electoral vote. The party struggled after the election, due in large measure to the absorption of its issues by the two major parties. Jesse Ventura, a former professional wrestler, shocked the political establishment with his successful run for the Minnesota governorship as a Reform Party candidate, but he broke his ties with the party shortly after he was elected. The party nominated a candidate in the 2000 election, but he received just 1 percent of the popular vote. The Reform Party has since withered away.

The Tea Party "Movement" or Tea Party "Party"?

Not long after the election of Barack Obama, conservative activists across the United States began to organize. By the summer of 2009, a new group had been formed—dubbed Tea Party Activist. The "tea party" reference was to the Boston Tea Party in 1773, when the Sons of Liberty stormed merchant ships docked in Boston Harbor and threw tons of imported tea over the side into the harbor to protest the newly imposed "tea tax." The 2009 group set its sights on what it perceived to be the growing scope of the federal government under Democratic control, particularly the economic stimulus bill and the proposed health care reform initiative. The group's membership list swelled, as did its coffers. By February of 2010, the group held its first convention, with its keynote speaker being former Alaska governor and vice presidential candidate Sarah Palin. The event was widely covered by the media.

There was no doubt that the Tea Party group had a dramatic impact in the 2010 election. The party moved quickly to organize local chapters, to raise money, and to endorse conservative candidates in Republican primaries. Roughly one-half of the Tea Party–endorsed candidates were successful in GOP primaries in 2010, most notably U.S. Senate candidates Christine O'Donnell of Delaware, Joe Miller of Alaska, and Sharron Angle of Nevada. Yet many of these candidates, including O'Donnell, Miller, and Angle, lost the general election. By most accounts, the results of the 2010 election were "mixed" for the Tea Party movement. Thus the question of whether this group would move toward the development of a third party or remain a "movement" within the Republican Party is unclear. Many, including Palin, argued that they should remain Republicans, but others argued a clean break was needed.

MINOR PARTIES AT THE LOCAL LEVEL

Most studies on the viability of minor parties have focused on national party organizations. An important study by Christian Collet, for example, explores national public opinion over time, finding increased support for minor-party candidates. Those focusing on the weight of institutional forces, such as John Bibby and L. Sandy Maisel,[19] also use the entire nation as the unit of analysis. Conversely, few studies have attempted to chart local minor-party dynamics. There are many state-based case studies, such as those dealing with Bernie Sanders of Vermont, Angus King of Maine,

---

[19]Bibby and Maisel, *Two Parties or More?*

Jesse Ventura of Minnesota, and Joe Lieberman of Connecticut, but it is difficult to make general assessments from these few works.

The problem with using the nation as the unit of analysis is that it is likely that local, state, or regional nuances will be lost. While it is true that minor parties and third-party candidates face an uphill battle everywhere in the United States, they clearly do better in some states and in some communities than in others. We might take, for example, Ross Perot's election results in 1992. Perot ran a nationwide campaign; there is little evidence to suggest that his campaign targeted particular states or regions. Given his widespread use of earned and paid network television (his oft-cited "infomercials"), one would be hard-pressed to discern a particular geographic focus. Nationwide, Perot received 19 percent. But when looking at the state level, a great deal of variance emerges. In some states, his share of the vote languished far behind the national average: Arkansas (10%), Georgia (13%), Louisiana (12%), Mississippi (9%), Tennessee (10%), and so on. But in other states, Perot's percentage was much larger than the national average: Alaska (28%), Idaho (27%), Kansas (27%), Maine (31%), Nevada (26%), Oregon (24%), Vermont (23%), and Washington (24%), among others. Some of this variation was likely due to Perot himself, as his rogue style and approach seemed to resonate with voters in particular states, such as Alaska and Idaho. But it also seems likely that a good bit was due to differences in voter receptivity to minor-party candidates.

It is revealing that the correlation between Perot's state-by-state vote share in 1992 and Ralph Nader's share of the vote as a Green Party candidate in 2000 and in 2004 is rather high. While we might suggest both candidates were "reformers" of sorts, the similarities are limited beyond this. In most respects, they were very different candidates, appealing to different constituencies. Then what would explain this surprisingly high state-based correlation?

Two scholars, C. Dan Myers, and the author of this text, Daniel M. Shea, created an "index of minor party support" based upon three important factors: major-party dynamics, institutional factors, and demographics.

Major-Party Dynamics   Likely one of the most important forces shaping minor-party success is the overall party culture. A host of studies detail significant differences in state and local party dynamics. On the most basic level, certain states have a tradition of aggressive party activity while others do not. Some communities have local party organizations that are vastly more effective than those in other communities. The degree to which the major parties claim the allegiance of average voters (i.e., the number of hardcore partisans) is also an important part of local electoral culture. In some communities voters are accustomed to highly competitive elections, where Democratic and Republican candidates stand on an equal footing. Here we would expect the wasted-vote syndrome to be significant. In other communities, one party dominates, which used to be true in the South, although recent evidence suggests the emergence of highly competitive elections in this region again.

Institutional Factors   As noted earlier, institutional factors are key in maintaining the two-party system throughout America. Yet, not all of these factors are the same in every state. The first-past-the-post, single-member-districts system and the electoral college are universal, but other laws and regulations are state-specific. One of the most important of these forces deals with direct primary nuances. Unlike most democracies, where party leaders choose the candidates who will run under the party's banner, in the United States, rank-and-file party members are allowed to select candidates. The direct primary system also allows anyone to run in a primary with or without the blessing of party leaders. Successful primary candidates gain all the advantages of major-party sponsorship in the general election. Groups seeking a policy or candidate different than what their party's leadership is offering have the option to pursue their agenda *without* leaving their party. Revolutions or rebellions in the party are handled internally; the dissenter stays with the party. Also, since both major parties use primaries, candidates representing a spectrum of beliefs are available within the two-party system— further reducing the likelihood of voters bolting to a minor party. As John Bibby and Sandy Maisel suggest, "The direct primary system makes American parties particularly porous and susceptible to external influences and in the process reduces the incentive to create additional parties."[20] Of course the key aspect of direct primaries is that while every state uses direct primaries to pick party candidates, *regulations vary greatly*. In some states, the system is vastly more "open" than in other states (see Chapter 6).

A second state-level institutional variable is ballot access. Once again, ballot access is often pointed to as one of the many legal barriers that minor parties confront nationwide. But there is significant state-by-state variance (see Table 5.4). Access to the general election ballot is easier in some states than in others. For instance, it requires roughly 50 times the number of voter signatures for minor parties to list their presidential candidate in Florida than it does for minor parties in Minnesota. Other stipulations, such as the requirement that signatures be collected in a set amount of time or from people registered as members of a minor party, produce even more variance.

A final institutional issue is fusion. In a small number of states, candidates are allowed to run on numerous party lines, and add up the results on Election Day. In New York, for example, Democratic candidates often try to run on the Working Family Party line as well, and Republican candidates will sometimes try for the Right to Life Party endorsement. Writing about a Supreme Court case, *Timmons v. Twin Cities Area New Party (1997)*, in which the Court ruled that fusion can be rejected by the state, scholar David Ryden notes, "The decision foreclosed a rare avenue of tangible minor party inroads into the two-party duopoly."[21] Only three states use fusion, and it is prohibited in 40 states.

Demographics   Studies of political behavior have long noted the importance of demographic factors. They have been key to our understanding of modes of participation, voter choice, trust, efficacy, attitudes toward partisanship, and the party system more generally, and much else. In *American Voter*, an immensely important book on numerous aspects of individual voting behavior written in 1961, the authors spend a great deal of time exploring the relationship between a host of demographic factors and party identification in the United States.[22]

---

[20]Bibby and Maisel, *Two Parties or More?*

[21]David K. Ryden, "The Good, the Bad, and the Ugly: Judicial Shaping of Party Activities," in John C. Green and Daniel M. Shea, *The State of the Parties*, 3rd ed. (Lanham, MD: Rowman & Littlefield, 1999).

[22]Angus Campbell, Philip Converse, Warren Miller, and Donald Stokes, *The American Voter* (New York: John Wiley and Sons, 1961).

More recently, Martin Wattenberg[23] explored demographic trends and the rise of nonaffiliated voters. In short, few would dispute the importance of individual characteristics in attempting to discern the existence of a minor-party culture.

Figure 5.4 lists the results of the index of minor-party support at the state level. One is immediately struck by the variation. Those states with voters most receptive to minor-party candidates are as widely varied as Alaska and Maine; and they are geographically disparate, including California, Hawaii, New York, and Oklahoma. Interestingly—with the exception of Oklahoma—no Southern states are classified as "most supportive." Kansas ranks as "somewhat supportive"; the remainder are "unsupportive." This is due in part, no doubt, to the generally more restrictive ballot access laws and traditionally uncompetitive elections in the South. In brief, it seems clear that local and state variation in minor-party performance is significant. It seems that minor-party candidates do better in some parts of the country than others. It is difficult to break these reasons down comprehensively, but they have much to do with the wide variances in state laws and voter attitudes.

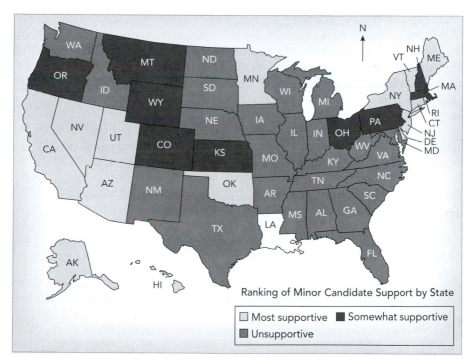

FIGURE 5.4 Ranking of Minor Candidate Support by State

Note: Louisiana does not have a primary system score because of its unique system in 2004.

Source: C. Daniel Myers and Daniel Shea, "Local Political Culture and Support for Minor Parties." Paper presented at the Midwest Political Science Association (April 17, 2004).

---

[23]Martin P. Wattenberg, *The Decline of American Party Politics, 1952–1980* (Cambridge, MA: Harvard University Press, 1998).

Conclusion

Given the challenges that minor parties confront in the American system and the limited success they have had at the polls throughout American history, one might be tempted to conclude that they are a waste of time; they play no role in changing the course of government. But nothing could be farther from the truth. Minor parties have played a significant role in shaping public policy by drawing attention to particular issues and by threatening to divert support from the major parties. Indeed, it has often been minor parties' success that has led to their downfall: Once a new party draws attention to an issue, and thus gains popularity, one or both of the major parties will pick up the issue and the voters will fall back in line. The minor party falters, but the issue has new life. As noted by one observer, "Established parties rarely develop ideas or present new issues on their own." The major parties are reinvigorated precisely because minor parties nip at the edges of the process.

Minor parties have historically played a significant role in bringing more citizens into the political process. Voters often begin to feel distrustful of the major parties—or at the very least ill-represented by them. They slowly withdraw from the process altogether, only to be drawn back in by the energy and excitement of minor-party activity. When minor parties are most active, the number of people heading to the polls increases.

As noted in this chapter's introduction, support for minor parties appears to be on the rise. Survey after survey suggests that Americans are ready for more alternatives on Election Day, and other data tell us that the number of minor-party candidates is also on the rise. It might be some time before America moves to a genuine multiparty system—and likely many institutional adjustments will have to be made—but a change does seem to be under way. Minor parties have always been avenues for change, and perhaps in the years ahead they will prove to be an even more potent force in American politics.

Critical Thinking

1. Does the U.S. Constitution itself inherently favor a two-party system? In thinking about this question, you might consider the various checks and balances. What might help different parts of the system work together?
2. If first-past-the-post, winner-take-all elections favor the major parties, why does Canada boast a viable multi-party system? After all, it also uses a winner-take-all, first-past-the post system.
3. Are ballot access laws and other restrictions undemocratic, or do they simply streamline the election process? Should the United States, as a democracy, embrace third parties?

On the Web

If you are interested in learning more about minor parties or would like to follow their developments in the news, visit: www.independentpoliticalreport.com, a website dedicated to covering America's third parties and independent candidates.

6

The Nomination Process

After reading this chapter, you should be able to understand these core concepts and explain their significance:

- King Caucus
- Types of Primaries
- McGovern–Fraser Commission
- The Invisible Primary
- Frontloading

- Proposed Reforms
  - National Primary Day
  - The Delaware Plan
  - The Ohio Plan
  - Rotating Primary Plan

I n Chapters 4 and 5, we introduced party politics and underscored the role that major parties play in American electoral politics, as well as the impact of minor parties. You have read that parties serve a host of functions, not the least of which are a range of services to voters like providing information, helping them to the polls on Election Day, and providing a cognitive shortcut when it comes to making a decision in the polling booth. This chapter deals with another important party service: the process of picking candidates to appear on the general election ballot under the party's name—the nomination process. We begin with a discussion of the primary system more generally, but quickly turn our attention to presidential nominations. The way major parties select presidential candidates for the general election has varied over time and is today one of the most controversial aspects of American elections.

WHY NOMINATE CANDIDATES?

Nominations represent an important step in the electoral process and serve a number of functions. For voters, party nominations narrow their choices on Election Day. Without nominations, voters might confront dozens or even hundreds of candidates on each ballot. In the 2003 California recall election, for example, some 135 candidates appeared on the ballot because party nominations were unnecessary. This was a rare occurrence, but a vivid demonstration of why nominations can help voters.

In many places, without a party's backing, candidates can only be "written in" on Election Day, making winning highly unlikely. This might seem a bit unfair to some, but others would say that if a candidate is not strong enough to garner a party's backing, he or she is probably not the best person for the office. Nominations by direct primary also extend the democratic process from simply voting on candidates to also selecting those candidates. Prior to the advent of primaries, party bosses typically handpicked nominees—a decidedly undemocratic method. Nominating contests, additionally, can encourage competition in otherwise solidly single-party areas by allowing intra-party challenges.

So, while most would agree that some sort of party nomination process is quite useful, exactly how to go about it has been a source of contention. During the early years of the American political system, a handful of party leaders simply chose their candidates. They argued that as heads of private organizations, "nominatin'" was their business, and few disagreed. After all, if the voters did not like the candidates chosen by the party leaders, they could vote for the other party's nominee. There was a built-in incentive to offer the best possible candidate in the general election. Why nominate poor candidates only to lose the election?

Thoughts about the nomination process changed during the Progressive Era, as noted in Chapter 5. By picking the nominee, party bosses could limit voter options, which often meant that reform-minded and minority candidates never stood a chance. But how might one break the grip of party elites in the nomination process? The solution was to pass laws mandating the selection of candidates through widespread voter input, a process Americans now call the direct primary. Average members of the party, the rank-and-file voters, would go to the polls and pick a nominee. Party elites were more or less shut out of the process. Today, both major parties and most minor parties choose their candidates by letting their members cast a ballot in the primaries.

VARIATIONS IN PRIMARY SYSTEMS

The direct primary first emerged in Crawford County, Pennsylvania, in 1842—the home of this author. Frustrated by a series of contentious nominating conventions that left their local party divided and out of office, Crawford County Democrats sought a means of nomination that would have public legitimacy and would unite the party behind a single candidate.[1] This approach caught on throughout the rest of the country

---

[1]Essays by Howard Reiter, Robert Kolesar, J. Morgan Kousser, John F. Reynolds, Jon Enriquez, and Thomas Coens, "H-Pol's Online Seminar: The Presidential Nominating Process," *SSHA Politics Network New* (Fall 1996). Accessed at: www.h-net.org/~pol/ssha/netnews/f96/reynol2.htm

for a variety of reasons. Many urban areas were controlled by corrupt party machines, and the direct primary proved to be a popular, powerful weapon against these organizations. The Democratic Party dominated Southern politics following the Civil War, and reformers pushed for the direct primary as a way to encourage competition in an otherwise single-party region.[2] The Progressive Party added support for the direct primary to its platform around the turn of the 20th century for ideological reasons (more involvement implied a healthier democracy), and by 1920, direct primaries were used in nearly every state.[3]

Not every state uses the same primary system, however. To the contrary, the diversity of approaches is significant. "It is probable," write William J. Keefe and Marc J. Hetherington, "that no nation has ever experimented as fully or fitfully with mechanisms for making nominations as has the United States."[4] Roughly one-half of the states now use what is called a closed primary system. In such states, only registered party members are allowed to vote in their own primary. In some states, the declaration of one's party registration must occur well in advance of the primary election—often 30 days—while in other states, it can be done on primary day. The latter is often called a partial or semi-closed system. Either way, states that rely on this system mandate that only members of the party can play a role in selecting the nominees.

Most of the other states use an open primary system. In these states, voters are allowed to participate in the primary election without declaring membership in a party. On primary day, the voter can simply choose to vote in the Republican primary or the Democratic primary, and no record is kept. Table 6.1 details the different types of primaries, and Figure 6.1 shows the primary system of each state.

A few states—Alaska, California, and Washington—have explored precisely how open their systems might be. Several years ago, they introduced blanket primaries where voters are allowed to participate in the primaries of both parties at the same time. For example, an Alaskan might support a Republican candidate for governor and a Democratic candidate for the Senate in the same primary election. Each of these states seemed to be responding to voter concerns for a less partisan system, but the major parties have not been especially pleased—as you might expect. For one, they argue crossover voters in blanket primaries may sabotage the opposition by supporting an inferior candidate. There is little hard data to support this claim, but many party operatives can point to anecdotal evidence of strategic crossover voting. Second, and more to the point, blanket primaries strip the nomination process from the party organization, so nonparty members, even non-partisan voters, can pick the nominees for a party.

Several parties in California challenged the blanket primary system on the grounds that it was a violation of free association rights under the First Amendment of the Constitution. The case was *California Democratic Party et al. v. Jones et al.* (2000). The parties argued that they are private organizations, comprised of their own

---

[2]L. Sandy Maisel, *Parties and Elections in America: The Electoral Process*, 3rd ed. (Lanham, MD: Rowman & Littlefield, 1999), 193.

[3]Ibid.

[4]William J. Keefe and Marc J. Hetherington, *Parties, Politics, and Public Policy in America,* 9th ed. (Washington, DC: CQ Press, 2003), 59.

TABLE 6.1 Types of Primaries	
Type of Primary	**What This Means**
Binding	The results of the election legally bind some or all of the delegates to vote for a particular candidate at the national convention.
Non-Binding	May select candidates to a state convention, which then selects delegates.
Open	Any voter may vote in any party's primary; however, a voter may participate in only one primary but not both.
Semi-Open	All voters may vote in any single primary, but must publicly declare which primary they will vote in before entering the voting booth.
Closed	Only voters registered with a party can vote in that party's primary.
Semi-Closed	Voters unaffiliated with a party (independents) may choose a party primary in which to vote.
"Top Two"	Voters receive a ballot with all candidates running for office; the two candidates with the highest vote total move on to the general election regardless of which party the candidate belongs to.
Blanket	Voters could vote for one candidate in multiple primaries, however, this system was ruled illegal by the Supreme Court in 2000.
Run-Off	A primary in which the ballot is not restricted to one party and the top two candidates advance to the general election no matter what their party affiliation is.

members, and that blanket primaries allow nonmembers to decide the groups' leaders (candidates). Among other things, this intrusion would have detrimental impacts on the long-term viability of party organizations, a harmful turn for democratic politics.[5] The Supreme Court agreed. Writing for the majority of the Court, Justice Antonin Scalia stated:

> [California is] forcing political parties to associate with those who do not share their beliefs. And it has done this at the crucial juncture at which party members traditionally find their collective voice and select their spokesman . . . The burden [California's primary system] places on [the political parties'] rights of political association is both severe and unnecessary.[6]

Since the Court's decision, these three states have scrambled to find a system that both meets the new judicial muster and satisfies most voters for a truly "open" primary system.

---

[5]John K. White and Daniel M. Shea, *New Party Politics: From Jefferson and Hamilton to the Information Age,* 2nd ed. (Belmont, CA: Wadsworth, 2003), 218.

[6]503 U.S. 567 (2000). See also the Associated Press, "Supreme Court Throws Out California's Blanket Primary" (June 26, 2000).

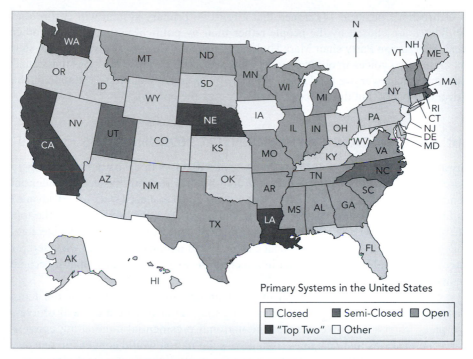

FIGURE 6.1 **Primary Systems in the United States, as of 2010**

Note: (a) District of Columbia has closed primary elections. (b) The "Other" category refers to a state where the two major political parties hold different types of primaries/caucuses: Iowa—Democrats: open, Republicans: semi-open; New Jersey—Democrats: closed, Republicans: semi-closed; and West Virginia—Democrats: semi-closed, Republicans: closed. (c) Some states have a different type of primary for presidential elections than for all other primary elections: Kentucky, Nevada, and Washington have closed presidential primaries for both major political parties: California—Democrats: semi-closed, Republicans: closed; Montana—Democrats: open; Republicans: closed.

Source: Compiled by the author. Data from Nina Kasniunas and Daniel M. Shea, *Campaign Rules: A 50-State Guide to Campaigns and Elections in America* (Lanham, MD: Rowman & Littlefield, 2010) with updates on California and Washington from their respective secretary of state websites, and the update on the District of Columbia from its Board of Elections and Ethics website.

In some states, effort has been directed to more or less jettison party-based nominations altogether. In 2004, the voters in the state of Washington passed a ballot initiative to create a "top two" nomination process. Here, any number of candidates are allowed to run in an initial contest, but only the top two are placed on the general election ballot. These two candidates might be of a different party, or they might not. Louisiana has had a similar system for years. In Nebraska, it is used only for the state's nonpartisan legislature and for some statewide races. In 2010, voters in California made a similar switch. Numerous organizations and party leaders disagreed over the benefits of the new primary system. Governor Arnold Schwarzenegger, a supporter of California's position 14, argued that a top-two primary system will ensure that candidates are chosen by the people rather than by political parties.[7] On the other hand, Libertarian Party chair Mark Hinkle suggested, "This top-two system will shut out all but two voices in our November elections, which are the elections that count. Now more than ever, we need more political voices and broader representation on the November ballot, but this proposition will do just the opposite."[8]

THE SPECIAL CASE OF PRESIDENTIAL NOMINATIONS

Given that the American political system began without political parties and that there were great hopes that parties would not take hold in the new system, presidential nominations were deemed unnecessary. It was assumed that each state would advance its favorite son, and men of high intellect and good character would rise to the top. Members of Congress would then suggest a small set of candidates for the electoral college to consider. The congressional caucus-based nomination system was used for three decades and was so important in selecting the eventual president that it became known as King Caucus.

To many, the Corrupt Deal of 1824 underscored the elitism of the King Caucus. Many began to push for something that better reflected the will of average party voters. The outcome was the national presidential nominating convention. The idea was that delegates from across the nation would convene in one city to discuss the strengths and weaknesses of potential candidates, and after a few days, they would settle on one candidate—the party's best candidate for the general election. It would also be an opportunity to develop a party platform, or list of policies that the party supports, as well as rules for conducting party business. Major parties held their first national conventions in 1832 and have done so every four years since.

The birth of the national nominating convention was an important turn in the history of popular elections in America. Reflecting on this change, the late political scientist V. O. Key suggested,

> The destruction of the caucus represented more than a mere change in the method of nomination. Its replacement by the convention was regarded as removal from power self-appointed oligarchies that had usurped the right to nominate . . . Sharp alterations in the distribution of power were taking place [in the 1830s], and they were paralleled by the shifts in methods of nomination.[9]

---

[7]Arnold Schwarzenegger, "Press Release: Governor Schwarzenegger Discusses New Era of Government with Passage of Proposition 14," Office of the Governor (June 11, 2010). Accessed at: http://gov.ca.gov/press-release/15347/

[8]"Libertarian Party Chair Mark Hinkle Opposes Proposition 14," *Independent Political Report* (June 3, 2010). Accessed at: www.independentpoliticalreport.com/2010/06/libertarian-party-chair-mark-hinkle-opposes-proposition-14/

[9]V. O. Key, *Politics, Parties, and Pressure Groups,* 4th ed. (New York: Thomas Y. Crowell, 1958), 373.

This is not to say the early convention model was completely democratic. One of the sticking points was how delegates would be chosen from their communities and what role they might play at the convention. A few states developed mechanisms to let rank-and-file party members select delegates, but most simply allowed state and local party bosses to handpick them. Once at the convention, these delegates were obliged to follow the orders of their local party leaders. This often led to high drama at party conventions, as party bosses used their delegates as negotiation chips, looking to play a central role in nominating the candidate—looking to play the role of kingmaker. Rules were established to mandate that successful candidates—the eventual nominees—had to receive at least 50 percent of the delegate votes. Given that several candidates were considered, this often leads to numerous ballots. (In 1924, it took the Democrats 103 ballots to finally nominate John Davis of West Virginia.) Conventions were about selecting the presidential nominee and making deals. This system, often referred to as the days of "smoke-filled rooms," lasted for nearly 140 years.

The strain between party bossism and average party followers came to a head in a fight over the 1968 Democratic presidential nomination. Early that year, most had assumed that the sitting president, Lyndon B. Johnson, would accept his party's nomination. Yet there seemed to be a groundswell of opposition to Johnson within the Democratic Party over the American involvement in the Vietnam War, so Johnson decided to step out of the race. A sharp division emerged between the party leaders, who backed Vice President Hubert Humphrey, and the "anti-war Democrats," who supported either Minnesota Senator Eugene McCarthy (not to be confused with Joseph McCarthy of Wisconsin, leader of the anti-communist witch hunts of the 1950s) or New York Senator Robert Kennedy. As the nomination season progressed, Kennedy and McCarthy drew wide support, yet the party bosses continued to back Humphrey. Robert Kennedy's assassination after the California primary added a greater sense of urgency to the anti-war Democrats. Faithful to their bosses, delegates at the nomination convention in Chicago nominated Humphrey. Thousands of anti-war Democrats filled the streets in protest outside the convention hall. To make matters even worse, Mayor Richard Daley of Chicago, one of the top Democratic bosses, ordered his police force to break up the protests, and the violence of the clash was broadcast to living rooms across the United States. Although he won the nomination, Humphrey went on to lose the general election against Richard Nixon. The Democratic Party seemed in shambles.

A reform panel was established and was called the McGovern–Fraser Commission (after its two chairmen, Senator George McGovern of South Dakota and Congressman Donald Fraser of Minnesota). Their report, "Mandate for Reform," forever changed the way presidential nominations would be conducted. The report argued that the Democratic nomination process must be "open, timely, and representative." A number of mechanisms were devised to achieve these goals; the most important pertained to the process of selecting delegates. Binding primaries were established in most states. Similar to the direct primary, this is a process where voters head to the polls to pick delegates who have pledged their support for a particular presidential candidate. The winners in each state are sent to the convention, where they vote to nominate a candidate.

Another way to pick delegates, used in about 15 states, is a nomination caucus. Here average party followers attend a local meeting, share ideas and concerns about particular candidates, and cast a ballot for pledged delegates to attend a statewide meeting. The same process takes place at the state level, and the delegates who win at the state level are sent to the national party convention. The key difference between primaries and caucuses is that the former is an election and the latter a series of town hall–like meetings.

Later Democratic Party reforms, such as those proposed by the 1976 Mikulski Commission, contributed in no small part to the drawn-out 2008 Democratic primary. The Mikulski Commission, co-chaired by Senator Barbara Mikulski (D, MD), recommended the proportional allocation of delegates, among other things. This meant that if a candidate netted 25 percent of the vote from a state, he or she should get 25 percent of the delegates. The Republicans, on the other hand, rely mostly on a winner-take-all system; if a candidate wins the state, he or she gets all the delegates from that state. It also led to the creation of a special category of participants called superdelegates, where 15 percent of Democratic delegates are chosen by party leaders. The idea was to select Democratic elected officials, such as mayors, members of Congress, and state legislators, so they would come to the convention and bond with other party officials. Superdelegates do not have to declare their support for a candidate until the convention.

The Democrats first used the open delegate selection process in 1972 when they nominated George McGovern as their candidate. McGovern was badly defeated by Nixon in that election, but the idea of allowing average citizens the right to pick delegates caught hold. Soon state Republican parties began using the same mechanism. Today, 35 states hold presidential nomination primaries for both parties, and the remaining number boast nomination caucuses. Table 6.2 provides the nomination calendar for the 2012 presidential election.

TABLE 6.2 2012 Presidential Primary Schedule	
January 3, 2012	Iowa (caucus)
January 10, 2012	New Hampshire (primary)
January 21, 2012	South Carolina (primary)
January 31, 2012	Florida (primary)
February 4, 2012	Nevada (caucus)
February 4–11, 2012	Maine (caucus)
February 7, 2012	Colorado (caucus)
	Minnesota (caucus)
February 28, 2012	Arizona (primary)
	Michigan (primary)
March 3, 2012	Washington (caucus)

(continued)

March 6, 2012	Alaska (caucus)
(Super Tuesday)	Georgia (primary)
	Idaho (caucus)
	Massachusetts (primary)
	North Dakota (caucus)
	Oklahoma (primary)
	Tennessee (primary)
	Texas (primary)
	Vermont (primary)
	Virginia (primary)
March 6–10, 2012	Wyoming (caucus)
March 10, 2012	Kansas (caucus)
	U.S. Virgin Islands (caucus)
March 13, 2012	Alabama (primary)
	Hawaii (caucus)
	Mississippi (primary)
March 17, 2012	Missouri (caucus)
March 20, 2012	Illinois (primary)
March 24, 2012	Louisiana (primary)
April 3, 2012	Maryland (primary)
	Washington, DC (primary)
	Wisconsin (primary)
April 24, 2012	Connecticut (primary)
	Delaware (primary)
	New York (primary)
	Pennsylvania (primary)
	Rhode Island (primary)
May 8, 2012	Indiana (primary)
	North Carolina (primary)
	West Virginia (primary)
May 15, 2012	Nebraska (primary)
	Oregon (primary)
May 22, 2012	Arkansas (primary)
	Kentucky (primary)
June 5, 2012	California (primary)
	Montana (primary)
	New Jersey (primary)
	New Mexico (primary)
	South Dakota (primary)
June 12, 2012	Ohio (primary)
June 26, 2012	Utah (primary)

THE LIMITS OF PRIMARIES AND CAUCUSES

Although many agree that nominations should not be held in smoke-filled rooms, the open delegate selection system also has problems, to be sure. Opening the primaries to the entire population may have helped with transparency, but it is not clear if the primary system has become a true reflection of the electorate as yet.

Primary elections are notorious for their low turnout. Even in the record-setting 2008 elections, few states recorded a primary or caucus turnout of greater than 35 percent of the voting-eligible population. Gubernatorial and municipal primary elections have even more meager turnout rates, and rarely break double digits. Table 6.3 compares the primary and general election turnout rates (as a percentage of registered voters) in the 2008 presidential election.

TABLE 6.3	Voter Turnout 2008	
State	**2008 Primary %**	**2008 General %**
United States		61.6
Alabama	32.2	61.4
Alaska	5.0	67.7
Arizona	24.2	55.1
Arkansas	26.8	52.6
California	40.0	61.2
Colorado	5.4	70.2
Connecticut	20.5	67.4
Delaware	23.8	66.5
District of Columbia	30.1	61.7
Florida	34.0	66.9
Georgia	32.0	61.5
Hawaii	N/A	50.5
Idaho	17.7	63.7
Illinois	33.8	63.2
Indiana	37.3	59.3
Iowa	16.1	69.7
Kansas	2.9	62.0
Kentucky	29.2	57.9
Louisiana	17.7	61.1
Maine	4.9	70.9
Maryland	31.5	67.4
Massachusetts	38.2	65.9
Michigan	20.0	68.4
Minnesota	7.4	77.7
Mississippi	27.5	61.4
Missouri	33.0	67.2

(continued)

State	2008 Primary %	2008 General %
Montana	38.7	66.8
Nebraska	20.5	63.4
Nevada	9.7	58.6
New Hampshire	53.6	71.1
New Jersey	29.2	67.2
New Mexico	19.3	61.7
New York	19.5	58.3
North Carolina	32.8	66.1
North Dakota	5.9	64.3
Ohio	42.4	66.6
Oklahoma	29.1	56.3
Oregon	43.2	67.5
Pennsylvania	34.0	63.7
Rhode Island	28.4	61.9
South Carolina	30.3	58.5
South Dakota	28.4	64.1
Tennessee	26.1	57.0
Texas	28.4	54.4
Utah	24.7	54.5
Vermont	40.7	67.2
Virginia	26.9	67.5
Washington	30.6	66.5
West Virginia	32.5	50.7
Wisconsin	37.1	72.1
Wyoming	2.6	64.5

Source: Michael P. McDonald. "Voter Turnout" *United States Elections Project* (2011).
Accessed at: http://elections.gmu.edu/voter_turnout.htm on June 5, 2011.

A second concern is that the current nomination process might *not* reflect the will of average party members because those who do turn out to vote or caucus might be different than average party followers. Scholars have been debating this issue for some time. For example, John G. Geer has found that primary voters for both parties have less education and less income than regular party followers.[10] On the other hand, Alan Abramowitz suggests that, on an ideological measure, primary voter and general election voters were very similar (see Table 6.4).[11] This surely bucks traditional

---

[10]John G. Geer, "Assessing the Representativeness of Electorates in Presidential Primaries," *American Journal of Political Science*, 32, no. 4 (November 1988), 929–945.
[11]Alan Abramowitz, "Don't Blame Primary Voters for Polarization," *The Forum*, 5, no. 4 (2008). Accessed at: www.themonkeycage.org/Abramowitz.Primary.Voters.pdf

TABLE 6.4	Ideological Liberalism of Democratic and Republican Voters in 2000 Presidential Primaries	
State	**Democrats**	**Republicans**
Iowa	70	16
New Hampshire	73	31
Connecticut	70	34
Delaware	64	23
Massachusetts	74	40
Maryland	70	28
Maine	76	32
New York	72	32
Rhode Island	70	32
Vermont	82	38
Arizona	—	23
California	71	22
Colorado	66	22
Michigan	—	36
Missouri	70	28
Ohio	66	34
Florida	64	25
Georgia	66	24
Louisiana	56	16
Mississippi	57	22
Oklahoma	52	19
Tennessee	54	22
Texas	60	22
Virginia	—	28
Primary Average	66	27
General Election Average	62	28

Note: Ideological liberalism = liberal percentage + half of moderate percentage.

Source: Alan Abramowitz, 2008. "Don't Blame Primary Voters for Polarization," *The Forum: Politics of Presidential Selection* 5, no. 4 (2008): Article 4.

wisdom, which suggests that only the most ideological members of the party turn out to vote in primary elections. Anecdotal evidence from 2010 House and Senate primary contests would suggest the wings of each party are more engaged during these contest than the moderates. In nearly a dozen contests, for example, moderate Republicans were knocked off by more conservative, often Tea Party–backed, candidates.

A related issue is the extent to which delegates to presidential nomination conventions reflect average voters. In a famous study of delegates attending the 1972

Democratic and Republican conventions, political scientist Jeane Kirkpatrick found them to be largely unrepresentative of the American electorate: 56 percent of the Democratic delegates had a college degree; 59 percent of the GOP (Grand Old Party) delegates also had college degrees.[12] At the time, only 13 percent of the electorate had a college degree.[13] Given this data, it was not surprising that George McGovern, the most liberal Democrat nominated for the presidency since William Jennings Bryan in 1896, received the Democratic nomination in 1972.

In a time-series study conducted by John Jackson and John C. Green in 2008, the convention delegates were found to be much more polarized on ideology and numerous political issues than the general public (see Figure 6.2). While the Democratic delegates were more liberal than the Republican delegates, the Democrats were spilt—between liberal and moderate factions—but the Republicans stayed together under the conservative label. The authors also asked about social welfare, foreign policy, and cultural issues to study the polarization of the parties' elites. The delegates supported their respective party platform and showed that some factions do occur within the party.[14]

Because candidates win or lose based on how citizens feel about them, the nomination process has become very expensive, time-consuming, and often negative. Candidates who can raise the most money (especially those who can do it quickly) have a significant advantage. This money can be used to attack the other candidates—who are all part of the same party, of course. Some of the harshest

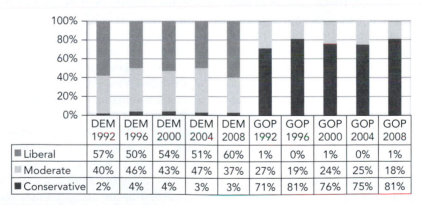

	DEM 1992	DEM 1996	DEM 2000	DEM 2004	DEM 2008	GOP 1992	GOP 1996	GOP 2000	GOP 2004	GOP 2008
■ Liberal	57%	50%	54%	51%	60%	1%	0%	1%	0%	1%
▨ Moderate	40%	46%	43%	47%	37%	27%	19%	24%	25%	18%
■ Conservative	2%	4%	4%	3%	3%	71%	81%	76%	75%	81%

FIGURE 6.2 Delegates and Ideology, 1992–2008
Source: John Jackson and John C. Green, "The State of Party Elites: National Convention Delegates 1992–2008" in John C. Green and Daniel J. Coffey, eds., *The State of the Parties: The Changing Role of Contemporary American Parties*, 6th ed. (Lanham, MD: Rowman & Littlefield, 2011).

---

[12]Jeane M. Kirkpatrick, *Dismantling the Parties* (Washington, DC: American Enterprise Institute, 1978).

[13]American National Election Studies, "Education of Respondent: 1948–2004." Accessed at: www .electionstudies.org/nesguide/toptable/tab1a_4.htm

[14]John Jackson and John C. Green, "The State of Party Elites: National Convention Delegates 1992–2008" in John C. Green and Daniel J. Coffey, eds., *The State of the Parties: The changing Role of Contemporary American Parties*, 6th ed. (Lanham, MD: Rowman & Littlefield, 2011).

attacks against presidential candidates occur during the primaries, not during the general election.

On top of this, candidates able to garner media attention before and during the primary season do much better—unfairly advantaging well-known candidates. The process is drawn out, but at the same time puts a premium on winning early primary and caucus contests—which, of course, helps raise money and draw media attention. Some argue that states like New Hampshire and Iowa, which hold their events early in the process, are provided a disproportionate role in selecting the eventual nominees.

The current system also allows anyone the opportunity to run for office. While this might seem like a good idea, some suggest that some sort of screening mechanism should filter out unworthy candidates. To put it a bit differently, it has been argued that in today's system anyone with a hefty bank account and a good team of campaign consultants can run for office and do quite well regardless of his or her knowledge, experience, background, and character.

A great deal of emphasis is put on the very early stages of the nomination contest—what scholars have dubbed the "invisible primary." Which candidates have raised the most funds or garnered the most high profile endorsements early in the process? For the 2008 presidential election, fund-raising began two years prior. Some observers claim that, barely half a year into Barack Obama's first term, the invisible primary had already begun for the 2012 Republican nomination. Indeed, several prominent Republican leaders, like Governors Bobby Jindal, Haley Barbour, and Mike Huckabee, found excuses to make trips to Iowa during the first few months of 2009. (The precise meaning of Sarah Palin's trip to Iowa in the fall of 2010 and her "One Nation" bus tour in the spring of 2011 was widely debated.)

The early start has led to front-loading—moving the state's nomination contest up in the election calendar in order to be relevant to the final outcome. In the 2000 election, for example, Texas Governor George W. Bush and Vice President Al Gore had essentially locked up the Republican and Democratic nominations by March although voters in 33 states had not yet cast their primary ballots![15] If these contests are deemed "over" after a few early contests, why not move your state's primary or caucus date up? So it should come as no surprise that many states have moved their primaries and caucuses forward. The 2008 pre-primary season saw an intense leapfrog contest, leading to a dramatic rearrangement of the primary calendar. Both Iowa and New Hampshire have passed legislation protecting their first-in-the-nation primary status, and the Democratic National Committee (DNC) continues to support these states. In 2008, DNC rules stipulated that no state should hold its nomination contest before Iowa and New Hampshire, at the risk of having its delegates barred from the national convention; the DNC went so far as to strip one-half of the delegates of Michigan and Florida because these states scheduled their events in January (under DNC rules, only Iowa, New Hampshire, South Carolina, and Nevada are allowed a January primary). Despite the many threats and regulations, the 2008 primary leapfrog contest quickly

---

[15]"The Report of the National Symposium on Presidential Selection," The Center for Governmental Studies at the University of Virginia (2001). Accessed at: www.centerforpolitics.org/downloads/rnsps.pdf

took on aspects of the absurd. One state would schedule its nominating contest earlier, only to be leapfrogged by another state—and in response, the first state would again move up its date. The results were nothing short of chaos. South Carolina, for example, decided to move its contest earlier in order to have the distinction of being the first primary in the South. Nevada made a similar move. But in spring of 2007, Florida changed its primary date to January 29, reasoning, why shouldn't Florida be the first in the South? In response, both South Carolina and Nevada pushed their dates even earlier in order to be ahead of Florida.

Several additional problems sprung from this turbulent leapfrog process. It put even more pressure on the early stages of the nomination process and led to an unprecedented early campaign season. Nearly all candidates in both parties had declared their intentions to run a full 18 months before the general election. Indeed, Fred Thompson was criticized for his late entry into the race—early September 2007—and in 2011 Texas Governor Rick Perry got the same rap, and he entered the race in early August of that year! In past presidential elections, few candidates had formally declared their intentions until after Labor Day.

Another implication has been the importance of early fund-raising. Money has been critical in presidential elections for many years; the rapid succession of primaries means that without a very large bank account, a candidate cannot compete.

REFORMING THE PROCESS FOR 2012 AND BEYOND

Is the nomination process too demanding on the candidates and downright harmful to the electoral process? Many people are beginning to question the utility of the current system and to explore solutions. Despite the official standing of Iowa and New Hampshire in the primary season among both Republicans and Democrats, there is increasing concern that these states have undue influence over the electoral process and that their voters have an unfair advantage over the rest of the country; indeed, it is these concerns that helped to drive the leapfrogging of 2008 and 2012. Many state legislators and party officials are starting to ask why Iowa and New Hampshire should be first. Sure, it might be good for those states, but is it really the best move for the nomination process? Why shouldn't their states move their contests to the head of the process and get all that attention from candidates and the media? The outcome has been a rapid succession of states making moves to hold their contests earlier in the nomination calendar.

To combat the front-loading process, both of the national party committees established reform commissions in 2009. The DNC commission recommended stringent rules to limit early contests in 2012. It suggested that the Iowa caucus should be held on February 6, the New Hampshire primary on February 14, the Nevada contest on February 18, and the South Carolina primary on February 28. All other states should hold their contests after March 6. (Many recognized, however, that the four-day gap between the New Hampshire primary and the Nevada caucuses violates New Hampshire law, which requires a seven-day cushion). Rule changes adopted by the Republican National Committee (RNC) were a bit more flexible; in short, the RNC allows Iowa, New Hampshire, South Carolina, and Nevada to "begin their processes at any time on or after February 1" while other states can hold contests starting the first Tuesday in March.[16]

But how do you get state legislatures and state party committees to adhere to national party committees' rules? Both parties have adopted incentives to encourage states to hold their events later in the process. For example, Republicans adopted a rule that requires states holding contests prior to April 1 to allocate delegates on a proportional basis; states holding contests on April 1 and after can use the winner-take-all system, which gives them more clout. Democrats developed a model with clusters of dates: March 6–31, April 1–30, and May 1–June 12. States that hold their events in the last two stages will gain from 10 percent to 20 percent more delegates. The DNC also made moves to encourage regional clustering—such as the so-called 2008 Potomac Primary, which encompassed Washington, DC; Maryland; and Virginia. States that cluster can get upward of 15 percent more delegates.[17]

But that still might not be enough to dissuade states from front-loading. The Florida legislature, in particular, seems set on an early primary date. In response, South Carolina Republican Party chair Karen Floyd wrote a letter to RNC noting, "If Florida refuses to move its primary date into compliance with RNC rules, I am respectfully requesting that the Committee convene a special task force to select a new site for the 2012 Convention outside the state of Florida."[18] In Arizona, on September 12, 2011, Governor Jan Brewer (R) signed a proclamation setting the primary date at February 28 (Brewer had been leaning toward moving the primary up to January 31). This date violates both RNC and DNC rules. In the fall of 2011, the Michigan state legislature began moving on a measure that would shift their date to the fourth Tuesday in February. This is just the tip of the iceberg. Some states have decided to move their contests to very late in the season, such as in June, with the hopes of highlighting their relevance. Other states, like Washington, seem fed up with the entire process; Washington has suspended the state presidential primary, saving $10 million in general fund expenditures.

The end result is continued chaos. By October of 2011, an official calendar of nomination contests had yet to be set. A tentative schedule is offered in Table 6.2, but it seems entirely likely that if Florida continues to make moves to be the first in the election process, New Hampshire and Iowa will leapfrog to December.

In the long range, most agree that a coherent plan makes the most sense. Several models have been suggested in recent years. One approach would be to have one national primary day. Just as with the general election, voters from across the United States would pick their party's nominee on the same day. For all intents and purposes, as front-loading increases as a trend, the country seems to be naturally moving in the direction of what amounts to a national primary, so why not formalize this process?[19] Many suggest that this plan would increase turnout because more people would feel that their vote could make a difference (recall that in the current system the nominee is

---

[16]P2012.org, "Race for the White House," September 23, 2011. Accessed at: www.p2012.org/chrn/othp12.html
[17]Ibid.
[18]Ibid.
[19]"National Symposium on Presidential Selection."

often determined after a few weeks, leaving some states without a say in the process). But others have argued that the "retail" (meaning intimate, face-to-face) electioneering common in many early states, particularly New Hampshire and Iowa would be lost. In its place would be one massive national media campaign.

The Delaware Plan would group four "blocks" of states according to population to determine the order of primaries. The smallest 12 states and the District of Columbia would go first, then the next 13, then 13 medium states, followed by the largest 12 states (see Figure 6.3). States would remain free to decide between a primary and a caucus, and could schedule their events for any time during their appointed period. This plan addresses the problem of front-loading, and supporters argue that it would encourage voter participation and increase grassroots campaign efforts while giving small states—historically not influential—a chance to participate. On the other hand, opponents argue that in this plan money would still play a large role, and instead of a single winner, the plan could produce multiple winners in the many competitions. The main concern is that the four blocks would effectively be four media-centered campaigns.[20] Again, retail campaigning would be lost.

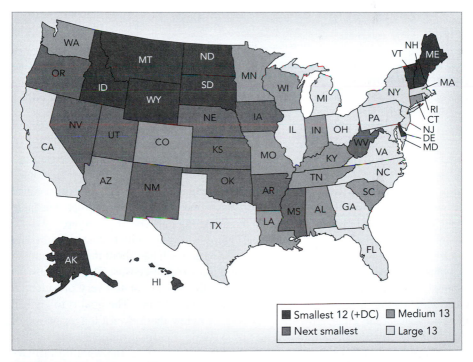

FIGURE 6.3 The Delaware Plan

Source: "Fix the Primaries: The Delaware Plan." Accessed at: http://fixtheprimaries.com/solutions/delawareplan/

---

[20]"National Symposium on Presidential Selection."

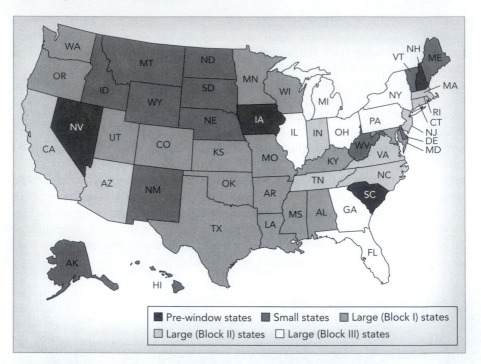

FIGURE 6.4 The Ohio Plan

Source: "The Ohio Plan," adapted from http://bp1.blogger.com/_4u9lzZ9sqJk/SCYGlIrtkQI/AAAAAAAAAHM/-O3IAEBarPs/s1600-h/Ohio+Plan.gif

In the wake of the 2008 election, the RNC voted in favor of implementing a similar system called the Ohio Plan. While not used in 2012, if the Ohio Plan were adopted in subsequent elections, states would be split into three tiers—early states (also called pre-window states), small states, and large states—and will vote in that order. The large states would be further broken down into three rotating clusters[21] (see Figure 6.4).

Under a rotating primary plan (see Figure 6.5), the United States is split into four regions—Northeast, Midwest, West, and South. Each has about the same number of votes in the electoral college, based on the most recent census. This plan has the same structure as the Delaware Plan; however, the blocks rotate every presidential election, allowing different regions to be influential each time. The goal is to give all the candidates a fair chance by allowing voters to view them over a longer period of time, and therefore to let a more diverse group choose the front-runners.

This regional lottery system uses the blocks created in the rotating primary plan, with the main differences being that the order is determined by a lottery, and leadoff states are not allowed. Scholar Larry Sabato argues, "The key to this plan is

---

[21]Chris Cillizza, "The Fix: GOP Weighs Calendar Changes for 2012," *Washington Post* (April 2, 2008). Accessed at: http://voices.washingtonpost.com/thefix/republican-party/republicans-weigh-calendar-cha.html

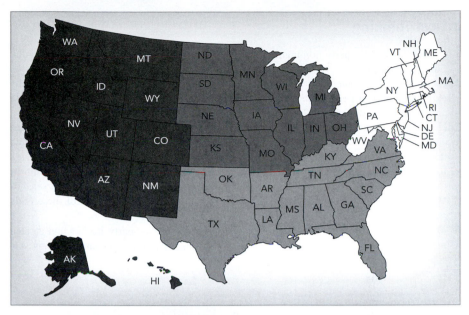

FIGURE 6.5 **Proposed Regional Nomination Map**
*This figure notes what many believe to be a logical division of the nation into four regions.
Source: "The Report of the National Symposium on Presidential Selection,"
The Center for Governmental Studies at the University of Virginia (2001).
Accessed at: www.centerforpolitics.org/downloads/rnsps.pdf

the lottery used to determine the order each region will participate in the nominating process. Because candidates are unable to know more than a few months in advance which region will lead off the calendar, homesteading is eliminated and candidates are forced to focus equally on all areas."[22]

Conclusion

Most would balk at the prospects of returning to a boss-centered system, but at the same time, there is an acknowledgment that the current process is rife with problems. Changes designed to make the system more "open, timely and representative" have moved things in the right direction, but have also created a new set of issues. One has to wonder whether some of America's greatest presidents—such as Abraham Lincoln, with his odd appearance and shy demeanor, and Franklin D. Roosevelt, bound to a wheelchair at a time when disabilities were not well received—would have won their parties' nomination in today's process.

---

[22]"National Symposium on Presidential Selection."

Critical Thinking

1. Should we think of party nominations as private affairs, and therefore beyond the regulation of government?
2. It is said that candidates must appeal to primary voters who seem to be more ideologically extreme than their general election counterparts. How has this changed both the process and the outcome of elections?
3. How might a single national primary affect the "invisible primary"? How might it affect the chances of a lesser-known candidate—would it favor the establishment candidate, or would it simply cut down the influence of states like Iowa and New Hampshire?
4. Iowa's and New Hampshire's respective places in the primary process have been a political tradition for decades. Do these states deserve their prime slots in the nomination season? Why or why not? Would American democracy benefit by regular rotation of these early states?
5. The Democrats' nominating process involves superdelegates—party leaders and elected officials who can cast their votes irrespective of the outcome of the primary elections. Are superdelegates undemocratic?

On the Web

To learn more about the frontloading process, as well as the most recent information regarding presidential primary and caucus dates, consider visiting Frontloading HQ, at: http://frontloading .blogspot.com/

New Players in the Election Process: Consultants, Interest Groups, and LCCs

No review of the players in contemporary elections in America would be complete without a discussion of important new actors, namely new-style campaign consultants, interest groups, and legislative campaign committees (LCCs). During most of America's history, candidates relied on the help of friends, relatives, and amateur party operatives, often called "hacks," to aid their efforts. During the 19th century, for example, if candidates collected money for their campaign, it was immediately turned over to the party leaders to disburse as the leaders saw fit. Given that the foremost means of connecting with voters was interpersonal, often on one's doorstep or at one's factory gate, there seemed to be little need for sophisticated, professional assistance. Elections were volunteer oriented, and candidates depended on party leaders to reach voters.

But things have changed a great deal, of course. This chapter takes a look at the transformation of campaigns from being purely party centered to the new system characterized by a coalition of allied actors. Parties remain at the center of contemporary elections, but they work very closely with campaign consultants, interest groups, LCCs, and other actors. As noted by University of Maryland scholar Paul Herrnson, "These coalitions include actors not often considered components of the party; namely, party-connected committees and party allies . . . The inclusion of these actors highlights the parties' ability to adapt to their political environment."[1]

We begin with the roots of the change and then move to the rise of campaign consultants and some of the services they provide. We then spend a bit of time discussing ethical issues, which will lead us to another important turn in modern campaign: the rise of attack advertising. Next we'll move to the rise of interest groups and finally to the emergence of LCCs. The chapter ends with a brief discussion of how these new actors have altered electoral politics in America.

CAMPAIGN CONSULTANTS

Campaigns began to change at the presidential level only around the 1950s. By this time, a growing number of Americans had televisions in their living rooms, and millions more had radios, telephones, and daily newspaper subscriptions. Political operatives soon realized that new media technologies offered candidates the potential to reach millions of voters simultaneously; connecting through the "tube" was more efficient and effective than the person-to-person electioneering of previous decades. Dwight Eisenhower ushered in the age of television campaigning with a series of 60-second commercials that invited viewers to get to know him. Eisenhower's 1952 presidential campaign can largely be credited as the first truly modern political campaign. A business Republican, Eisenhower called upon several friends—"Madison Avenue" marketing executives and other product marketing professionals—to run his campaign. While he was criticized by his opponents for trying to sell his candidacy like a household product, there seemed no denying the significance of professional campaign help. Slowly but surely, campaign management caught the attention of statewide, congressional, state-legislative, and even municipal candidates; by the late 1970s, nearly every significant campaign involved a campaign consultant.[2]

Media technologies were not the only developments to affect political campaigns. During the 1940s, a new means of accurately discerning public opinion was perfected: survey research, also called public opinion polls. Politicians quickly learned not only that polls can be accurate tools for measuring voter attitudes and beliefs, but that they also require a high level of technical sophistication to construct and implement. Early campaign consultants typically served only as general advisors

---

[1]Paul S. Herrnson, "The Role of Party Organizations, Party-Connected Committees, and Party Allies in Elections," *Journal of Politics* 71 (2009): 1207–1224.

[2]David A. Dulio, *For Better or Worse? How Political Consultants Are Changing Elections in the United States* (Albany, NY: State University of New York Press, 2008), 6.

and devised broad campaign strategies. The advent of survey research required candidates to hire narrowly defined consultants with specific technical expertise; they were the first of a new breed who would gradually supplant the original broad-focus consultants.

By the 1970s, a growing number of Americans had rejected party labels; events like the 1968 Democratic National Convention, the Vietnam War, and the Watergate scandal led to disillusionment with party politics and the largest number of self-identifying independents in decades, as noted in Chapter 5. This led to volatility in the electorate; a higher level of campaign prowess was necessary to overcome this uncertainty. All told, the electoral system was ripe for the emergence of a new profession.

Indeed, according to the author of a book entitled *High-Tech Grass Roots*, by the early 1970s, "the flood of technologically oriented campaigns became a deluge."[3] By the early 1980s, numerous college campaign management programs had sprung up, each turning out a new generation of highly skilled campaign operatives. Another scholar of the election process has noted that the breadth of new-style campaigning is so great that elections in the United States might be described as "consultant-centered."[4] Today, few serious candidates for office head into the campaign trenches without well-trained, well-paid assistance.

Types of Campaign Consultants

It is difficult to put a figure on the number of professional consultants in the United States, as there are no official requirements, regulations, or registration procedures to conduct campaign work. Unlike accountancy, law, medicine, plumbing, and even auto repair in some states, no certification is required for campaign consulting. Many have suggested that this is a problem and that some sort of professional guidelines need to be established. In 1969, the American Association of Political Consultants (AAPC) was formed, essentially a trade group of media consultants, pollsters, campaign managers, professors, fund-raisers, and an array of campaign product venders. Today the AAPC boasts some 1,100 members. It holds regular conferences, hands out numerous awards, and pushes its members to adhere to a code of ethics. But this is all voluntary, and the AAPC membership captures only a fraction of the new profession.

Many think that campaign consultants are little more than pollsters and strategists, but in reality, a wide array of specialized consultants can be found working on one campaign. In the 1960s, political consultants started narrowing their scopes from general information and media proficiency to specific areas of communications, single resource allocation, and individualized areas of expertise.[5] Today, individuals and firms lend their skills to research, fund-raising, advertising, and other significant

---

[3]J. Cherie Strachan, *High-Tech Grass Roots: The Professionalization of Local Elections* (Lanham, MD: Rowman & Littlefield, 2003), 3.

[4]Daniel M. Shea, *Campaign Craft: The Strategies, Tactics, and Art of Political Campaign Management* (Westport, CT: Praeger, 1996), 13.

[5]James A. Thurber, "The Study of Campaign Consultants: A Subfield in Search of Theory," *PS: Political Science and Politics* 31, no. 2 (1998): 145–150; Expanded Academic ASAP (February 12, 2004).

areas. Hiring the right professional for a specific strategy or task is important to a campaign, and the diversity of consultants in operation today makes that specialized assistance increasingly available.[6]

Campaigns & Elections Magazine, essentially a trade journal for consultants, boasts a directory of political consultants that includes over 60 categories, in its 2010 edition.[7] On its list, even traditional consultant jobs are broken down into specific areas. For example, the polling category is narrowed into firms specializing in focus groups, firms conducting survey research and analysis, and web-based firms. Consultants specializing in individual media and public relations tactics are also well represented, each with a specific asset to offer. For example, direct mail strategists boast effective methods for reaching voters through informative and attractive postal mailings and e-mailings. Internet consultants promise to increase fundraising, reach potential voters, and spawn grassroots activism through tactical uses of websites. Targeting consultants, another type of specialist, are available to help candidates reach a specific demographic or subset of voters that may be crucial to a campaign. Other consultants include speechwriters, field operators, and media consultants.[8] Although not every campaign necessitates a specialized firm for every task, the availability of experts to assist with areas in need is a helpful addition to the traditional general consultant.

Consultants and Ethical Issues

Campaign consultants have no formal ethical guidelines to steer their conduct on the campaign trail. There is no book of consultant bylaws to be referenced before campaign decisions are made. However, the absence of a strict ethical code does not imply that consultants are free to make outlandish, untrue, or inappropriate statements without facing repercussions. After all, the public is watching, and mean-spirited campaigning can lead to the alienation of voters.[9] There are three general practices that campaign consultants seem to agree upon. Although these principles are vague and not formally enforced, they do provide a preliminary check on potentially unethical behavior.

The first standard holds that the information to be presented must be true and verifiable.[10] This component is easy for consultants to agree upon, as the dissemination of falsified information to the public ultimately benefits no one. This includes untrue assertions about a consultant's own candidate as well as claims made against an opponent. Doctored photographs or images are also unethical.[11] The truthfulness of a statement should be easy to prove, making violations easy to detect. The second standard follows from this and states that all research must be legally obtained public information.

---

[6]Ibid.

[7]"The Political Pages 2010," *Campaigns & Elections*. Accessed at: www.politicsmagazine.com/resources/the-political-directories

[8]Ibid.

[9]Shea, *Campaign Craft*, 95.

[10]Ibid.

[11]Whit Ayres, "Can Campaign Advertising Be on the Level?" *Campaigns & Elections* 22, no. 8 (2001), 20; Expanded Academic ASAP (February 11, 2004).

BOX 7.1 Types of Consultants

Following is a list of the top ten types of consultants and what their jobs on the campaign entail. Remember that these categories are very broad and that numerous subcategories exist. For a full list of political consulting firms in the United States, go to the Political Pages directory at www.politicsmagazine.com/resources/the-political-directories.

Direct Mail consultants create all forms of mailing from the basic campaign flyer to fund-raising letters. Each piece is targeted to a specific audience that is determined by using demographics, consumer interests, and other micro-targeting techniques. The consultant strategizes the most influential way to stay on message, attract the audience, and receive the correct response. Simple things, such as how the envelope is addressed, can make a recipient read the mailer or throw it away without a glance. There are consultants who specialize in creating, strategizing, printing, and processing.

Field consultants focus on the creating the best ground effort for a candidate. These consultants first collect signatures to get the candidate on the ballot. Other field operations include finding and setting up offices, hiring and training field organizers, and drafting plans for canvassing, phone-banking, and get-out-the-vote. There are also consultants who provide mailing and telephone lists and others who provide maps for canvassing.

Fund-Raising consultants are trained to bring in money through events, mail, telephone, and the Internet. There are consultants for getting PAC (political action committee) money and others who know the campaign finance laws and deal with the Federal Election Commission.

Internet consultants do multiple tasks including designing candidates' websites, creating web ads, and writing blogs. Computer sharing software and e-mail services for campaigns' headquarters are also provided by Internet consultants.

Media consultants produce television and radio ads, buy broadcast time, and target their ads to a specific audience. Some consultants focus on the presentation of the candidate by giving public speaking and camera training. A television or radio ad must be very effective in the delivery, imagery, and time placement, so there are advertising strategists who come up with the idea and production consultants who make it happen.

Polling consultants analyze all aspects of the campaign from how strong the candidate's campaign message is to which issues are of the highest concern for each demographic. Polling comes in numerous types, including focus groups and Internet polls, but most commonly telephone polls. Tracking polls are often conducted in big campaigns, such as the presidential. These polls occur every day and are compared to other days' results in order to view changes in the electorate and to measure the effectiveness of campaign events, for instance releasing a television advertisement. Consultants write and analyze the polls, and report the findings to the candidate.

Research consultants are used to find out information about the candidate's opponent. Often, candidates will also conduct research on themselves in order to know what information the opposition may use against them. Every word the candidate says must be true, or the media will have a feeding frenzy, so campaigns will hire research consultants who focus on legislation and issues.

Strategy consultants create and keep a campaign theme and message in all aspects of the campaign. Having a consistent message helps voters understand the candidate's positions and create name recognition. Every element should have a similar theme, including the look of direct mail, television ads, and the campaign website. Strategy consultants also help

(continued)

BOX 7.1   Types of Consultants   *(continued)*

with crisis management by giving the candidate quick advice about how to respond effectively to negative attacks and minimize the amount of damage to his or her reputation.

Speech writing and press consultants draft the candidate's public addresses. These consultants compose the candidate's issue positions in a clear way, so the public understands the problems and the candidate's idea on how to fix them. Press consultants deal with writing press releases, granting interviews, and setting up press areas at all the campaign events. Consultants also provide political coaching on how to talk to the press.

Targeting consultants look for the best way to connect the campaign message with different demographics. Through polling, U.S. Census, and state data, targeting consultants obtain a pretty good idea of the makeup of the electorate. The consultant needs to then find the best way to target specific demographics. Through micro-targeting techniques, such as using magazine subscriptions, demographics of television programs, and organization membership lists, consultants can narrow down voter interests and then select which issue will best resonate with a particular group of voters. Targeting consultants also find out the number of party supporters and swing voters in the electorate.

City, county, and even state public records include a wealth of information that is readily available to the average person.[12] The use of this information ensures legitimacy and accuracy, and makes verification relatively easy for the voter.[13]

The third unofficial standard, unlike the first two, is rather ambiguous. It states that the information should be relevant to the electoral race.[14] It is difficult to pinpoint violations of this standard, as particular information may be important to one voter, while irrelevant to the next. However, there is some information that can be generally agreed upon as irrelevant, and thus unethical, in any campaign. For example, an event that occurred many years ago and has not recurred since is often deemed irrelevant. Condemning a candidate based on the weaknesses of a family member and other such information is also considered unethical due to its irrelevance to campaign issues. Asking whether or not the information is related to or would affect the performance of the job the candidate is seeking is a practical guideline to use in instances of uncertainty.[15]

Although there are no legal punishments for violating any of these standards, consultants generally agree to abide by them for the benefit of the campaign, their candidate, and their own reputation. For many of the same reasons, the AAPC has devised its own list of guidelines for ethical behavior. As a member of the AAPC, consultants pledge to abide by these rules, but, like the previously mentioned guidelines, there is no punishment for their violation. In accepting the principles included in the AAPC "Code of Ethics," members agree to, among other things, be honest in their relationship with the news media; not participate in any activity that would "corrupt or degrade the practice of political consulting"; not appeal to voters based

---

[12]Shea, *Campaign Craft*, 95.

[13]Ayres, "Can Campaign Advertising Be on the Level?" 20.

[14]Shea, *Campaign Craft*, 95.

[15]Ayres, "Can Campaign Advertising Be on the Level?" 20.

on racism, sexism, or unlawful discrimination of any form; and not support any individual or organization that acts in violation of the code.[16] This last stipulation helps to ensure, in the absence of enforced discipline, the continuation of these ethical guidelines. Although unofficial, these types of standards do provide some structure to the competitive practice of political campaigning.

Consultants and Political Parties

Many academics and commentators have noticed that the rise of campaign consultants seemed to occur at the very same time that local political parties began to decline. Some contend, more dramatically, that consultants may have caused the decline of party structures outright. But this is hardly true. Instead, a confluence of factors—from the emergence of new media technologies to the decline in partisan identification to the civil service and nomination reform that broke up party machines—made possible and encouraged the rise of campaign consultants. "Consultants did not arrive on the campaign scene when the parties were at their strongest and push them to the side of electioneering, but rather appeared to meet a need that both candidates and parties faced."[17]

Today, campaign consultants and political parties work as partners, not rivals, in the election process. Consultants provide some of the services that political parties traditionally supplied and fill roles that were previously unnecessary or nonexistent, while the parties act as fund-raising vehicles and financiers, for the most part. An occasional consultant will work for candidates of both parties, but generally speaking, most work with only Democratic or only Republican candidates. It is also common to find party operatives playing a matchmaking role between consultants and candidates. A novice candidate might not know reputable consultants, and the party can provide that information. For example, when a candidate signs on with a known, respected consultant (one suggested by the party), it can appear to potential contributors that the candidate is serious, perhaps worthy of support.

Consultants and Negative Advertising

No discussion of modern campaign consultants would be complete without brief mention of negative campaigning.[18] Very few subjects stir passions like negative campaigns; voters dislike them; political consultants adore them; and political scientists scrutinize them. Many believe, at least at a gut level, that negative campaigns have serious consequences for American democracy. Yet for all of the emotional attachment to the subject, research into the effects of negative campaigns provides inconsistent conclusions. In fact, reviews of this research indicate that the findings quite often

---

[16]"Code of Ethics," American Association of Political Consultants (2010). Accessed at: www.theaapc.org/about/code/

[17]David Dulio and James A. Thurber, "The Symbolic Relationship between Political Parties and Political Consultants: Partners Past, Present, and Future," in John C. Green and Rick Farmer, *The State of the Parties*, 4th ed. (Lanham, MD: Rowman & Littlefield, 2003), 215.

[18]Portions of this section is from Kelly D. Patterson and Daniel M. Shea, "Local Political Context and Negative Campaigns: A Test of Negative Effects across State Party Systems," *Journal of Political Marketing* 3, no.1 (2004).

BOX 7.2   American Association of Political Consultants Code of Ethics

As a member of the American Association of Political Consultants, I believe there are certain standards of practice that I must maintain. I, therefore, pledge to adhere to the following Code of Professional Ethics:

- I will not indulge in any activity that would corrupt or degrade the practice of political consulting.
- I will treat my colleagues and clients with respect and never intentionally injure their professional or personal reputations.
- I will respect the confidence of my clients and not reveal confidential or privileged information obtained during our professional relationship.
- I will use no appeal to voters that is based on racism, sexism, religious intolerance, or any form of unlawful discrimination, and will condemn those who use such practices. In turn, I will work for equal voting rights and privileges for all citizens.
- I will refrain from false or misleading attacks on an opponent or a member of his or her family and will do everything in my power to prevent others from using such tactics.
- I will document accurately and fully any criticism of an opponent or his or her record.
- I will be honest in my relationship with the news media and candidly answer questions when I have the authority to do so.
- I will use any funds I receive from, or on behalf of, my clients, only for those purposes invoiced in writing.
- I will not support any individual or organization that resorts to practices forbidden by this code.

Source: "Code of Ethics," American Association of Political Consultants (2010). Accessed at: www .theaapc.org/about/code/

---

differ; some studies find significant effects on voter behavior while others find little or none.[19]

When one considers the role of negative campaigning in the American political system, and the role that consultants might play in using these types of campaigns, two somewhat contradictory points become evident: First, attack advertising has been with us for a long time. A common misconception is that campaigns have turned negative only in recent years and that the elections of America's forefathers were shining examples of civil discourse. To the contrary, the mudslinging and dirty tricks of some 19th-century presidential elections could put recent ones to shame. Thomas Jefferson, for example, was called an amoral atheist and an adulterer who would lead the country to sin and ruin; Andrew Jackson was accused of murder and of marrying a woman who was not yet divorced; and Grover Cleveland was tarred as having

---

[19]Scott L. Hale, "Attack Messages and their Effects on Judgments of Political Candidates: A Random-effects Meta-Analytic Review," paper presented at the annual meeting of the Midwest Political Science Association, Chicago (1998); Richard Lau, Lee Sigelman, Caroline Heldman, and Paul Babbitt, "The Effects of Negative Political Advertisements: A Meta-Analytic Assessment," *American Political Science Review* 94, no.4 (December 1999).

fathered an illegitimate child. Negative campaigning, indeed, is as old a tradition in America as democracy itself. There have been some dramatic changes in the delivery of these messages, especially since the advent of television, but for the most part, smearing your opponent is an old tune in the American electoral system. Upon visiting America in the late 1880s, Lord Bryce suggested that campaigns are best described as a "tempest of invective and calumny."[20] We must note, however, that in terms of the research done on its effects, "negative campaigning" does not actually refer to mud-slinging, dirty tricks, and unsubstantiated personal attacks; rather, negative advertising is a "sort of advertising in which the focus is on criticizing the opponent's record rather than promoting one's own record."[21] Admittedly, the distinction between mud-slinging and advertisements of this kind is often blurred, as candidates often deliberately mischaracterize their opponents' records (for example, John McCain's 2008 advertisement in which he accused Barack Obama of supporting comprehensive sex education for kindergarteners).

Second, the effects of these attacks, both intended and unintended, remain unclear. Numerous studies have examined negative advertising, but the variation in findings remains one of the most prominent features of this area of inquiry. Researchers have sought to measure the effects of negative campaigns on the attitudes of voters toward the candidates and vote choice, on feelings of civic duty and trust in government, and most recently on political participation. With regard to attitudes toward the candidates and vote choice, the results have been mixed. Campaign consultants generally believe that attack ads can work to pry voters away from a popular candidate. This is especially important, they argue, when running against an incumbent. Yet scholars Stephen Ansolabehere and Shanto Iyengar found that during primary campaigns, attack ads tended to work less effectively than advocacy spots.[22] During a general election campaign, however, the attack ads helped the candidate more than advocacy ads. After a careful and exhaustive review of this type of research, Richard Lau and Lee Sigelman concluded that there is no real consensus on the effectiveness of attack ads versus other kinds of ads at persuading individuals to vote in a particular way.[23] A later study of 109 Senate elections found no significant benefits from negative campaigns, and concluded that whatever small benefits they might have would come at substantial risk and cost.[24]

Negative ads have also been blamed for a decline in civic engagement and trust and for a rise in cynicism about politics and government. These effects are often referred to as unintended consequences. Here again the results are mixed. Some

---

[20]Lau et al., "Effects of Negative Political Advertisements."

[21]Michael M. Franz, Paul B. Freedman, Kenneth M. Goldstein, and Travis N. Ridout, *Campaign Advertising and American Democracy* (Philadelphia: Temple University Press, 2008), 20.

[22]Stephen Ansolabehere and Shanto Iyengar, *Going Negative: How Political Advertisements Shrink and Polarize the Electorate* (New York: Free Press, 1995).

[23]Richard Lau and Lee Sigelman, "Effectiveness of Negative Political Advertising," in *Crowded Airwaves: Campaign Advertising in Election,* James A. Thurber, Candice J. Nelson, and David A. Dulio, eds. (The Brooking Institution, 2000).

[24]Richard R. Lau and Gerald M. Pomper, *Negative Campaigning: An Analysis of U.S. Senate Elections* (Lanham, MD: Rowman & Littlefield, 2004).

studies find that exposure to ads does not affect the trust a citizen has in government[25] or his or her sense of political efficacy,[26] while many others find the opposite.[27] Franz et al. conclude that—to the surprise of many—exposure to a proliferation of campaign advertising actually serves to *increase* public trust in government and belief in the necessity and importance of elections.[28]

What about voter turnout? Do negative ads turn people away from politics? Traditional wisdom suggests negative ads "demobilize" the electorate, especially those less partisan.[29] But here again researchers have come to different conclusions. Ansolabehere and Iyengar found that negative ads tend to turn off some voters—particularly younger citizens and those not emotionally connected to a candidate or a party.[30] Yet another study found that exposure to ads actually increases turnout in gubernatorial elections,[31] and a second study reached similar findings for Senate elections.[32] Still another found that negative ads produce no significant effect on aggregate turnout in presidential elections.[33] There are probably several reasons the precise impact of negative campaigning is unclear. Whether this amalgam of contradictory studies relating negativity to trust and voter turnout favors a positive or negative trend in any given cycle, most studies tend to agree that the effects either way are mild. One study, conducted by scholar John Geer, found only modest effects, as noted in Table 7.1.[34]

One explanation for the lack of consensus on each of these issues might be the complexity of the phenomenon itself, as voters are exposed to countless messages during a campaign period. Sorting through the precise weight of different ads is no simple task. Another may be the selection of television as the preferred medium for assessing the effects of negative campaigns. An overwhelming number of recent studies have centered on television advertisements—either their impact on actual voters or in an experimental setting. The selection of television makes good sense because a majority of attacks now reach voters via this medium. But a television-based analysis creates significant difficulties for the researcher. First, if researchers want to study real-life

---

[25]Michael D. Martinez and Tad Delegal, "The Irrelevance of Negative Campaigns to Political Trust: Experimental and Survey Results," *Political Communications* 7, no. 1 (January 1990): 25–40.

[26]Kenneth M. Goldstein, "Political Advertising and Political Persuasion in the 1996 Presidential Campaign," paper presented at the annual meeting of the American Political Science Association, Washington, DC. (1997).

[27]For a sharp review of the state of negative campaign research, see Franz et al., *Campaign Advertising and American Democracy.*

[28]Franz et al., *Campaign Advertising and American Democracy*, 104.

[29]Stephen Ansolabehere, Shanto Iyengar, Adam Simon, and Nicholas Valentino, "Does Attack Advertising Demobilize the Electorate?" *American Political Science Review* 88 (December 1994): 829–838.

[30]Ansolabehere and Iyengar, *Going Negative.*

[31]Paul Freedman and Kenneth M. Goldstein, "Measuring Media Exposure and the Effects of Negative Campaign Ads," *American Journal of Political Science* 43 (October 1999): 1189–1208.

[32]Kim Fridkin Kahn and Patrick J. Kenney, "Do Negative Campaigns Mobilize or Suppress Turnout? Clarifying the Relationship between Negativity and Participation," *American Journal of Political Science* 93 (December 1999): 877–889.

[33]Stephen E. Finkel and John Geer, "A Spot Check: Casting Doubt on the Demobilization Effect of Attack Advertising," *American Journal of Political Science* 42 (April 1998): 573–595.

[34]John G. Geer, *In Defense of Negativity: Attack Ads in Presidential Campaigns* (Chicago and London: Chicago University Press, 2006), 144.

TABLE 7.1	Impact of Negativity on Trust, Faith, and Turnout			
	Political Trust	Faith in Elections	VAP[b]	VEP[c]
Overall negativity	0.000[a]	0.001	−0.009[a]	0.006[a]
	(0.002)	(0.002)	(0.14)	(0.13)
Issue negativity	0.001	0.001	−0.22	−0.18
	(0.003)	(0.002)	0.17	0.16
Trait negativity	−0.006	0.003	0.17	0.16
	(0.004)	(0.003)	(0.31)	(0.34)

Notes: These estimates all come from a simple multivariate model that seeks to explain the dependent variable (the top row of the table) by a measure of issue, trait, or overall negativity and a lagged dependent variable. The text explains the reasons for this choice.

(a) These three estimates include data from 2004. Estimates in parentheses are the standard errors for these coefficients

(b) VAP uses the usual estimate of the voting age population to estimate the rate of turnout in presidential elections.

(c) VEP uses the Popkin-McDonald revised measure of voting age population that corrects for the number of illegal immigrants, prisoners, and other errors in the count.

Source: John G. Geer, In *Defense of Negativity: Attack Ads in Presidential Campaigns,* 2006.

campaigns, then building a large sample of districts becomes difficult. In order to tag one race negative and another positive, television spots from both races must be compiled and analyzed. Second, different assessments of what is and what is not negative are inevitable. Indeed, exactly how one defines a "negative ad," juxtaposed a "comparative ad" likely accounts for some of the inconsistency in the research. A spot might be labeled negative, but the number of times that the campaign actually uses the commercial is difficult to discern.

More important, reach, or the number of voters exposed to the commercials, is critical, but these data have proven especially difficult to obtain. The researcher would have to first review spots to determine their negativity, then get a list of the stations where the spot was used, and then find out the number of times it was aired. Next, he or she must get a breakdown of the times when each of the spots was used for each station and then overlay ratings information. This provides an estimate of the number of viewers for the program that surrounds the commercial. Finally, the researcher would have to make some sort of estimate as to the number of potential *voters* who would be exposed, given the projected demographics and size of the audience. With much effort, this process is possible, of course, but the true difficulty is the one identified earlier—expanding the sample size beyond a few districts.

The author of this text teamed up with Brigham Young University scholar Kelly Patterson to conduct an analysis aimed at what they believed to be a missing element in the research on negative advertisements.[35] Specifically, they hypothesized that

---

[35]Kelly D. Patterson and Daniel M. Shea, "Local Political Context and Negative Campaigns: A Test of Negative Effects across State Party Systems, *Journal of Political Marketing* 3, no.1 (2004).

studies that rely upon respondents or subjects from one local electoral culture may yield findings entirely different than studies that rely upon people from another area. Perhaps subjects from New Jersey might have a different take on negative advertising than a group from Utah, for instance.

Patterson and Shea first created a measure of negativity by surveying newspaper editors and reporters who covered the 1998 congressional campaigns. They then merged this information with the 1998 American National Election Studies to measure the effects on respondents in different electoral subcultures. In short, they found that a host of unintended effects of negative campaigns are more pronounced in U.S. states with little or no history of partisan competition.

Other studies have found that the consequences of negative advertisements aren't always negative. Franz et al. demonstrate, for example, that negative advertisements can "increase the store of [accurate] information about campaigns," and that "there is limited evidence that ads serve to improve assessments of politics and campaigns."[36] Franz et al. further conclude that there is reasonable evidence to suggest that, if anything, advertising can increase voter turnout and engagement.[37]

It is clear that negative campaigns are prominent features of the American political landscape—and will remain so for a long time. Many scholars and pundits believe—even though bodies of research beg to differ—that negative campaigning distorts the process. Surely it is changing voter perceptions about candidates, the electoral system, and the political process—but in what ways and among which citizens? Campaign consultants—those who make their living in the political trenches—tell us that the effects are real. But is this equally true in all circumstances—among all types of voters? Indeed, the range of opinions and the intensity of beliefs make this a fascinating area of inquiry.

INTEREST GROUPS

A second new player in contemporary American elections, a critical piece of any election coalition, is interest groups. Interest groups have been a dominate feature of American politics since the very beginning. To be sure, James Madison warned anyone who would listen about the dangers of factions (interest groups) in *The Federalist Papers*. But the entrance of interest groups into the electoral process—as key players—is relatively new.

The 1960s and 1970s were difficult years for parties. During this time, hundreds of state and national special interest groups entered the political fray. There had always been factions in American politics, but the nature and volume of the interest groups represented drastically changed during those years. Groups representing consumers, environmentalists, professionals, women, the elderly, business, and labor, among others, mushroomed. For example, the National Organization for Women was founded in 1966, and by 2010, it had more than 550 local chapters and 550,000 contributing members. Environmental groups have experienced similar growth. Membership in the Sierra Club, which hovered at 114,336 in 1970, ballooned to more 1.3 million by

---

[36]Franz et al., *Campaign Advertising and American Democracy*, 103.
[37]Ibid., 115.

2010. The National Rifle Association went from about 500,000 members in the 1960s to some 4.3 million members in recent years. Many of these organizations articulate policy demands and engender fierce loyalties among their members.

The number of issue advocacy groups in Washington has risen exponentially since 1960. Back then, there were approximately 5,000 associations; that number doubled by 1965, tripled by 1975, and by 2010 had reached well above 25,000. These organizations include a wide ranging list of business, labor, racial, religious, consumer-oriented, and environmental groups. Their involvement is often far reaching, and the political coalitions they assemble vary dramatically from issue to issue. In 1989, for example, when the Supreme Court heard the case *Webster v. Reproductive Health Services* that permitted states to place restrictions on abortion, 74 interest groups submitted briefs to the justices (24 supporting restrictions on abortion; 50 opposed). These interest groups included the American Family Association, the Knights of Columbus, the National Association of Evangelicals, and the National Right to Life Committee in favor of restrictions. The American Civil Liberties Union; American Medical Association; American Nurses Association; Brooklyn Women's Martial Arts; Gay Men's Health Crisis; YWCA USA; and the United Electrical, Radio, and Machine Workers of America opposed restrictions. A similar interest group explosion has occurred in each of the 50 state capitals, with equally wide-ranging interest group involvement in a variety of local issues.

There are numerous explanations as to why this change occurred. One possibility is that as the whir of government activity increased, for example with Franklin Roosevelt's New Deal and Johnson's Great Society, interest groups organized to get a larger slice of the pie. Often, they were created in response to new government initiatives. And as an interest group on one side of the issue achieves some success, the opposing side takes notice and moves to create its own organization. This might be called the "two can play at that game" strategy.

Another possibility, touched upon early in this chapter, is that by the 1960s, Americans had become dissatisfied with traditional modes of activism. Interest groups seemed a less partisan and more acceptable way to alter public policies. Moreover, the legacy of the civil rights and anti-Vietnam War movements suggested that citizens could change the course of government without the aid of parties, as long as they worked together.

A third explanation has been dubbed the "post-materialist" perspective. This view suggests that as Americans entered into a post-industrial society, they were so prosperous that a broader set of issues such as human rights, environmental protection, and consumer affairs emerged. The parties, historically preoccupied with economic concerns, seemed a poor choice to advance these post-materialist issues. Sociological changes, including increased levels of education following World War II and the exodus from the cities to the suburbs, resulted in an issue-oriented politics that did not include a role for traditional parties.

Perhaps the greatest impetus to the interest group explosion was changes in the Federal Election Acts of the early 1970s that permitted political action committees (PACs). As discussed in greater detail in Chapter 8, PACs are the money-raising arms of interest groups. Their growth, graphically illustrated in Figure 7.1, gave candidates new sources of campaign funds and reduced the need for party money. Also discussed in

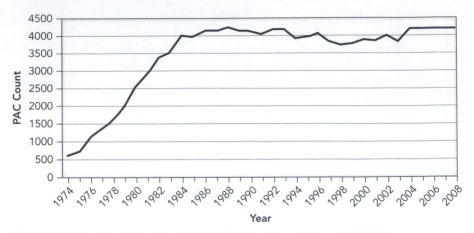

FIGURE 7.1 **Number of Registered Political Action Committees, 1974–2008**

Source: Federal Election Commission. Accessed at: http://www.fec.gov on November 16, 2010.

greater detail in Chapter 8 is the latest interest group innovation called 527 organizations, named after Section 527 of the Internal Revenue Code, which regulates their practices.

   The growth of organized groups vying for power and influence in American politics stunned both Democrats and Republicans, and shocked students of American politics. Prior to this period, many believed that parties best served the public interest because they set their sights on winning elections and consequently drew ordinary citizens into the political process. Interest groups, concerned with changing policy and not the outcome of elections per se, seemed to have less reason to bring average citizens into the electoral fray. In fact, at times it may be to their advantage to keep politics private. Scholars now understand that interest groups generally work closely with political parties. For example, one of the time-tested links between a major party and an interest group is the tight relationship between the Democratic Party and labor unions. This stretches back to the 1940s. "Led by the Congress of Industrial Organizations (CIO), unions provided campaign funds to candidates, mobilized voters, and sought to influence public opinion."[38] In recent years, a similar pattern has emerged between the Democratic Party and groups like AFL-CIO (American Federation of Labor—Congress of Industrial Organizations), EMILY's List (pro-choice women), National Education Association (a teachers' union), Sierra Club, National Abortion Rights Action League, and the Trial Lawyers Association. For the Republicans, the interest coalition includes Americans for Tax Reform, the U.S. Chamber of Commerce, National Rifle Association, National Right to Life Committee, National Beer Wholesalers Association, a number of conservative religious organizations, several anti-gay marriage groups, and many others. Table 7.2 lists contribution totals for various interest

---

[38]John F. Bibby, "Party Networks: National–State Integration, Allied Groups, and Issue Activists," in John C. Green and Daniel M. Shea, eds., *The State of the Parties*, 3rd ed. (Lanham, MD: Rowman & Littlefield, 1999), 76.

TABLE 7.2	Top Interest Groups Giving to Members of Congress in 2010 Election Cycle				
Rank	**Interest Groups**	**Total ($)**	**Democratic Percentage**	**GOP Percentage**	**Top Recipient**
1	Lawyers/Law firms	59,298,447	81	18	Harry Reid (D-NV)
2	Retired	37,402,970	55	44	Barbara Boxer (D-CA)
3	Health professionals	35,152,278	58	42	Mark Kirk (R-IL)
4	Securities/ Investment	30,191,664	64	36	Charles E. Schumer (D-NY)
5	Real estate	29,305,144	61	38	Charles E. Schumer (D-NY)
6	Insurance	22,888,602	53	47	Charles E. Schumer (D-NY)
7	Leadership PACs	20,085,323	64	35	Roy Blunt (R-MO)
8	Lobbyists	17,879,832	68	31	Harry Reid (D-NV)
9	Democratic/ Liberal	17,345,795	100	0	Joseph A. Sestak Jr (D-PA)
10	Pharmacy/ Health products	15,336,195	58	42	Richard Burr (R-NC)
11	Electric utilities	13,474,915	60	37	Rick Boucher (D-VA)
12	Public sector unions	13,396,486	92	8	Steny H. Hoyer (D-MD)
13	TV/Movies/ Music	13,369,556	70	30	Barbara Boxer (D-CA)
14	Misc. finance	12,769,052	57	43	Charles E. Schumer (D-NY)
15	Business services	11,837,937	70	29	Harry Reid (D-NV)
16	Oil and gas	11,724,822	36	62	Blanche Lincoln (D-AR)
17	Building trade unions	11,128,060	93	6	Joseph A. Sestak Jr (D-PA)
18	Commercial banks	10,974,615	47	53	Roy Blunt (R-MO)

(continued)

TABLE 7.2   Top Interest Groups Giving to Members of Congress in 2010 Election Cycle   (*continued*)

Rank	Interest Groups	Total ($)	Democratic Percentage	GOP Percentage	Top Recipient
19	Hospitals/ Nursing homes	10,564,112	68	32	Charles E. Schumer (D-NY)
20	Transport unions	10,199,067	88	12	James L. Oberstar (D-MN)
21	Computers/ Internet	9,887,505	65	34	Patty Murray (D-WA)
22	Misc. Manufacturing/ Distribution	9,801,626	53	47	Charles E. Schumer (D-NY)
23	Crop production	9,252,388	59	40	Blanche Lincoln (D-AR)
24	Air transport	8,403,976	54	45	John L. Mica (R-FL)
25	Pro-Israel	8,401,916	68	31	Mark Kirk (R-IL)

Source: "Top Industries Giving to Members of Congress, 2010 Cycle." Opensecrets.org.
Accessed at: www.opensecrets.org/industries/mems.php

groups and the percentage given to each party in the 2009–2010 election cycle. As you can see, some of these figures are most impressive. (Democrats were clearly the biggest recipients in this cycle because they controlled both chambers of Congress.) As noted by a lead scholar of parties and elections in America, John Bibby, "Interest groups have long been involved in electoral politics, but in recent years an expanding number of groups have developed close ties with the [parties] and become integral parts of the party network and campaign apparatus."[39]

LEGISLATIVE CAMPAIGN COMMITTEES

Another important development has been the creation of branch party organizations designed to finance and manage legislative contests.[40] At the national level, these organizations are called the Hill Committees because of their origins within the halls of Congress (Capitol Hill). There are four units, one for each party in each house of Congress: the Democratic Congressional Campaign Committee (DCCC), the Democratic Senatorial Campaign Committee (DSCC), the National Republican Congressional Committee (NRCC), and the National Republican Senatorial Committee (NRSC). Roughly 40 states now boast similar organizations, dubbed

---

[39]Ibid., 84.
[40]Portions of this section are excerpted from John K. White and Daniel M. Shea, *New Party Politics*, 2nd ed. (Boulder, CO: Wadsworth, 2004), 112–116.

legislative campaign committees (LCCs). In Illinois, for example, there is the Illinois House Republican Organization, the Illinois Republican State Senate Campaign Committee, the Illinois Democratic Majority Committee, and the Illinois Committee to Elect a Democratic Senate.

Each of these new organizations consists of elected members serving in the corresponding house of the legislature. These organizations hire professional staff to oversee campaign efforts—paying particular attention to those members seeking reelection, those contesting open seats, and competitive challengers. These LCCs are office- and level-specific: House organizations help House candidates; Senate organizations aid only Senate candidates.

Few organizational developments have had a greater impact on parties than the ascendance of LCCs. LCCs epitomize the merger of high-technology, candidate-centered elections and centralization into a single political unit. Because there are modest differences between state and national organizations, a brief review of each follows. In each case, however, important questions remain: To what extent have these committees transformed party politics—and at what cost?

The Hill Committees

The first congressional campaign committees emerged in the House of Representatives in 1866. During that year, a struggle ensued between Andrew Johnson, who became president after Lincoln's assassination, and the Radical Republicans, most of whom were from the Northeast. Johnson, a Tennessean, was hesitant to support many of the political goals espoused by the radicals, especially bills seeking reprisals against the South following the Civil War. Johnson opposed legislation that would have helped former slaves—including passage of the Fourteenth Amendment and the establishment of the Freedmen's Bureau. Because Johnson controlled the RNC (Republican National Committee) by virtue of his holding the presidency, Radical Republicans feared political reprisals. They retaliated by establishing the NRCC. Not to be outdone, a group of pro-Johnson Democrats created the DCCC. Senators had little need for these legislative party organizations until the Seventeenth Amendment was passed in 1913, instituting direct election of senators. Shortly thereafter Senate campaign committees were established by both parties.

Until the 1970s, these committees were seemingly unimportant players, often serving merely as fund-raising apparatuses for incumbents to collect money in Washington and channel it back to local districts. No professional staff or permanent headquarters existed for these "poor sisters" in the party hierarchy. All that began to change as the cost of campaigning began to escalate, television came to play an important role, and partisan loyalties weakened. Incumbents felt they could no longer take their victories on Election Day for granted. Their fears increased as progressive reformers stripped local parties of much of their patronage, with the result that fewer volunteers showed up at party headquarters. Accordingly, members of Congress turned to the congressional campaign committees for help. The Senate and House Republican campaign committees soon devised extensive direct mail programs. Other "inside the Beltway" fund-raising schemes were pursued, including holding extravagant dinner parties in Washington, DC. The result was an avalanche of cash. Indeed, NRCC receipts quintupled from less than $12 million in 1978 to $58 million in 1984. The NRSC posted an even greater gain, with receipts ballooning from $2 million in 1978 to $82 million in 1984. By the late 1990s, combined receipts for both GOP (Grand Old Party) Hill Committees approached the $200 million mark, where it more or less remained through the 2010 election.

Democrats followed a similar path. After losing the Senate in 1980 and seeing their majority wither away in the House, sweeping reforms were instituted. Under the aggressive leadership of California Representative Tony Coelho, the DCCC implemented scores of new fund-raising programs. Coelho made it a practice to visit hundreds of business and trade associations asking for contributions. According to Representative Barney Frank, "Tony Coelho was very good at explaining the facts of life to PACs: If you want to talk to us later, you had better help us now." Thanks to these strong-arm tactics, DCCC receipts jumped from less than $3 million in 1980 to $10.4 million four years later. The DSCC also saw its war chest expand. By 2008, the combined resources of the Democratic Hill Committees topped $350 million.

With both the Democratic and Republican Hill Committees awash in cash, they began spending on professional campaign managers and strategists, holding training seminars, and compiling computerized data to target voters. Today, the Republican congressional organizations conduct frequent in-house polling, and Democrats have forged agreements at bargain prices with private survey research firms that assist their candidates. Both parties have assembled vast files of research on their opponents that are circulated to candidates and media outlets in targeted districts. The Hill Committees also issue briefings on local, state, and national issues to would-be candidates. Their national headquarters are outfitted with state-of-the-art radio, television, and Internet facilities that can generate generic advertisements that are easily customized to specific localities. Candidates also receive help from professional event coordinators, who prepare them for large galas and rallies. Just about anything needed to run a professional campaign can be provided by the Hill Committees.

Services are one thing; but as California state treasurer Jesse Unruh said many years ago, "Money is the mother's milk of politics."[41] Here, too, the Hill Committees provide immeasurable assistance. While there are modest restrictions on the amount that the Hill Committees can give directly to House and Senate candidates, considerably larger sums can be spent on behalf of individual candidates. These "coordinated expenditures" are made in conjunction with a candidate's campaign. Typically, these expenditures are payments for services that candidates would have to otherwise purchase, such as polling or producing television advertisements. Because Hill Committees have a vast array of in-house staff, facilities, and equipment (such as computers, print presses, and editing rooms), the itemized contribution per service rendered is

---

[41]Burr Van Atta, "Jesse Unruh, 64, Calif. Treasurer; Once 'Big Daddy' of State Politics," *Inquirer* (August 6, 1987). Accessed at: http://articles.philly.com/1987-08-06/news/26169142_1_assembly-speaker-politics-friends-and-foes on June 7, 2011.

small, but coordinated expenditures have enabled them to become modern-day political powerhouses.

Perhaps the biggest asset the Hill Committees bring to the fund-raising table is what has been termed their brokerage role, meaning that they serve as intermediaries between special interest groups and needy candidates. At meet-and-greet events, often organized in Washington, DC., congresspersons and heads of PACs commingle. Like a blind date, the goal is to help candidates hit it off with the PAC representatives. To aid in this process, Hill Committees provide candidates with "PAC kits," which are tailored appeals to potential contributors. Afterwards, representatives from the congressional campaign committees spend hours on the telephone convincing would-be potential donors that their candidates stand a good chance of winning and will not forget their friends after Election Day.

Finally, the Hill Committees send reams of data to the editors of the *Cook Political Report* and the *Rothenberg Political Report*—important newsletters that handicap individual congressional races and are closely read by political operatives. If it is reported that a particular challenger has a good, or even fair, chance of winning, interest groups take notice and start sending checks. Poor notices in these newsletters are often the death knell for candidates, as contributors dry up, and hapless challengers stand no chance of getting their messages out.

Not every candidate benefits from the inner workings of the Hill Committees. Although they are influential in close races, because even a marginal effort may make a difference, non-endangered incumbents often receive little or no help. Likewise, challengers with little or no chance of winning are left to their own devices. If the hill committee will not help, interest groups won't either. As one would-be congressional candidate described his first encounter with the DCCC: "All they did was show me a list of PACs and then tell me that the PACs wouldn't talk to me until I was the designated candidate. They promised me nothing. I could count on no help from them at all."[42]

State Legislative Campaign Committees

State LCCs have been around since the 1970s—first sprouting up in large states like New York, Illinois, Wisconsin, California, Pennsylvania, and Minnesota, and later spreading to 40 other states.[43] As with the congressional campaign committees, the heightened costs of state elections and a weakening of partisan ties have prompted the proliferation of state legislative party committees. They, too, dispense much-needed funds and provide state-of-the-art services, often concentrating their resources on close contests. Because most states do not limit campaign contributions, the result has been the transfer of considerable sums of cash from the state LCCs to a few candidates. In 1986, for example, the California Assembly

---

[42]Linda L. Fowler and Robert D. McClure, *Political Ambition: Who Decides to Run for Congress* (New Haven: Yale University Press, 1989), 37.

[43]Daniel M. Shea, *Transforming Democracy: Legislative Campaign Committees and Political Parties* (Albany, NY: State University of New York Press, 1995), 18.

Democratic Committee spent $589,000 on one Sacramento area open seat, which accounted for 67 percent of that candidate's budget. The New York Republican Senate Committee targeted 12 races out of 61 in 1992, infusing each with massive resources.[44] In 1996, there were a handful of House races in Ohio where state legislative committee contributions approached the $500,000 mark.[45] In recent years, these transfers have continued to grow and are today a critical part of state legislative campaigns.

An interesting difference between state-level LCCs and the Hill Committees is in the way staff members are paid. Hill Committees have large, year-round staffs consisting of full-time professionals. Most state committees do not have these resources, opting instead to call upon state employees who use vacations, sick time, or leaves of absence during election time to work for the legislative committee. By the late 1980s, such practices had become a serious legal problem. In 1987, Democratic operatives in New York were accused of conducting campaign activities on state time. The Democratic majority leader of the Senate was indicted on 564 counts of conspiracy, grand larceny, and related charges. One accusation claimed that an LCC employee was paid up to $10,000 per month by the state for conducting campaign activities. State courts dismissed the indictment, saying that, although the hiring of legislative employees for campaign work might be unethical, no law prohibited it. Two decades later, in Pennsylvania, several legislators and their staff came under investigation for the alleged use of state time and money on campaigns. One of the legislators, the former majority leader, was convicted and sent to jail in 2010 for masterminding a scheme to use public monies for Democratic candidates to the state house.[46]

LCCs and Traditional Political Parties

A key issue surrounding all of these new organizations is how they fit into the traditional party rubric. In the past, most textbooks have placed the national committees at the top of a pyramid-like structure with the congressional and senatorial committees below them as subordinates. Similar characterizations were made for state LCCs. Today, the picture is much more complex. As one former congressional campaign committee director said: "We take our instructions from the chairman and the other congressmen [*sic*] on the committee. They are selected by party members in the House and are responsible to them, if anyone. While members of the national committee may occasionally consult with the members of the committee, they certainly don't give them orders . . . and they don't tell us what to do either."[47]

---

[44]Anthony Gierzynski, *Legislative Party Campaign Committees in the American States* (Lexington, KY: University Press of Kentucky, 1992), 73, 90.

[45]Shea, *Transforming Democracy*, 27.

[46]Mario Cattabiani, "Veon Convicted in Bonusgate Trial," *Philly.Com* (March 22, 2010). Accessed at: www.philly.com/philly/news/breaking/20100322_Bonusgate_jury_deadlocked_.html

[47]Paul S. Herrnson, *Party Campaigning in the 1980s* (Cambridge, MA: Harvard University Press, 1988), 40.

The author of this text has spent a good bit of time investigating these new organizations, including interviewing more than 300 state- and county-level party leaders. His research finds that these new entities more closely resemble campaign consulting firms than traditional party organizations. Although some state LCCs work closely with the formal party structures, most do not. Indeed, in some states, a growing hostility has developed between local party officials and LCCs because these new organizations are stripping local parties of their historic functions in running election campaigns. Whereas local parties once controlled most congressional and state legislative races, today's organizations, centered in the state capitals and in Washington, fund and oversee these campaigns. Operatives from national or state headquarters are dispatched into targeted areas, creating a "party presence" of sorts. They are central part of the party network. But this is a far cry from local party activist knocking on doors asking for support of the entire party ticket. And when the election is over, the campaign committee technicians leave—maybe to return for the next election, but perhaps not.

Conclusion

If there is a truism in the story of elections in America, it is that the system continues to evolve. Steadfast characteristics of one age give way to new approaches, tactics, strategies, and players. In the not-too-distant past, roughly the post–World War II period, local party committees were at the epicenter of elections in America. Candidates relied on these structures to raise funds and connect with voters. It was basically unheard of that a candidate would "go it alone." But things changed. Today, parties are important players (perhaps a bit less so at the local level), but they are aided by new players—most notably consultants, interest groups, and LCCs. Consultants have brought new ideas, techniques, and skills; interest groups added money and aggressive voter outreach methods; and LCCs helped broker connections between candidates and various additional actors. These pieces have merged to create a powerful campaign network. Candidates still do not go it alone, but neither do they simply turn to local party leaders for help. Behind the scenes we now find a vast coalition of actors—all working to influence the outcome of each election.

Critical Thinking

1. Should there be an effort to somehow regulate the activities of campaign consultants, starting with some sort of licensing requirement?
2. Some argue that negative campaign ads are effective in influencing voters while others argue that they push potential voters away from the system. Which is true from your experience? Do negative advertisements make you less likely to vote?
3. What does the new style of professional political consulting mean for the future of campaigns?

4. Years from now, do you suspect we will still refer to parties as the center of campaign networks, and that the other key players are consultants, interest groups, and LCCs? Will there be other important players? If so, who or what?
5. How might "net-root" campaigns impact the role of these campaign actors in the years ahead?

On the Web

If you are interested in discovering which committees and special interest groups have contributed money to political candidates, visit www.opensecrets.org, where all of this and more is documented for your access to transparent information.

CHAPTER

8

Political Participation in the United States

In previous chapters, we charted the ambivalence the framers had about broad-based political participation. On the one hand, they realized that citizen involvement in the conduct of government was a prerequisite for democracy, but on the other hand, they feared mob rule—what one called the "excesses of democracy." They created a system that allowed for participation, but also one with clear limits. We also outlined the explosion of civic and political participation after the Corrupt Deal of 1824, a period called Jacksonian Democracy. The mid-19th century was indeed the highpoint of electoral participation in America, as eight in ten eligible voters cast their ballots each election. But the breadth of eligible voters was limited to white men. With the exception of convicted felons in most states, today all citizens aged 18 and older have the legal opportunity to vote.

We now turn to levels of electoral participation. To what extent do Americans take advantage of their right to participate, their right to be players in the election process? As you will read, while many steps have been taken to broaden the opportunities to participate in the election process, levels of engagement remain modest. Americans believe elections are critically important, but in most elections, only a minority of citizens become involved. And when it comes to involvement in ways other than voting, the percentages are stunningly meager.

ELECTORAL PARTICIPATION DEFINED

There are numerous ways average citizens can shape the course of government. The same applies to participation in the electoral process, as there are many ways citizens can become involved in campaigns and elections.

Individualistic versus Collective Participation

Voting is generally considered the principal means for involvement in the electoral process. Many have suggested that voting is the base of electoral participation; very few become involved with "higher" activities, such as attending political events or sending a check to a candidate, without first being a voter. This is probably not true, however. For one thing, it is likely that many citizens are politically active, but do not vote. For some Americans, nonvoting is either a statement of contentment or a form of political protest. Second, even if there may be some sort of pyramid of electoral participation, voting should probably not be considered the base. Talking about different candidates with friends and family, for example, and reading news stories or watching programs about election happenings are important forms of electoral participation. In fact, any action broadly linked to the conduct or outcome of an election can be considered electoral behavior. We might add to the list: helping with a campaign; donating money; joining an election-centered group; attending election-centered rallies, dinners, or meetings; placing a yard sign in front of one's house or a bumper sticker on one's car; or even wearing a button. And this is only a partial list. The point is that citizens can become involved in the election process in many ways—voting being just one of them.

Another way to think about forms of political participation is to consider the difference between individualistic and collective participation. Individualistic participation is where the citizen engages in activity aimed at changing the outcome of government action (public policy) without interacting with other citizens. Examples are voting, giving money to a candidate or party, watching political news on television, and writing a letter to an elected official. Collective participation is where the citizen's action is in collaboration with other like-minded citizens, such as attending a rally, discussing politics with friends and family, working at a party or candidate headquarters, joining others in a protest, or attending a town hall meeting. Although each can be seen in the American setting, it is clear that individualistic participation occurs more often. Some would argue that our individualist tendencies are unfortunate. Many of the most significant changes in public policy, such as workers' rights, civil rights, and environmental legislation, stemmed from collective action efforts. Some scholars have even suggested that Americans' focus on individualistic forms of political participation serves to buttress an cut throat, oppressive economic system.[1] Perhaps dramatic assaults on the corporate power structure are possible only when citizens merge with other like-minded citizens. But for most Americans, politics is a private matter. Consider the writings of a prominent scholar of elections in America:

> People whose only political activity is voting are left to infer that politics is intensely personal and private, almost shameful. We vote not only individually, but often in booths with curtains, like Roman Catholics confiding their sins in the confessional. Instead of treating politics as the most public of activities, because it is concerned with the future of all of us, we treat it as something to be hidden.[2]

Precisely why most people in the United States focus their political energies to individualistic acts is an open question. Most, however, point to childhood socialization.

Voting and Childhood Socialization

Why would anyone engage in electoral participation? Surely there are more interesting, more entertaining things one might do with his or her time. Yet Americans are drawn to elections for many reasons. Many Americans believe that the outcomes of elections matter, that elections are an important tradition, and that they are, yes, even interesting and entertaining. Americans also believe involvement in elections is part of their civic duty. Polling data suggest that about 90 percent of Americans believe it is the duty of "good citizens" to become involved in the election process.[3]

This begs the question of how individuals come to learn what is expected of them in civic life. Socialization is the process by which new members of a society come to learn the norms, values, and customs of their country. Most times these new members are children; socialization implies the passing on of customs, beliefs, and values from one generation to the next. Yet socialization can also take place for newly arrived adults. Socialization agents refer to the avenues through which this information is transmitted. The principal socialization agent in the American setting has been the family, followed by schools, peer groups, and religious institutions. These days, the media has also become quite important.

There are many interesting and telling socialization components in the United States. For one, youngsters are taught to revere the American economic system (capitalism) and structure of government (republicanism). Even the youngest citizens are deferential to political authorities; Americans become trustful of government and

---

[1]See, for example, Howard L. Reiter, *Parties and Elections in Corporate America* (New York: St. Martin's Press, 1987).

[2]Ibid., 8.

[3]William H. Flanigan and Nancy H. Zingal, *Political Behavior and the American Electorate*, 9th ed. (Washington, DC: Congressional Quarterly Press, 1998), 12.

governmental leaders at an early age. "Initially, the emphasis is on obedience: The good citizen obeys the law, just as good children obey their parents."[4] From here, children learn about the importance of voting. "A good citizen is one who votes."[5] The final step is the belief that voting is more than a duty; it is also a true opportunity to change the outcome of government.

Some time ago, scholars Gabriel Almond and Sidney Verba set out to chart the socialization process in numerous countries. Their book *The Civic Culture*[6] set the bar for scores of subsequent studies. They found that the socialization process in the United States does a better job in promoting the importance of voting and political participation than that of any other Western democracy.[7] There is some variation due to social class, levels of education, and race (poor African-Americans were less sure about voting than were affluent white citizens), but for the most part, Americans are socialized to be involved.

The Civic Culture was published in 1963, with most of its data originating in the 1950s. Much has changed since then in the United States. It is fair to say that while new members of American society are still taught the importance of voting and elections, there is a counterforce at work: Data suggest that a growing number of Americans believe that elections no longer matter and that their involvement is a waste of time. In the early 1960s, for example, the American National Election Studies found that about 65 percent of the public felt that elections made the government pay attention to what people wanted, "a good deal." By 2008, that figure had dropped to 47 percent.[8] In the 1950s, about 30 percent of the public agreed with the statement, "I don't think public officials care what people like me think." Recently, that figure has shot up to 60 percent.[9] Other variables suggest the same: a general decline in faith in the election process.

Why would Americans be less optimistic about the virtues of voting and elections now? One answer might be related to levels of education. In 1956, some 37 percent of Americans had only a grade school education. That figure dropped to just 3 percent in 2008. The percentage that has at least some college education went from 19 percent to 61 percent during the same time period.[10] Perhaps as levels of education rose an appreciation for the limits of voting and elections spread. Stated a bit differently, maybe the "myth of elections" was shattered as more and more citizens went to college. The only problem with this explanation, however, is that those with a college education are significantly *more* likely to get involved in elections than those without one.

---

[4]Flanigan and Zingal, *Political Behavior and the American Electorate*, 20.

[5]Ibid.

[6]Gabriel Almond and Sidney Verba, *The Civic Culture: Political Attitudes and Democracy in Five Nations* (Princeton, NJ: Princeton University Press, 1963).

[7]As cited in Flanigan and Zingal, *Political Behavior and the American Electorate*, 20.

[8]The American National Election Studies, "Elections Make the Government Pay Attention 1964–2008," Table 5C.2. Accessed at: http://electionstudies.org/nesguide/toptable/tab5c_2.htm on June 7, 2011.

[9]The American National Election Studies, "Public Officials Don't Care What People Think 1952–2008," Table 5B.3. Accessed at: http://electionstudies.org/nesguide/toptable/tab5b_3.htm on June 7, 2011.

[10]Alan I. Abramowitz, *The Disappearing Center: Engaged Citizens, Polarization, and American Democracy* (New Haven, CT: Yale University Press, 2010), 35.

Some speculate that the root of the change is that the generation of Americans who were first turned off to politics—the "counterculture" protest generation of the 1960s—have passed along their ambivalence for traditional modes of activism to their children. To many in the 1960s, elections and political parties were deemed "part of the problem," and a means to maintain the status quo, the white male-dominated system. Other modes of activism, like protests and demonstrations, seemed more effective, especially for traditionally disenfranchised groups (such as women and blacks). And as the protest generation aged, they passed along their lackluster interest in voting to their children. These children, now adults, continue to doubt the utility of elections.

Another theory is that the media has become the primary socialization agent—and that it offers a recurring negative view of politics. Numerous studies have found, for example, that the media tends to focus on candidate transgressions much more than on positive developments or policy matters. And the focus on the horse race (which candidate is ahead and by how much) trumps all other forms of coverage. As noted by two scholars of media and politics,

> From the point of view of a well-functioning democracy polity, the horse race focus . . . seems particularly troubling. . . . Simply put, horse race dominated coverage shortchanges candidates who are trying to talk about issues, and voters who are trying to talk about issues, too.[11]

Much related, scandal-based news reporting by the news media, what one scholar has dubbed the rise of "feeding frenzies,"[12] has bombarded all Americans with the dark side of politics. According to Larry Sabato of the University of Virginia, "The new media's greatest impact on voters is not in the winnowing of candidates but in the encouragement of cynicism."[13] It is no wonder that levels of pessimism and alienation have skyrocketed precisely at the same time that a burgeoning number of news outlets vie for higher ratings.

THE SCOPE OF THE ELECTORATE

In thinking about levels of political participation in any democratic system, scholars and observers often look at election turnout. This is the ratio of those who actually vote divided by those who are legally able to participate. For example, if 1 million residents are allowed to vote in a given election but only 600,000 do so, the turnout rate is 0.6, or 60 percent. Again, the number of citizens or residents of a nation does not factor into the ratio; rather, it is the number legally eligible to vote on Election Day. If a resident is legally entitled to vote, but does not register and thus cannot vote on Election Day, he or she would still be within the denominator. Today, the denominator in the United States would include all citizens 18 years of age and older—roughly 210 million citizens.

---

[11]Stephen J. Fransworth and S. Robert Lichter, *The Nightly News Nightmare* (Lanham, MD: Rowman & Littlefield, 2003), 71.

[12]Larry Sabato, *Feeding Frenzy: How Attack Journalism Has Transformed American Politics* (New York: Free Press, 1993).

[13]Ibid., 207.

Levels of Participation throughout American History

As discussed in Chapter 1, there was not a great deal of interest in federal elections in the early days of the republic. Turnout for presidential elections reached only into the teens until 1800, when it jumped to 31 percent. It slipped again during the "Era of Good Feelings" to roughly 25 percent, but after the Corrupt Deal of 1824, it rose dramatically. In 1828, turnout was 57 percent, and by the 1840s, it had leveled off at around 80 percent, where it remained until the 20th century.

By the turn of 20th century, election turnout had begun to slip. There are a number of likely causes. For one, a flood of immigration during this period caused a population boom in most urban areas. While they would soon be assimilated into the political process, many of these new Americans did not or could not immediately vote. Second, as part of the Progressive Movement, most states passed strict voter registration laws, residency requirements, and other laws. On the surface, these new laws seemed designed to reduce voter fraud, which was rampant during the party machine heyday. But below the surface, these changes made it harder for a certain group of citizens to participate: the lower class. As noted by a team of scholars,

> Voter registration arrangements were targeted specifically at the cities where the immigrant working class was concentrated. Literacy tests, stricter naturalization procedures, and burdensome voter registration procedures were not so likely to bar the rich as they were the poor, or the well-educated as they were the uneducated.[14]

Much of the decline in turnout in the 20th century can be explained by these "reforms."

The Nineteenth Amendment to the Constitution granted women the right to vote in 1920, but some women were slow to exercise their voting rights, thus pushing turnout numbers down. The percentage of women voting gradually improved, increasing overall turnout through the midpoint of the 20th century, but as noted by one scholar, "Even as late as 1960, turnout among women was nearly 10 percentage points below that of men."[15] The 2008 election was the first time in American history when the percentage of women coming to the polls outpaced the percentage of men who voted.

In the 1960 contest between Vice President Richard Nixon and Senator John F. Kennedy, some 63 percent of the electorate turned out to vote. This was lower than the heyday of political participation in the late 19th century, but most agree that a turnout of nearly two-thirds of the electorate at the polls suggested faith in the process. Between that election and 2004, however, there was a consistent decline, as noted in Figure 8.1. For example, throughout the 1980s and 1990s, turnout for presidential elections hovered around 50 percent. Turnout in the 2004 and 2008 election increased to roughly 55 percent. While this might be encouraging, it still means that roughly 100 million

---

[14]Frances Fox Piven and Richard A. Cloward, *Why Americans Still Don't Vote: And Why the Politicians Want It That Way* (Boston: Beacon, 2000), 43.

[15]Thomas E. Patterson, *The Vanishing Voter: Public Involvement in an Age of Uncertainty* (New York: Knopf, 2002), 6.

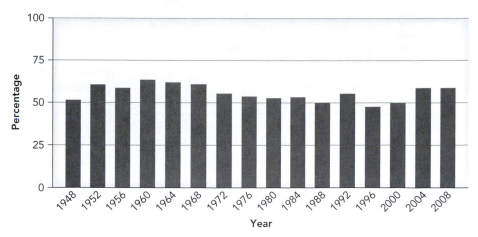

FIGURE 8.1 Voter Turnout in Presidential Elections

Source: International Institute for Democracy and Electoral Assistance, "Voter Turnout: United States."
Accessed at: www.idea.int/vt/graph_view.cfm?CountryCode=US

citizens decided to sit on the sidelines in the two most recent presidential elections. The turnout in presidential primaries has declined as well. In the early 1970s, when average citizens were first granted the opportunity to select party nominees through binding primaries, turnout was roughly 30 percent. In recent presidential primaries (since 1996), that number has shrunk to about 15 percent, with the 2008 Democratic primary being an exception due to the tight, prolonged battle between now-Secretary of State Hillary Clinton and now-President Obama, as noted in Figure 8.2. On the Republican side, the numbers remained meager.

As shown in Table 8.1, the picture of participation in midterm congressional elections is even worse. (These are the elections between presidential election years;

TABLE 8.1   Voter Turnout in Federal Elections over Time

National Voter Turnout in Federal Elections: 1960–2010

Year	Voting Age Population	Voter Registration	Voter Turnout	Turnout of Voting Age Populations (percentage)
2010	235,809,266	NA	90,706,582	37.8%
2008	231,229,580	NA	132,618,580	56.8
2006	220,600,00	135,889,600	80,588,000	37.1
2004	221,256,931	174,800,000	122,294,978	55.3
2002	215,473,000	150,990,598	79,830,119	37.0
2000	205,815,000	156,421,311	105,586,274	51.3
1998	200,929,000	141,850,558	73,117,022	36.4

(continued)

| TABLE 8.1 | Voter Turnout in Federal Elections over Time | *(continued)* |

National Voter Turnout in Federal Elections: 1960–2010

Year	Voting Age Population	Voter Registration	Voter Turnout	Turnout of Voting Age Populations (percentage)
1996	196,511,000	146,211,960	96,456,345	49.1
1994	193,650,000	130,292,822	75,105,860	38.8
1992	189,529,000	146,211,960	96,456,345	49.1
1990	185,821,000	121,105,630	67,859,189	36.5
1988	182,778,000	126,379,628	91,594,693	50.1
1986	178,566,000	118,399,984	64,991,128	36.4
1984	174,466,000	124,150,614	92,652,680	53.1
1982	169,938,000	110,671,225	67,615,576	39.8
1980	164,597,000	113,043,734	86,515,221	52.6
1978	158,373,000	103,291,265	58,917,938	37.2
1976	152,309,190	105,037,986	81,555,789	53.6
1974	146,336,000	96,199,020[a]	55,943,834	38.2
1972	140,776,000	97,328,541	77,718,554	55.2
1970	124,498,000	82,496,747[b]	58,014,338	46.6
1968	120,328,186	81,658,180	73,211,875	60.8
1966	116,132,000	76,288,283[c]	56,188,046	48.4
1964	114,090,000	73,715,818	70,644,592	61.9
1962	112,423,000	65,939,751[d]	53,141,227	47.3
1960	109,159,000	64,833,096[e]	68,838,204	63.1

NA = not available.

Notes: Presidential election years are in bold.

(a) Registrations from Iowa not included.

(b) Registrations from Iowa and Missouri are not included.

(c) Registrations from Iowa, Kansas, Missouri, Montana, Nebraska, and Wyoming are not included. District of Columbia did not have independent status.

(d) Registrations from Alabama, Alaska, District of Columbia, Iowa, Kansas, Kentucky, Missouri, Montana, Nebraska, North Carolina, North Dakota, Oklahoma, South Dakota, Wisconsin, and Wyoming are not included.

(e) Registrations from Alabama, Alaska, District of Columbia, Iowa, Kansas, Kentucky, Missouri, Montana, Nebraska, New Mexico, North Carolina, North Dakota, Oklahoma, South Dakota, Wisconsin, and Wyoming are not included.

Sources: Federal Election Commission. Data drawn from Congressional Research Service reports, Election Data Services Inc., and State Election Offices.

Information Please Database, 2007 Person Education, Inc. All rights reserved.

Accessed at: www.infoplease.com/ipa/A0781453.html

Michael McDonald, 2010 Election Turnout Rates, George Mason University's United States Election Project. Accessed at: http://elections.gmu.edu/Turnout_2010G.html

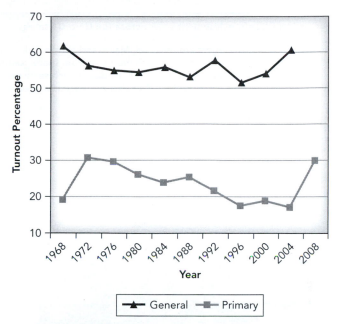

FIGURE 8.2 **Relationship between Primary Turnout and General Election Turnout: 1968–2008**

Source: Curtis Gans, *2008 Primary Turnout Falls Just Short of Record Nationally, Breaks Records in Most States,* America University Center for the Study of the American Electorate (May 19, 2010).
Accessed at: http://domino.american.edu/AU/media/mediarel.nsf/1D265343BDC2189785256 B810071F238/C34358140EBD07B88525744E005AC5A6?OpenDocument

for example, 1998, 2002, 2006, and 2010.) In the 1960s, about 50 percent of Americans made it to the polls for these elections. By the 1970s, the number had dropped to just over 40 percent and has since shrunk to just over one-third. With only one-third of eligible Americans going to the polls, there are two people who do not vote in congressional elections for every one person who does. Moreover, the decline in participation in state and local elections has been much the same—or worse. Many cities have seen their voter turnouts for municipal posts, such as mayor and city councilperson, drop to their lowest ever.

Given this data, one might be surprised to hear an argument that the decline in turnout might be a "myth" or, at the very least, less significant than what it might appear on its face.[16] A team of scholars argue that turnout figures are based on U.S. Census Bureau estimates of the adult population, but this figure often includes individuals who cannot legally vote, such as prison inmates and convicted felons. As demonstrated in Figure 8.3, many states do not allow inmates or those with prior convictions to vote. It is difficult to know precisely how many people this adds up to,

---

[16]See, for example, Michael McDonald and Samuel Popkin, "The Myth of the Vanishing Voter," paper presented at the annual meeting of the American Political Science Association (Washington, DC: August 30–September 3, 2000), as cited in Patterson, *The Vanishing Voter,* 198.

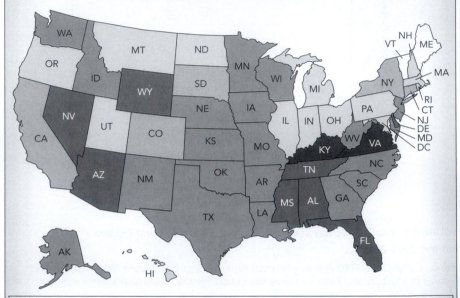

Criminal Disenfranchisement Laws across the United States

States vary widely on when voting rights are restored. Maine and Vermont do not withdraw the franchise based on criminal convictions; even prisoners may vote there. Kentucky and Virginia are the last two remaining states that permanently disenfranchise all people with felony convictions, unless they receive individual, discretionary, executive clemency.

■ Permanent disenfranchisement for all people with felony convictions, unless government approves individual rights restoration: KY, VA

■ Permanent disenfranchisement for at least some people with criminal convictions, unless government approves individual rights restoration: AL, AZ, DE, FL, MS, NV, TN, WY

■ Voting rights restored upon completion of sentence, including prison, parole, and probation: AK, AR, GA, ID, IA, KS, LA, MD, MN, MO, NE*, NJ, NM, NC, OK, SC, TX, WA, WV, WI

□ Voting rights restored automatically after release from prison and discharge from parole (probationers may vote): CA, CO, CT, NY, SD

□ Voting rights restored automatically after release from prison: DC, HI, IL, IN, MA, MI, MT, NH, ND, OH, OR, PA, RI, UT

□ No disenfranchisement for people with criminal convictions: ME, VT

*Nebraska imposes a two-year waiting period after completion of sentence.

FIGURE 8.3 Disenfranchised Citizens

Source: Brennan Center for Justice at New York University School of Law, "Voting after Criminal Conviction: Criminal Disenfranchisement Laws across the U.S." Accessed at: www.brennancenter.org/page/-/Democracy/09.03.31.disenfranchisement .map.png

but one estimate is roughly 4 million citizens.[17] On top of this, there has been a liberalization of immigration laws since the 1960s, which has led to one of the largest influxes of immigrants since World War I: "Non citizens were two percent of the population in 1960 and today they account for seven percent."[18] Simply put, these scholars argue that when adjusted for ineligible adults, the picture of turnout in America is less stark—and in fact suggests stability since the 1960s.

But other scholars are ready with a response. In a provocative book entitled *The Vanishing Voter*, Harvard political scientist Thomas Patterson makes several interesting points. First, even when adjusted for ineligible voters, the picture is still one of decline—perhaps not as steep, but a decline nonetheless. Second, on top of this, "there would still be the puzzling question of why gains in education and registration have not produced the 15–20 percent rise in turnout that voting theories would have predicted."[19] We might add that other forms of electoral participation, where eligibility laws do not apply (such as watching debates on television or talking about politics with friends and family), have declined sharply as well. Finally and perhaps most significant, prior to the 1960s, Southern Blacks and many poor whites were disenfranchised. Patterson writes,

> [T]he clearest picture of what's been happening with turnout in recent decades emerges from a look at non-Southern states only. There, turnout among eligible voters exceeds 70 percent in the 1960s. By 1972 it has dropped to 60 percent, and, in 1996, barely topped 50 percent. The non-South voting rate is now near the levels of the 1820s, a time when many eligible voters could not read or write and had to travel by foot or on horseback for hours to get to the nearest polling place . . . [T]he flight from electoral politics is not illusory.[20]

FACTORS INFLUENCING VOTER TURNOUT

A robust debate in recent years has centered on the cause(s) of lackluster electoral participation. As noted earlier, turnout has been sliding since the 1890s. Yet the recent decay period appears to be much longer and more significant than earlier periods, and it has also occurred during a time in which one might expect voting levels to actually *increase*. More Americans than ever attend college (higher education seems correlated with higher levels of turnout), registration barriers have been lowered (see the discussion of the motor-voter bill in Chapter 3), and the civil rights movement has opened the door to greater African-American involvement (also see Chapter 3). With so many positive changes, why would levels of electoral participation be on the slide? There is no clear answer, but there are many theories.

---

[17]Ibid.

[18]Patterson, *The Vanishing Voter*, 8.

[19]Ibid., 9.

[20]Ibid.

Attitudinal Change Perspective

One possibility might be dubbed attitudinal change perspective. This parallels our discussion of changes in the socialization process noted earlier in this chapter. In sum, this approach holds that the decline is based on changing attitudes toward politics and elections. Increased cynicism, distrust, alienation, and the like are often pointed to as the roots of the problem. Young Americans, in particular, seem less efficacious—they are less sure about their own role in changing the course of government. Additional survey data seem to support the claim that negative attitudes about politics have been on the rise since the 1950s. For instance, in the mid-1950s, about 75 percent of Americans might have been described as "trustful" of their government to "do what is right all or at least most of the time." This number plummeted to just over 20 percent by the early 1990s, but has since moved back up a bit—to roughly the 40-percent range. About 24 percent of Americans in the 1950s thought "quite a few" politicians were crooked. That number jumped to 50 percent in the mid-1990s and in 2011 stands at about 40 percent. Numerous other indicators suggest Americans are less assured about government and politics than in previous times.[21] But can one link these attitudes to lower levels of electoral participation? Most scholars agree that these changes likely have an impact on levels of participation, although the size of this impact is uncertain. It would simply make sense that as citizens feel worse about the entire political system, they would be less willing to join the fray.

Lifestyle Change Supposition

Another perspective is what we might call the "lifestyle change" supposition. Simply put, life today is simply busier and offers more distractions. According to Robert Putnam, author of *Bowling Alone: The Collapse and Revival of American Community*, "I don't have enough time," and "I'm too busy" are the most often heard excuses for social disengagement.[22] Let us examine, for instance, the number of dual-income families. Today, a majority of families have two wage earners, a massive shift from the 1950s when few women worked outside the home. "[A]nd since there are only 24 hours in the day," writes Putnam, "something had to give . . . [and] it seems plausible that the cutbacks also affected community involvement."[23] The same sort of argument is often made with regard to the shrinking number of nonworking hours for all Americans. The argument also suggests that Americans are too distracted by new technologies, namely television (and now the Internet), to be heavily involved in politics. Television competes for people's scarce time. Indeed, studies suggest that "TV watching comes at the expense of nearly every social activity outside the home."[24] Once again, these changes likely play some role in the decline, but many, including Putnam, are quick to caution against overstating the case. With regard to women in the workplace, for

---

[21]This data, and much else, can be found at the National Election Study Cumulative Data File, 1952–2004. Accessed at: www.umich.edu/~nes/nesguide/nesguide.htm

[22]Robert D. Putnam, *Bowling Alone: The Collapse and Revival of American Community* (New York: Simon and Schuster, 200), 189.

[23]Ibid., 194.

[24]Ibid., 237.

example, while it may be true that they have less time to vote, they also have more opportunities to vote, given that they are pulled outside the home on Election Day by work. Moreover, it seems that employed women are actually more involved in civic life than are stay-at-home women.[25] As for television, Putnam's best guess is that around 15 percent of the decline in civic participation, more generally, can be attributed to Americans' love affair with television screens.[26]

Local Parties, Partisanship, and Polarization

While change at the individual level—be it more pessimistic attitudes about politics or less time to join the political process—is part of the decline phenomena, many suggest that the causes of the problem lie elsewhere. A strong possibility would be the political party–centered argument. As noted in Chapter 4, political parties seem to be heading in two directions at the same time. State and national party organizations, such as the Republican National Committee and the Democratic National Committee, are as vibrant and as well funded as ever. Party organizations at this level are thriving. But at the local level, party organizations seem to be withering. It is here that the problem lies: Local political parties historically have been the institutions that pulled citizens to the polls on Election Day. Legions of party workers, nearly always volunteers, would keep track of which party members had voted and which had not. By dinnertime on Election Day, those who had yet to vote would receive a telephone call or perhaps even a visit from one of these workers and would be "gently" reminded to vote. Indeed, political scientists have set their sights on testing the relationship between local party vitality and levels of turnout. The data are convincing: Turnout is much higher in communities that still have strong local parties.[27] The problem, however, is that fewer and fewer communities have such organizations. And even this argument may not get at the heart of the problem, because the decline in local party activity itself can be linked more broadly to the same general decline in civic engagement.

Along similar lines, there was a dramatic increase in the number of non-partisan voters, particularly from the 1950s to the end of the 1990s. Again referring to the American National Election Studies, in the 1950s, about 7 percent of Americans had no party identification and did not lean to either of the two parties (a group often referred to as "pure independents"). By the mid-1970s, that figure had more than doubled—to roughly 17 percent—and throughout the 1980s and 1990s remained at roughly 13 percent. Is it just a coincidence that the number of independent citizens rose at precisely the same time fewer voters came to the polls? Scholars have long noted a strong relationship between one's partisan intensity and voting: Those individuals most committed to a party are also the ones most likely to vote. Thus, it is quite likely that changing attitudes toward party identification have had a bearing on turnout levels. Along similar lines, in

---

[25]Ibid., 196.

[26]Ibid., 284.

[27]See John P. Frendreis, James L. Gibson, and Laura L. Vertz, "Electoral Relevance of Local Party Organization," *American Political Science Review* 84 (1990): 225–235; Stephen Brooks, Rick Farmer, and Kyriakos Pagonis, "The Effects of Grassroots Campaigning on Political Participation," paper presented at the 2001 Annual Meeting of the Southern Political Science Association (Atlanta, Georgia: November 8–10, 2001).

his study of thousands of citizens during the 2000 election, Patterson found that those who believed that the parties are alike were much *less* likely to vote.[28]

Most recently, there appears to be an increase in partisan polarization. Indeed, "party polarization" seems to be one of the defining characteristics of American politics in the early part of the 21st century. Figure 8.4 offers a geographic look at partisanship in the United States, where light grey indicates areas of Republican strength, darkest grey denotes Democratic strength, and the shade in between, an even balance. Clearly, there are distinct partisan regions in the country, but there are also numerous areas that are evenly matched.

Beyond geographic differences, the exact dimensions of the recent partisan polarization are a bit unclear. Some scholars, such as Stanford political scientist Morris Fiorina, have suggested the root of the change stems from activists at the ends of the ideological spectrum; hard-core liberals and hard-core conservatives have become especially informed, vocal, and engaged. Most citizens remain moderate, but the wings of the party have become loud and very active. And because hard-core activists are more likely to vote, particularly in primary elections, the winners tend to be more ideological than their constituent base. Ironically, as middle-of-the-road citizens see their member of Congress and state legislature as firmly committed to either far-left or far-right policies, they may stay away from the process. They also notice that the tone of politics, given this polarization, has become shrill. It is possible, then, that this type of polarization is actually contributing to lower levels of voting. True ideologues turn out, to be sure, but moderates, who tend to be much less engaged

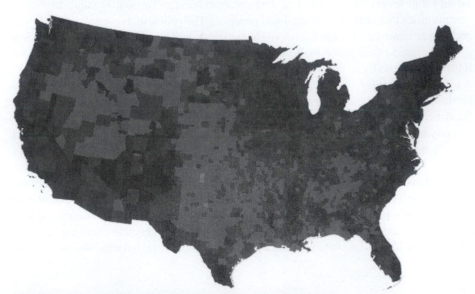

FIGURE 8.4 Geographic Look at Partisanship in the United States

Source: Mark Newman, "Map of the 2008 U.S. Presidential Election Results." Accessed at: www-personal.umich.edu/~mejn/election/2008/

---

[28]Patterson, *The Vanishing Voter*, 59.

in the process, may be staying home on Election Day. In his book *Disconnect: The Breakdown in Representation in American Politics*, Fiorina writes,

> [C]ross-sectional evidence does not rule out the possibility that the long-term decline in voting by independents and ideological moderates is relative to the growing negativity of contemporary politics . . . [O]rdinary Americans are turned off by the uncivil manner of many members of the political class, their emphasis on issues of limited importance to most people.[29]

Other scholars have suggested that the polarization is much more widespread than merely among those at the ideological extremes, and that this change has contributed to higher turnout in recent elections. Consider the writing of Emory University scholar Alan Abramowitz in his book *The Disappearing Center: Engaged Citizens, Polarization, and American Democracy*,

> Contrary to the claim that ordinary Americans have been losing interest in government and politics as a result of growing partisan animosity and ideological polarization, . . . [survey data] shows that Americans today are more interested in politics, better informed about politics, and more politically active than at any time during the past half century.[30]

So which perspective is correct? Has polarization been limited to those at the ideological extremes or has it been more widespread? Will this shift bring more people to the polls or keep higher numbers at home? Undoubtedly scholars will wrestle with these questions for some time. Either way, there are significant changes occurring in the electorate—adjustments will have a strong bearing on levels of engagement.

The Conduct of Campaigns and Turnout

Some suggest that the nature of campaigns in recent decades has contributed to the decline in voting. During the period of declining partisanship, candidates seemed ever anxious to pitch themselves to the center of the ideological spectrum. As voters found it harder and harder to distinguish policy differences between candidates, they withdrew from the electoral process. The opposite is precisely the argument being made by Abramowitz, noted earlier: As parties and candidates offer voters clear differences on important policy questions, voters are better able to make rational assessments and are thus more likely to come to the polls.

Campaigns, especially for the presidency, have become much longer, leading to voter burnout. "The long campaign of today runs in spurts, taxes people's attention, and dulls their sensibilities."[31] It used to be common for presidential candidates to kick off their campaigns in the fall, a year before the general election, but in 2008, all of the major candidates had done so by early spring of that year. Along with the length of

---

[29]Morris P. Fiorina with Samuel J. Abrams, *Disconnect: The Breakdown of Representation in American Politics* (Norman, OK: University of Oklahoma Press, 2009), 41.

[30]Abramowitz, *The Disappearing Center*, 19.

[31]Ibid., 127.

campaigns, the candidates have become impersonal, relying on radio, television, and Internet advertisements. In the not-too-distant past, much campaign work was done face-to-face, likely leading to greater interest among citizens and higher levels of turnout.

There is also the issue of negative campaigning. There is little question that the tone of campaigns has become more negative in recent decades. Hard-hitting, shrill campaigns have always been part of the political landscape in the United States, but the frequency these days, due in large measure to television, is unprecedented. Perhaps attack ads simply turn off voters. The first scholarly take on the issue seemed to confirm this theory, but upon closer inspection, the issue is more complicated. While many studies suggest that negative campaigning seems to turn voters off, an equal number find that turnout actually increases in negative races.[32] One impressive study suggests that while some voters (namely, less partisan ones) are turned off, others (the most partisan) are likely activated by negative campaigning.[33] Another promising line of research on this topic suggests that the effects of negative campaigning on voter turnout might be dependent upon the citizen's "local political culture."[34] A citizen in Provo, Utah, might respond differently to attack ads than, say, a voter in Newark, New Jersey. At present, however, there seems to be no scholarly consensus on the effects of attack ads on levels of turnout; one cannot simply tag negative campaigns as the culprit.

Media Effects

As noted earlier, some have suggested that the recent turn toward hyperinvestigative journalism—what one scholar has dubbed "attack journalism" or media "feeding frenzies"[35]—has turned off voters. In the past, a politician's personal transgressions were kept out of the news. Journalists, as well as average citizens, saw a wall between a politician's public and private matters. But today, likely due to the highly competitive nature of the news business, anything that draws the public's attention seems fair game to the media. This often means extensive coverage of matters once considered private. The result has been the negative portrayal of politicians—one scandal after another. Scholars have had a difficulty directly linking these media feeding frenzies with declining turnout, but most would agree that the connection seems plausible. Surely some voters would say, "If most politicians are corrupt, why should we become involved in the processes that put these crooks in office?"

Registration Laws and Early Voting

As noted in Chapter 3, in order to vote you must first be registered. Registration rules are set at the state level, but are capped by federal statute at no more than 30 days prior to an election. Many argue that this requirement, coupled with similar residency requirements, has served to limit the number of citizens who actually vote on Election

---

[32]For a meta-analysis on the topic—a study of the studies—see Richard Lau, Lee Sigelman, Caroline Heldman, and Paul Babbit, "The Effects of Negative Political Advertising: A Meta-analytic Assessment," *American Political Science Review* 93 (December 1999): 851–875.

[33]Stephen Ansolabehere and Shanto Iyengar, *Going Negative: How Political Advertisements Shrink and Polarize the Electorate* (New York: Free Press, 1997), Chapter 5.

[34]Kelly Patterson and Daniel M. Shea, "Local Political Context and Negative Campaigns: A Test of Negative Effect across State Party Systems," *Journal of Political Marketing* 3, no. 1 (December 2003): 1–20.

[35]Sabato, *Feeding Frenzy*.

Day because it requires two steps. The first step, registration, is considered more time consuming. As suggested by two lead scholars in a classic work called *Who Votes?*, "[r]egistration is usually more difficult than voting, often involving more obscure information and a longer journey at a less-convenient time, to complete a more complicated procedure. Moreover, it must usually be done before interest in the campaign has reached its peak."[36] In an effort to attract more voters on Election Day, the trend has been to shorten the period for registration. As of 2011, nine states allow voters to register to vote on Election Day. The data vary a bit, but generally speaking, about 13 percent of voters in these states register on Election Day.

Another step has been to lengthen the time for actual voting. Historically, citizens could cast votes prior to an election if they had a good reason for being away or unable to come to the polls. "Excuse-based" absentee voting allowed those who know they will be away or physically unable to come to the polls to cast a ballot by mail. This has been the foremost means for military personnel to vote, for instance. Generally, one had to apply for an absentee ballot at least 30 days in advance, and the completed ballot has to arrive at the election office before Election Day in order to be counted.

A trend in recent years has been to enhance early voting in four ways. First, many states now allow "no excuse" absentee voting. Here a voter has to apply for a ballot, but a reason as to why he or she cannot vote at the polls is not required. Second, in a few states, citizens can apply to become permanent absentee voters. Third, Washington and Oregon mail ballots to all voters. In this case applications are not required. Fourth, over half of the states now allow early, walk-in voting.

Explanations of the different types of early voting by state are noted below.[37]

"With Excuse" Absentee Ballot—Request to vote by paper mail-in ballot, but only if the voter has a valid reason why he or she cannot go to the polls on Election Day.

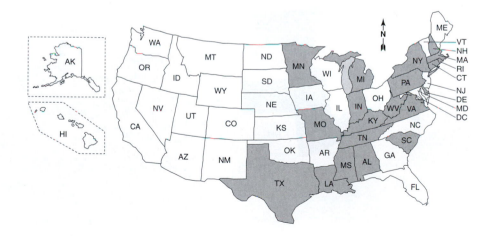

---

[36]Raymond Wolfinger and Steven Rosenstone, *Who Votes?* (New Haven, CT: Yale University Press, 1980), 6.

[37]The data to create these maps came from the National Conference of State Legislatures. Accessed at: www.ncsl.org/default.aspx?tabid=16604 on June 8, 2011.

"No Excuse" Absentee Ballot—Request to vote by paper mail-in ballot, but the voter does not need to provide a reason why he or she cannot go to the polls on Election Day.

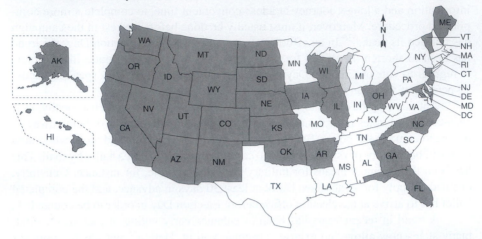

Early Mail-in Voting—In Washington and Oregon, all voters receive a ballot in the mail.[38] Voters in Washington have the choice of mailing in this ballot or going to their polling location on Election Day. Oregon conducts all its elections by mail-in voting.

Permanent Absentee Ballot—Voters may make a permanent request to have an absentee ballot sent to them each election. No excuse is necessary.

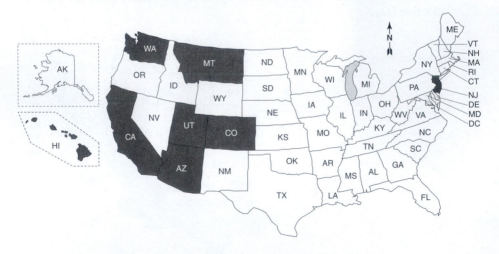

---

[38]The Early Voting Information Center, "Frequently Asked Questions: Voting by Mail (VBM)." Accessed at: http://earlyvoting.net/faq on June 8, 2011.

Early, Walk-in Voting—Voters are allowed walk in to their election office (or satellite location, i.e., shopping mall or library) and vote in person early. No excuse is necessary.

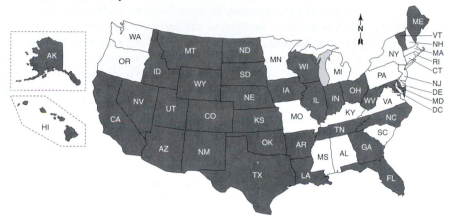

Military Voters—All states permit members of the military who are stationed overseas, their dependents, and other U.S. citizens living abroad to vote by absentee ballot.

The goal of these changes has been to lower the costs of voting (make it easier), and by doing so draw more citizens into the process. This would make sense, of course. Yet the scholarly evidence of the effectiveness of early voting is mixed, at best. Some studies have suggested a modest increase in turnout in states with same-day registration: an increase of roughly 5 percentage points.[39] But the research on the effects of extending the voting period (either by mail or walk-in) is inconclusive. We know that about one-third of the ballots in the 2008 election were cast early, and that in about a dozen states over one-half of the ballots are cast in advance of Election Day. Yet how many of these votes would have been cast under the traditional method is unclear. Several studies suggest overall turnout may have actually *decreased* because of these measures.[40] How could this be the case? It seems that early voting methods may detract voters from the excitement and energy of Election Day. When there is only one day to vote, there is energy and enthusiasm for fulfilling one's civic duty. As noted by a team of scholars from the University of Wisconsin–Madison, "Early voting dilutes the concentrated activities of Election Day itself that would likely stimulate turnout, an effect not counterbalanced by the increased convenience of voting prior to the election (which may only provide an alternative outlet for voters who would have voted in any case)."[41]

[39]Jan E. Leighley and Jonathan Nagler, "Electoral Laws and Turnout: 1972–2008," paper presented at the Fourth Annual Conference on Empirical Legal Studies, 2009, University of Southern California. Accessed at: http://papers.ssrn.com/sol3/papers.cfm?abstract_id=1443556

[40]John C. Fortier, *Absentee and Early Voting: Trends, Promises, and Perils* (Washington, DC: American Enterprise Institute Press, 2006).

[41]Barry C. Burden, David T. Canon, Kenneth R. Mayer, and Donald P. Moynihan, "The Effects and Costs of Early Voting, Election Day Registration, and Same Day Registration in the 2008 Elections," paper presented to the Pew Charitable Trusts, December 21, 2009. Accessed at: www.pewcenteronthestates.org/uploadedFiles/wwwpewcenteronthestatesorg/Initiatives/MVW/UWisconsin.pdf

An under-researched aspect of this debate centers on the type of citizens more likely to register the same day, or to use early voting opportunities. Clearly, young, more mobile citizens (such as college students) tend to use same-day registration, but it also appears that minority citizens may be more likely to do the same. It also seems that minority residents are more inclined to use early voting techniques. Given that these groups tend to vote Democratic, by the summer of 2011, a number of states controlled by Republican state legislatures were considering rescinding their early voting laws. As you might guess, this has been, and will continue to be, a controversial topic.

The Incumbent Advantage

Finally, congressional incumbent reelection rates have remained high during the very period that turnout has declined. In the past few decades, reelection rates have rarely dipped below 90 percent. Incumbents have numerous other advantages that help them win reelection, including name recognition, franking (mailings from their official office), campaign experience, professional staff, fund-raising skills, and a close relationship with the local media. It is also likely that careful redistricting can have a great impact on reelection rates. In any given congressional election year, only a handful of races are deemed truly competitive. Given that a vast majority of Americans do not live in districts with hard fought, tight campaigns, it is surely possible that many view their efforts as a waste of time. When an incumbent is unopposed or runs against a weak candidate, citizens ask, "What is the point of voting, when I already know who's going to win?" It is a near truism in American politics that turnout is higher in competitive races than in noncompetitive races. Reforms such as setting term limits for federal representatives and senators have been discussed as a way to increase participation and reduce incumbent advantage (see Chapter 10), but this would only apply to state and local elections.

TURNOUT AND DEMOGRAPHIC CHARACTERISTICS

As you might guess, not all groups of Americans participate in campaigns and elections at the same level. Legal restrictions originally limited participation to affluent white males, but even with the removal of these restrictions, not all groups participate equally. As Tables 8.2 and 8.3 show, there are some telling differences between different groups of voters. This section will take a close look a key demographic difference, with a keen eye to the importance of age.

Community Connectedness

Why would one group of citizens participate less than other groups? Here too the scholarly literature is extensive. One perspective that seems to carry a good bit of weight centers on "community connectedness." Simply put, it is theorized that the more someone is connected to his or her community, the more likely he or she is to vote. Demographic data suggest that poor people, for example, move more often than affluent folks, and are much less likely to own a home, suggesting they are less likely to be connected to a community. Not surprisingly, the level of political participation for this group is quite low. This perspective might also explain why younger Americans seem less engaged. Often, young folks have only modest connections to a particular community, as many

TABLE 8.2	Exit Polls by Demographics: Proportion of Total Electorate 2004–2010			
	2004 (%)	**2006 (%)**	**2008 (%)**	**2010 (%)**
Gender				
Male	46	49	47	48
Female	54	51	53	52
Race				
Whites	77	79	74	77
African-American	11	10	13	11
Latino	8	8	9	8
Age				
18–29	17	12	18	12
30–44	29	24	29	24
45–59	30	34	37	43
60+	24	29	16	21
Income*				
Under $15,000	8	7	6	
$15,000–30,000	15	12	12	17
$30,000–50,000	22	21	19	19
$50,000–75,000	23	22	21	21
$75,000–100,000	14	16	15	15
$100,000–150,000	11	13	14	19
$150,000–200,000	4	5	6	
$200,000 or More	3	5	6	8
Education				
No high school	4	3	4	3
High school graduate	22	21	20	17
Some college	32	31	31	28
College graduate	26	27	28	30
Postgraduate	16	18	17	21

* In 2010, $0–$15,000 and $150,000–$200,000 were not included as increments. Under $30,000 and $100,000–$200,000 were used instead.

Sources: Cable News Network website
2004: www.cnn.com/ELECTION/2004/pages/results/states/US/P/00/epolls.0.html
2006: www.cnn.com/ELECTION/2006/pages/results/states/US/H/00/epolls.0.html
2008: www.cnn.com/ELECTION/2008/results/polls/#USP00p1
2010: www.cnn.com/ELECTION/2010/results/polls/#USH00p1

TABLE 8.3	Political Participation by Demographics in 2008					
	Voted (Self-Reported) (%)	Tried to Influence How Others Vote (%)	Attended Political Meeting (%)	Worked for a Party or Candidate (%)	Wore a Button or Put a Sticker on the Car (%)	Gave Money to Help a Campaign (%)
Male	75	51	7	3	22	13
Female	78	45	7	3	19	13
Whites	80	51	8	4	22	15
Blacks	71	38	4	1	20	7
Born 1975 or later	65	56	8	3	23	4
Born 1959–1974	74	47	7	2	22	8
Born 1943–1958	83	49	8	4	20	17
Born 1927–1942	85	47	6	5	17	21
Born 1911–1926	71	25	6	0	20	17
Income 0–16 percentile	56	36	8	2	23	9
Income 17–33 percentile	68	40	5	1	19	6
Income 34–67 percentile	82	54	8	2	18	11
Income 68–95 percentile	90	55	9	6	27	16
Income 96–100 percentile	89	58	8	5	24	31
Grade school	51	20	9	0	13	0
High school	67	44	3	1	20	8
Some college, no degree	80	51	9	6	23	12
College degree/ Postgraduate	93	55	12	4	21	22

Note: This is the percentage of those who responded "Yes."
Also check out Table 4.5—Campaign Participation 1960–2008.

Source: The American National Election Studies, "Political Involvement and Participation in Politics: Campaign Participation," Tables 6B.1–6B.5.
Accessed at: www.electionstudies.org/nesguide/gd-index.htm#6

are in college and others are floating between jobs. While the logic of this perspective seems clear, the snag is encountered in explaining the decline: Are there more "disconnected" Americans today than in the past? While some data might lead us to this conclusion, much else, such as levels of home ownership, would suggest otherwise.

Education

Another perspective centers on the "cost/benefit" of participation. Voting happens only, this approach holds, when the benefits equal or exceed the costs. Believe it or not, there are some costs associated with voting: One has to register, find time to vote, and know enough about the candidates to make informed decisions. Although many would suggest these costs are minor, social scientists believe that they are enough to keep many voters from participating, particularly if the voter sees few benefits. They might ask, "Can I really make a difference by voting?" or "Do I really have a voice in the election process?" Perhaps if the voter has a community connection, the perceived benefits (which would also include fulfilling one's perceived civic duty) would outweigh the cost. An important characteristic here seems to be levels of education; the costs of voting seem to decline as one's level of formal education increases. Not only does awareness of the mechanics of elections increase with formal education, so too do the benefits of voting. Simply put, one's sense of civic duty seems to increase through education. As noted by a team of political behavior scholars, "Length of education is one of the best predictors of an individual's likelihood of voting."[42]

Ideology

In addition to differences in participation among different demographic groups, we find that people who hold certain ideological beliefs tend to participate more. Those who describe themselves as liberals or conservatives tend to participate more than those who describe themselves as moderates, as discussed earlier. There are several possible explanations for this. Traditionally, parties and candidates have relied on a core of supporters to give money, get volunteers, and spread the word. These core supporters are generally not moderates, as moderates tend to be less reliable supporters of a single party and its candidates. Many also suspect moderates have less deeply held views on policy issues, and are thus less likely to, for example, try to convince a friend whom to vote for.

Age

Simply stated, age has always been a solid predictor of election turnout, as noted in Figure 8.5. The likelihood of voting increases as a citizen gets older, probably because of a closer connection to the community. It remains quite high through one's later years, with a modest dip when the citizen becomes elderly.

Beyond this rather straightforward fact of American electoral politics are several interesting details related to young voters.[43] When 18-year-olds were first

---

[42]Flanigan and Zingal, *Political Behavior and the American Electorate*, 40.

[43]Portions of the following material are from Daniel M. Shea, "Obama Net-Roots Campaign, and the Future of Local Party Organizations," in John C. Green and Daniel Coffee, eds., *The State of the Parties*, 6th ed. (Lanham, MD: Rowman & Littlefield, 2010).

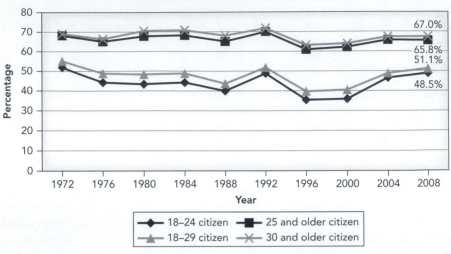

Presidential Voter Turnout by Age, 1972–2008

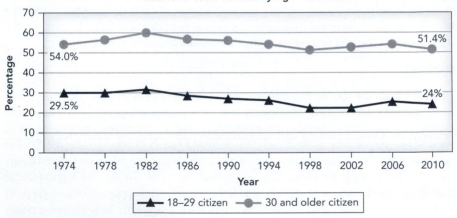

Mid-Term Voter Turnout by Age 1974–2010

FIGURE 8.5 Voter Turnout by Age

Source: "Youth Voting," The Center for Information Research on Civil Learning and Engagement.
Accessed at: www.civicyouth.org/?page_id=241

guaranteed the right to vote, in 1972, about 50 percent did so. By the 2000 election, that figure had dropped to just 35 percent. In midterm elections in the 1970s, the figure for those under 25 was about 40 percent, but by the end of the century, it was hovering around 20 percent. Clearly, young Americans were staying away from the voting booths.

The problem ran much deeper than nonvoting, however. According to the American National Election Studies, the number of young Americans (younger than 25) who were "very much" interested in campaigns stood at roughly 30 percent from the

1950s through the 1980s. By 2000, the figure had dropped to just 6 percent.[44] In 2002, 67 percent of all Americans cared "very much" or "pretty much" about the outcome of congressional elections in their area, but just 47 percent of those younger than 25 felt the same way.[45]

A poll of Americans in their late teens and early twenties conducted by the Pew Research Center found that less than 50 percent were thinking "a great deal about" elections in 2000. This compared to about two-thirds in 1992. Roughly 40 percent suggested that it did not matter who was elected president in 2000, twice as many as in 1992.[46] The UCLA (University of California, Los Angeles) study "Most of the Nation's College Freshman Embrace the Internet as an Educational Tool" drew attention to lackluster political participation. In 1966, some 58 percent agreed that "keeping up to date with political affairs" is very important, but by 1999, that figure had dropped to 26 percent. Only 14 percent of freshmen said they frequently discussed politics, compared with the high of 30 percent in 1968.[47]

Putnam, in *Bowling Alone,* summed up the issue this way:

> Very little of the net decline in voting is attributable to individual change, and virtually all of it is generational . . . [Moreover,] declining electoral participation is merely the most visible symptom of a broader disengagement from community life. Like a fever, electoral abstention is even more important as a sign of deeper trouble in the body politic than as a malady itself. It is not just from the voting booth that Americans are increasingly AWOL.[48]

At the same time, other data revealed that the same young Americans who were abstaining from politics were giving generously of their energy, time, and money to their schools, communities, and nation. A report by the Center for Information and Research on Civic Learning and Engagement (CIRCLE), for example, suggested young Americans were volunteering at significantly *higher* rates than were older Americans. Moreover, the frequency of pitching-in had increased: In 1990, some 65 percent of college freshmen reported volunteering in high school, and by 2003, that figure had risen to 83 percent. Rates of volunteer work for those under 25 were twice as high as for those over 55.[49]

---

[44]The American National Election Studies, "Interest in Current Campaign 1952–2008," Table 6D.6.3. Accessed at: www.electionstudies.org/nesguide/2ndtable/t6d_6_3.htm on June 7, 2011.

[45]The American National Election Studies, "Cares Who Wins in Congressional Election 1952–2008," Table 6D.8.2. Accessed at: www.electionstudies.org/nesguide/2ndtable/t6d_8_2.htm on June 7, 2011.

[46]Brooking Institute, "The American Voter 2000: Dissatisfied? Distracted? Or Just Don't Care?" Brookings Press Briefing: A new Survey from the Pew Research Center (2000). Accessed at: www.brookings.edu/events/2000/0714elections.aspx on June 9, 2011.

[47]Linda J. Sax, Alexander W. Astin, William S. Kom, and Kathryn M. Mahoney, "Most of the Nation's College Freshmen Embrace the Internet as an Educational Tool, UCLA Study Finds," 1998. Accessed at: www.heri.ucla.edu/pr-display.php?prQry=22 on June 9, 2011.

[48]Putnam, *Bowling Alone*, 35.

[49]Mark Hugo Lopez and Karlo Barrios Marcelo, "Volunteering among Young People," The Center for Information and Research on Civic Learning & Engagement (April 2007). Accessed at: www.civicyouth.org/PopUps/FactSheets/FS07_Volunteering.pdf on June 8, 2011.

These data have led many to question why a generation so eager to be involved in community would refrain from politics. Scholar Bill Galston suggested a plausible answer:

> Most young people characterize their volunteering as an alternative to official politics, which they see as corrupt, ineffective, and unrelated to their deeper ideals. They have confidence in personalized acts with consequences they can see for themselves; they have no confidence in collective acts, especially those undertaken through public institutions whose operations they regard as remote, opaque, and virtually impossible to control.[50]

In other words, young Americans were disengaged from the policy process because they felt marginalized within the political process.

And then things changed. The decline in partisanship and overall interest and faith in the electoral process took a dramatic turn in recent elections. As to why there has been such a dramatic turnaround, theories abound. Thomas Patterson, of Harvard's Vanishing Voter Project, points to the importance of issues and voter concerns. "Americans historically have voted in higher numbers when the nation confronts big issues. That was as true in the late 1800s and 1930s as it has been more recently. The meltdown in the financial markets [in the fall of 2008] likely confirmed Americans' belief that 2008 was a watershed election."[51] Another possibility is that the competitiveness and importance of the 2000 election drew new participants into the process. David Hill writes, "National elections in the United States since 2000 have been very competitive and thus it is possible that the cohorts entering the electorate during this period will create a footprint . . . and turnout will increase in future elections."[52] Still another possibility relates to the number of persuadable voters. Throughout much of the past three decades (since 1980), about one-fifth of the electorate "knew all along" whom they would vote for. That figure jumped to 33 percent in 2004. Conversely, about 7 percent of voters made up their minds on Election Day during the revival period. In 2004, this figure had shrunk to just 2 percent.[53] Establishing voting preference affects voter mobilization in two ways. First, as more and more voters establish voting preference early in the process, the number of voters who struggle with the "costs" of casting an informed vote declines. Second, and more importantly, as election activists confront a predisposed electorate, resources are shifted from persuasion to mobilization. If most voters make up their minds well before the election, then it makes sense to focus on getting the faithful to turn out. This might have been especially important for the mobilization of young voters.

But what about young voters? What was it that pulled them to the polls in 2004 and especially in 2008? A reasonable guess is that Barack Obama's "ground game" campaign had something to do with it. Obama's forces had four times as many paid

---

[50]William Galston, "Political Knowledge, Political Engagement, and Civic Education," *Annual Review of Political Science* 4 (June 2001): 224.

[51]Thomas Patterson, "Voter Turnout Approaches Some Records, Breaks Others," *Harvard University Gazette Online* (November 6, 2008).

[52]David Hill, *American Voter Turnout: An Institutional Perspective* (Boulder, CO: Westview, 2006), 5.

[53]The American National Election Studies, "Time of Presidential Election Vote Decision 1948–2004," Table 9A.3. Accessed at: www.electionstudies.org/nesguide/toptable/tab9a_3.htm on June 7, 2011.

local organizers than did John Kerry or Al Gore. This was especially true in swing states. For example, John Kerry had 10 field offices in New Mexico, whereas Obama had 39. As noted by one observer, "The architects and builders of the Obama field campaign have undogmatically mixed timeless traditions and discipline of good organizing with new technologies of decentralization and self-organization."[54] Indeed, the reach of the Obama net-root effort was massive. Consider the following:[55]

- Some 13 million addresses were compiled.
- 7,000 different e-mail messages to those on the email list, leading to a total of over one billion email messages.
- Over one million people signed up for Obama's text messaging program.
- Obama supporters were in undated with emails, getting an average of 20 texts per month during the campaign.
- All who signed up for alerts in battle ground states received three text reminders to vote on Election Day.
- Phone banks were used extensively, with roughly 3 million calls made during the final days of the race for the campaign. The Obama team used MyBO's virtual phone-banking system.
- Over five million people signed up as supporters of Obama on social network sites A vast majority of these were on Facebook.
- Over five million clicked the "I Voted!" button on these social network sites.
- The Internet was a boon for Obama fundraising, netting well over $500 million.

And of course the efforts seem to have paid off. According to a CIRCLE report, 64 percent of 18- to 24-year-olds and 43 percent of 18- to 29-year-olds were first-time voters. This compares to just 11 percent of all voters. Also, young voters were most likely to engage in online campaign activities supporting Obama on Election Day. In fact, the margin of victory for Obama from those under 30 was 68 percent to McCain's 32 percent. John McCain actually received a majority of votes from those over 45. Few were surprised to hear John McCain's daughter Meghan remark a few months after the election that the Republican Party was "on the precipice of becoming irrelevant to young people."[56] But of course a few years can be a lifetime in electoral politics, and by the 2010 election, the number of young Americans siding with the GOP (Grand Old Party) had significantly increased and was more or less on par with the number identifying with the Democrats.

TRENDS IN OTHER FORMS OF POLITICAL PARTICIPATION

As you might imagine, the trend of many other forms of political participation has paralleled what we have seen with elections. Take, for example, attending a political meeting or rally. Survey data suggest that roughly 9 percent of Americans

---

[54]Zack Exley, "The New Organizers: What's Really behind Obama's Ground Game," *Huffington Post* (October 8, 2008).

[55]Jose Antonio Vargas, "Obama Raised Half a Billion Online," *Washington Post Online* (November 20, 2008).

[56]As cited in Dan Gerstein, "The Republican Relevance Gap," *Forbes.Com* (April 1, 2009). Accessed at: www.forbes.com/2009/03/31/republican-relevance-gap-opinions-columnists-gop.html

attended some sort of political meeting during most of the 1960s and 1970s.[57] In 2011, that figure stands at about 5 percent. During the 1960s and 1970s, about 75 percent of Americans noted reading stories about political campaigns in newspapers and magazines; in 2011, that figure is just over 50 percent. The decline has been especially steep for younger voters. In the past, roughly 5 percent of young voters worked for a party or candidate, but in 2010, that number has barely risen above 2 percent. In the 1960s and 1970s, about 12 percent of the youngest voters attended political meetings; in the 2010 elections, this figure was just 4 percent. Again, Putnam notes,

> [S]ince the mid 1960s, the weight of the evidence suggests, despite the rapid rise in levels of education, Americans have become perhaps 10–15 percent less likely to voice their views publicly by running for office or writing Congress or the local paper, 15–20 percent less interested in politics and public affairs, roughly 25 percent less likely to vote, roughly 35 percent less likely to attend public meetings, both partisan and non-partisan, and roughly 40 percent less engaged in party politics and indeed political civic organizations of all sorts.[58]

It would be a mistake, however, to assume that all forms of political participation have declined. America has always been a nation of "joiners," and recent statistics suggest the number of groups vying for advantage in the policy process has skyrocketed during the past decade, as noted in Chapter 7. Also, another rather novel perspective suggests emergence of a new type of politics, dubbed lifestyle politics. Simply put, this view holds that while Americans may be less engaged in traditional forms of political action, they are increasingly involved in matters that concern their own well-being. At the forefront of this list of concerns is one's economic condition. As noted by a prominent scholar,

> The psychological energy (cathexis) people once devoted to the grand political projects of economic integration and nation-building in industrial democracies is now increasingly directed toward personal projects of managing the expressing complex identities in a fragmented society . . . For the vast majority, both the source of identity and the concerns of politics lay increasingly at home, and are, correspondingly, more removed from national and collective action.[59]

While many might suggest this perspective is little more than a "cop-out," at the very least it offers much to contemplate given the transformations brought upon by

---

[57]This data and the other statistics to follow, unless otherwise noted, are from the University of Michigan's American National Election Studies Commutative File, 1952–2004. Accessed at: www.umich.edu/~nes/nesguide/nesguide.htm

[58]Putnam, *Bowling Alone*, 46.

[59]W. Lance Bennett, "The Uncivic Culture: Communication, Identity, and the Rise of Lifestyle Politics," *PS: Political Science & Politics* 31, no. 4 (December 1998): 755, 758.

the information revolution and the "new economy." Some traditional forms of political participation have declined, but many Americans are finding new ways to stay active in politics and to fit politics into their busy daily lives. Small things, such as wearing a button or sticker, are up, and giving money has replaced attending political meetings for many people. Interestingly, the actual act of trying to influence others' votes has gone up significantly.

A CROSS-NATIONAL COMPARISON

The authors of *The Civic Culture*, discussed earlier, suggest that the socialization process in the United States does a better job at promoting the importance of voting and elections than in most other countries. Indeed, we have suggested at various places in the last few chapters that Americans are, in many ways, "election crazed." Yet since the start of the 20th century, a shrinking number has come out on Election Day. Can this paradox be explained by looking at the turnout rates at other countries? In other words, perhaps levels of involvement in the United States are less than perfect, but better than what we might find in other nations.

Unfortunately, this does not seem to be the case. Voting rates in the United States are low not only in historic terms but also in comparison to the rest of the world. Table 8.4 shows the average voter turnout since the 1990s in eight industrialized democracies, with the United States coming in near the bottom. This is not a new development. Turnout has declined in most of these nations during the last half of the 20th century, but the decline in the United States has been more pronounced and, when combined with traditionally lower levels of voting, places the United States comparatively near the bottom.[60]

There are a number of reasons for low voting levels in the United States—both structural and political. In the United States, registering to vote is the duty of each individual, while in many other nations, it is the duty of the state to compile voting lists.[61] In other words, in some countries, it is incumbent upon the government to register each citizen to vote, while in the United States, it is a job thrust upon the individual. Another structural difference is the day voting takes place. General elections in the United States take place on the first Tuesday after the first Monday in November. In many other nations, Election Day is a Saturday or Sunday, allowing citizens more flexibility in getting to the polls. In some nations, elections take place over two days. The Italians, for example, can vote on both Saturday and Sunday.[62] Both of these differences lower the "cost" of voting—the effort a citizen must expend to cast his or her vote.

Finally, some suspect that lower voter turnout is a result of limited political choices in the United States. Many other nations have a vibrant multi-party system. France, for example, elected representatives from 12 parties to its National Assembly in 2002, with no party winning more than one-third of the vote. While the two-party system offers many benefits, one negative result might be that voters who feel that neither major party speaks for them simply stay home.

---

[60]Rafael López Pintor et al., *Voter Turnout Since 1945: A Global Report* (Stockholm: International Institute for Democracy and Electoral Assistance, 2002), 78–85.

[61]Ibid., 25.

[62]Ibid., 116.

TABLE 8.4	A Comparative Look at Voting Rates Since 1992	
	Average Voter Turnout[a] (%)	**Compulsory Voting**
Greece	86.5	No
Italy	84.9	Yes
Belgium	84.6	No
Australia	82.8	Yes
Denmark	82.7	No
Sweden	79.7	No
Finland	78.6	No
New Zealand	78.1	No
Spain	77.8	Yes
Israel	77.2	No
Norway	75.5	No
Netherlands	75.4	Yes
Austria	74.9	No
Germany	73.3	No
France	73.0	No
United Kingdom	61.7	No
India	60.0	No
Japan	59.3	No
Canada	57.1	No
United States	53.3	No
Ireland	47.7	No
Switzerland	36.9	No

Source: International Institute for Democracy and Electoral Assistance, "Voter Turnout 2008," Accessed at: http://www.idea.int/vt/index.cfm, November 1, 2010.

Note: (a) Percentage of total voting-age population participating in election for highest-level office (president of the United States, for example).

The fact that Americans vote at lower rates than citizens of other industrial democracies tends to suggest that Americans are less politically involved overall—and one might expect that Americans would lag in other measures of political participation as well. Paradoxically, the opposite seems to be true. Surveys since the 1990s have consistently found that Americans lead the world in most forms of nonelectoral political participation, even though the trend has also been one of decline. Voting turns out to be a weak predictor of other forms of participation.[63] Some countries with the highest election turnout rates rank far behind in most other categories of participation, while the United States, with exceptionally low turnout, leads in most other categories.

---

[63]Samuel H. Barnes et al., *Political Action: Mass Participation in Five Western Democracies* (Beverly Hills: Sage Publications, 1979), 85.

These other forms of participation may be more common and important in the United States than in other countries because of its unique form of democracy. America features more elective offices, a clear separation of powers between branches and levels of government, and loose party discipline. One might conclude that individual elections matter less in America than they do in other countries. For instance, a British member of Parliament deals not only with national matters—concerns Americans generally associate with Congress—but also with many issues that Americans would consider within the scope of a state or local government, such as school issues and highway maintenance. From this perspective, a British voter's choice for Parliament is significantly more important than an American's vote for a member of Congress. Seeing that they cannot dramatically change public policy with a single vote, perhaps Americans try to influence the government in other ways.

Conclusion

What difference does it make that Americans seem only modestly interested in politics and that Americans, overall, vote less often than citizens in other democracies? Is this really something to care about?

One way to answer such questions is from a more practical point of view. In other words, what difference would it make in a policy sense if nonvoters joined the act? Would the government head in a different direction if turnout was higher? This issue has stymied political scientists for some time. Early studies suggested that, on the whole, the policy preferences of nonvoters essentially paralleled those of voters. There would be little policy change if the United States had full election turnout. More recently, studies suggest that who votes does matter. The low turnout in the 1994 election allowed the Republicans to capture control of both Houses of Congress, helped bring George W. Bush to the White House in 2000, and denied Democrats in the Senate their 60th vote by electing a Republican, Scott Brown, in the Massachusetts special election in 2010 replacing deceased Democrat Ted Kennedy (as noted in Chapter 1). In each of these cases, and many others, public policy shifts that followed these elections resulted in a more conservative, more Republican agenda than overall public opinion would have suggested. As two political scientists put it, "The idle go unheard: They do not speak up, define the agenda, frame the issues, or affect the choices leaders make."[64]

Another way to answer such questions is to refer to one's view of "democracy." On the one hand, perhaps precise levels of participation are unimportant. So long as there are enough citizens involved to make the process competitive, full participation is inconsequential. Moreover, the ones likely to refrain from involvement in politics are also the ones least informed. Perhaps Americans do not want these folks involved in the process; is an uninformed vote really preferable to abstention? Along similar

---

[64]Steven J. Rosenstone and John Mark Hansen, *Mobilization, Participation, and Democracy in America* (New York: Macmillan, 1993), 247; as cited in Patterson, *The Vanishing Voter*, 12.

lines, some speculate that less-informed citizens (the nonvoters) are more prone to radical policy shifts. As such, their abstention from the ballot box creates a degree of stability in public policy. Columnist George Will, in an article entitled "In Defense of Nonvoting," argues that good government is the fundamental human right, not the right to vote. He suggests that high voting rates in Germany's Weimar Republic enabled the Nazis' rise to power.[65] Declining turnout in America is surely no cause for worry. Such a perspective is often dubbed the elite democratic model. So long as there are guarantees of fairness and political opportunity, the system is healthy.

The popular democratic model, however, suggests that the character of any political system depends on not simply the outcomes of public policy but also the process by which policy is reached. This model places a premium on civic involvement. When this occurs, citizens develop an affinity for the system because they have a stake in the outcome. Systems of government designed to reflect the will of the people will better do so, and will be more stable in the long run, if average citizens join the political fray. Echoing this sentiment, political scientist and journalist E. J. Dionne, in a book entitled *Why Americans Hate Politics*, wrote, "A nation that hates politics will not long thrive as a democracy."[66] Another prominent scholar put it this way: "[A society of nonvoters] is potentially more explosive than one in which most citizens are regularly involved in activities which give them some sense of participation in decisions which affect their lives."[67]

Finally, there is a growing chorus of observers who suggest that voting and civic participation more generally can be linked to a community's ability to solve difficult problems, its economic development, the health of its residents, and even the level of crime. "[A]n impressive and growing body of research suggests that civic connections help make us healthy, wealthy, and wise . . . and better able to govern a just and stable democracy."[68] How we might connect these outcomes to voting is a bit fuzzy, but many would suggest the connections are surely there.

Critical Thinking

1. What do you think accounts for the fact that Americans are more involved than citizens of most nations in other forms of political participation, but have some of the lowest voting records? What can be done to change this?
2. Why do you think people don't vote as often in congressional midterm elections when the framers intended Congress to be the "people's branch"? What can be done to change the impression that midterm elections are not important?

---

[65]As cited in Patterson, *The Vanishing Voter*, 11.

[66]E. J. Dionne, *Why Americans Hate Politics: The Death of the Democratic Process* (New York: Simon and Schuster, 1991), 355.

[67]Seymour Martin Lipset, *Political Man* (Baltimore: Johns Hopkins University Press, 1981), 164; as cited in Thomas E. Patterson, *The Vanishing Voter*, 13.

[68]Putnam, *Bowling Alone*, 13.

3. Do you think the recent increases in partisanship will serve to increase turnout and political participation or do you think its effects will be detrimental to the American democracy?
4. Why do many young Americans give a great deal to their communities, but also sit on the sidelines on Election Day?

On the Web

To get an inside look at political participation in action, check out sites.allegheny.edu/cpp, the website for Allegheny College's Center for Political Participation, a center directed by this text's author that engages in a variety of student-centered programs, distinctive community outreach projects, and scholarly activities.

Campaign Finance

After reading this chapter, you should be able to understand these core concepts and explain their significance:

- FECA
- *Buckley v. Valeo*
- PACs
- Incumbency Advantage

- BCRA
- *Citizens United v. FEC*
- 527s and Super PACs

I t surely will not come as a surprise that with all the changes discussed so far in this book that campaigns have become expensive affairs. President George W. Bush raised a record-breaking $200 million during the primary election season in 2004, even though he was unopposed! Barack Obama was able to dwarf that amount in 2008, raising roughly $600 million. Following the election, the *Washington Post*, in a piece detailing Obama's use of the internet to raise funds, suggested Barack Obama raised half a billion dollars online in his run for the presidency, ushering in a new era in presidential fundraising.[1] And of course this change will spread to lower-level campaigns.

---

[1]Jose Antonio Vargas, "Obama Raised Half a Billion Online," *Washington Post Online* (November 20, 2008). Accessed at: http://voices.washingtonpost.com/44/2008/11/20/obama_raised_half_a_billion_on.html

Even at the local level, the cost of running for office has skyrocketed. One scholar has suggested that local campaigning has become an "arms race."[2] This money has to come from somewhere—nearly always special interest groups, labor unions, corporations, and individuals. This is an old tune in politics, but the fear that such donations give these groups and individuals undue influence in the policy process has grown in recent years. Do campaign contributions skew the policy process toward the will of the donors, rather than the will of the people? There is also a concern that declining public trust in government and the decline in political participation, discussed in Chapter 8, are intimately linked to a drive for ever-larger campaign war chests.

But can candidates really "buy" their way into office? Do wealthy donors and interest groups control elected officials with their campaign contributions? Does big money in elections lead to growing voter cynicism and distrust of American political institutions? Fewer and fewer Americans seem interested in politics these days, but is big money really part of the problem? Perhaps the opposite is true—that heavy campaign spending provides voters with more information and thus increases the likelihood that they will go to the polls. Isn't contributing money to a candidate a form of "advocacy," akin to political speech? If so, is it not protected by the First Amendment of the Constitution? Don't Americans want more participation in elections?

In previous chapters, it was noted that the legal barriers to participation have been lowered. The declining role of local political parties and the growing importance of consultants and interest groups suggest a transformation is under way. Added to these changes, as you will soon read, is the dramatic acceleration of the role of money in elections.

THE ROLE OF MONEY IN ELECTIONS

Many would be surprised to hear that money has *not* always played such a central role in the American election process. During the early days, there was simply less to spend money on. Candidates would often "treat" voters, meaning that they would sponsor lavish picnics and barbecues. George Washington, for example, was said to have purchased a quart of rum, wine, beer, and hard cider for every voter in the district when he ran for the Virginia House of Burgesses in 1751 (there were only 391 voters). In 1795, one would-be Delaware officeholder roasted a steer and half a dozen sheep for his friends, and another candidate gave a "fish feast."[3]

Four decades later, Ferdinand Bayard, a Frenchman traveling the United States, commented that "candidates offer drunkenness openly to anyone who is willing to give them his vote."[4] A candidate might also spend a good bit on newspapers—either buying space or perhaps starting or buying his own newspaper to push his candidacy.

---

[2]J. Cherie Strachan, *High-Tech Grass Roots: The Professionalization of Local Elections* (Lanham, MD: Rowman & Littlefield, 2003), 72.

[3]John Kenneth White and Daniel M. Shea, *New Party Politics: From Jefferson and Hamilton to the Information Age* (Boston, MA: Bedford/St. Martin's, 2000), 210.

[4]Robert Dinkin, *Campaigning in America: A History of Election Practices* (Westport, CT: Greenwood, 1989), 8.

Indeed, the most heated campaigns of the century were conducted through battling newspapers. Quite often when a wealthy individual was anxious to aid a particular candidate, he would simply publish a newspaper. Even Abraham Lincoln secretly purchased a small newspaper in Illinois in 1860.[5] On the whole, however, money simply did not play a pivotal role in elections because there were few ways to spend it.

By the election of 1896, things began to change. For one, William McKinley's closest advisor, Mark Hanna—considered to be the first campaign consultant—believed that Republicans could win by spending unprecedented sums on newspapers, pamphlets, buttons, billboards, parades, and speakers to travel across the nation, and so forth. For instance, 200 million pamphlets were mailed from a headquarters that housed over 100 full-time clerks. More significantly, for the first time in American

Mark Hanna (1837–1904) was a Cleveland industrialist who made his fortune in coal and iron. Hanna raised an election fund for McKinley from wealthy individuals and corporations and orchestrated the most expensive campaign ever seen at that time, undermining opponent William Jennings Bryan's grassroots campaign with hired orators and a flood of literature, all promising continued prosperity under McKinley.   *Source:* World History Archive/Newscom

---

[5]R. J. Brown, HistoryBuff.com—A Nonprofit Organization. Accessed at: www.historybuff.com/library/refrailsplit.html

history, corporations made contributions directly from their company treasuries. A massive sum was raised and spent—likely in the range of $7 million. The strategy worked, as McKinley narrowly defeated the popular Democrat, William Jennings Bryan.

As technology changed throughout the 20th century, so too did the cost of elections. Money became absolutely critical by the late 1950s. To many, the cost of running for office, at every level of government, was rising out of control. Five factors accentuated the increase in the importance of money by the midpoint of the century:

- *Decline of Local Party Organizations*—Given that parties had been primarily responsible for connecting with voters, candidates needed new ways of reaching out. Many of these new means were costly.
- *More Voters Up for Grabs*—Along with the decline of party organizations, fewer voters displayed steadfast loyalty to any political party. The number of "independent" voters grew during this period, leading to, among other things, greater uncertainty at election time. Nervous candidates were anxious to spend as much money as possible to feel more at ease about their chances on Election Day.
- *Television*—In the early 1950s, only a small percentage of homes boasted a television set; by the early 1960s, television had become nearly universal. Television transformed much of American life and changed the way campaigns were run. Running television advertisements requires huge sums of money.
- *Campaign Consultants*—Coupled with the growing importance of television were the professionals hired to create these commercials. Professional campaign consultants burst on to the political scene in the 1960s, bringing with them many other sophisticated technologies, such as direct mail and survey research. These techniques proved effective, of course, but they came with a hefty price tag.
- *Inflation*—The price of marketing all products has gone up over the years.

Figure 9.1 illustrates the rising costs of running for Congress. On average, the winning candidate spent roughly three times more in 2006 than in 1990 in both the House and Senate and the defeated candidate spent nearly six times more.

THE RAGE FOR REFORM

Efforts to control the flow of money in elections stretch back to the Progressive Era. The federal government and many states adopted laws that barred businesses and labor unions from giving money directly to candidates. The rationale behind these changes was to limit the likelihood of a quid-pro-quo relationship—that elected officials would feel obligated to "pay back" their campaign contributors with favored policies. Representatives were expected to look out for all citizens, not just the ones who flooded the campaign treasury with contributions. Given that the very politicians enacting these laws were often dependent upon such contributions to get reelected, it is not surprising that these laws had little real impact. The early reforms were filled with loopholes large enough to drive a truck through.

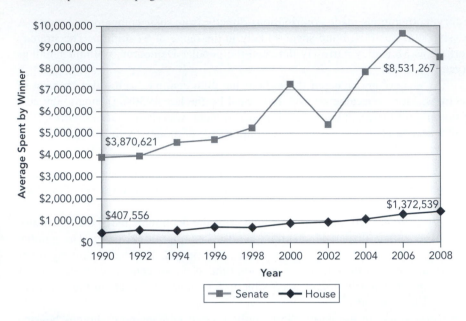

FIGURE 9.1 The Average Cost of Winning Election
Source: Data from Center for Responsive Politics, "Election Stats," OpenSecrets.org.
Accessed at: www.opensecrets.org/bigpicture/elec_stats.php?cycle=2008 on June 9, 2011.

Real reform came in the early 1970s, as members of Congress began to worry about the chances of being thrown from office by a candidate, perhaps a political novice, who would simply spend more money. The self-interest that inhibited meaningful reform during the progressive period lead to Draconian changes in the 1970s. The Federal Election Campaign Act (FECA) was signed into law in 1971. Three years later, a series of amendments was passed to make the law even more restrictive. Following is a partial list of FECA components:

- Limits on the amount of money candidates for federal office could spend
- Limits on the amount any individual or group could give to federal office candidates
- Limits on the amount of personal funds a federal office candidate could spend on his or her own campaign
- Limits on spending by independent groups (groups not connected to a candidate or campaign)
- Limits on the amount parties could spend on individual candidates and overall in an election year
- Requirements that federal office candidates disclose the source and amount of money given to their campaign
- Establishment of the Federal Election Commission to oversee campaign fundraising and spending in federal office campaigns, and to enforce election finance statutes
- Establishment of public funding for presidential elections

Few disputed that the provisions were real or that they would have a significant bearing on the way elections were conducted. Yet shortly after the amendments took effect, James Buckley, a conservative senator from New York, along with a group of politicians from both sides of the political spectrum, challenged the constitutionality of the law in the federal courts. Buckley and his colleagues argued that spending money was akin to free speech, and that limiting it would be an abridgement of one's First Amendment protections.

The case of *Buckley v. Valeo*, decided in 1976, was the most significant election-centered Supreme Court decision in American history. The Court, for the most part, sided with Buckley. It struck down provisions related to limits on overall spending, spending by the candidate, and spending by independent groups. It upheld public funding of presidential elections so long as it is voluntary. Surprisingly, however, the Court allowed limits on how much an individual or a group might give to a candidate. It stated, "The quantity of communication by the contributor does not increase perceptibly with the size of this contribution, since the expression rests solely on the undifferentiated, symbolic act of contributing."[6] In other words, when people give money to a candidate, they are expressing their support regardless of the size of the gift. Therefore, reasonable restrictions, designed to level the playing field a bit, are fine. Finally, the decision suggested that political parties were "special," given their role in the democratic process, and that few restrictions should be placed on their activities.

It is hard to overstate the ramifications of this decision. More than any other force, *Buckley* has shaped the nature of the election process since 1976. For one, the decision pushed candidates to raise money from numerous smaller sources, rather than from a pool of large donors. While this was the intent of the law, and while most Americans would applaud this change, candidates soon found much of their time—perhaps most of their time—was spent chasing donors. Not only has this made running for office less appealing but it has also greatly lengthened the time needed to invest in a campaign. Much related, an entire industry was born overnight: fund-raising consultants. Few candidates today head into the trenches without the aid of a high-priced fund-raising expert.

The role of political parties in elections was radically transformed by the reform movement and the subsequent Court decision. Candidates found that they could reach voters without the help of party workers, but because of FECA regulations and the special status afforded parties in the *Buckley* decision, state and national party organizations were reinserted into the process. Indeed, parties have since been placed at the center of the fund-raising process. In an effort to outdo the opposing party, new methods of stretching the legal system are devised in each election. The most significant of these loopholes was "soft money." While individuals and groups were limited in the amount they could contribute to a candidate by FECA, there were no restrictions when it came to giving money to a political party. Immense contributions were made—many over $1 million—which were filtered through the parties to support particular candidates. To many Americans, the soft-money loophole became little more than a money-laundering scam. Writing of this process in the late 1990s, scholar Anthony Corrado suggested that "An illness that has plagued previous elections has developed into an epidemic."[7]

---

[6]*Buckley v. Valeo*, 424 U.S. I, 44.

[7]Anthony Corrado, "Financing the 1996 Elections," *The Election of 1996: Reports and Interpretations*, Gerald M. Pomper, ed. (Chatham, NJ: Chatham House, 1997), 151.

Political Action Committees

Another spin-off of FECA and *Buckley* has been the proliferation of political action committees (PACs). Labor unions and corporations were barred from giving money to federal candidates by earlier acts of Congress. PACs were devised in the 1940s as a means to get around these restrictions. Here, none of the monies used to support a candidate came directly from a union or a corporation, but instead from their independent political units. Because FECA limits the amount that candidates might raise from an individual, candidates were forced to solicit help from a broad range of sources. The contribution limit for PACs was five times higher ($5,000), so their importance mushroomed. The number of groups exploded as well: In 1974, there were roughly 600 PACs; following the 2008 election, there were over 4,600.[8] Table 9.1 shows the

TABLE 9.1	Top 20 PAC Contributors to Candidates, 2009–2010		
PAC Name	**Total Amount ($)**	**Democratic Percentage (%)**	**Republican Percentage (%)**
National Association of Realtors	3,680,296	57	43
Honeywell International	3,569,700	55	45
AT&T Inc.	3,047,375	47	53
International Brotherhood of Electrical Workers	2,888,623	98	2
National Beer Wholesalers Association	2,708,000	56	44
American Association for Justice	2,654,000	97	3
American Bankers Association	2,637,404	33	66
American Federation of Teachers	2,282,250	99	0
American Federation of State/County/Municipal Employees	2,192,000	99	0
Operating Engineers Union	2,188,288	90	10
Teamsters Union	2,157,060	97	2
National Auto Dealers Association	2,133,400	47	53
Credit Union National Association	2,129,696	58	41

(continued)

[8]"Number of Federal PACs Increases," Federal Election Commission News Release (March 9, 2009). Accessed at: www.fec.gov/press/press2009/20090309PACcount.shtml

PAC Name	Total Amount ($)	Democratic Percentage (%)	Republican Percentage (%)
Boeing Co.	2,094,000	54	45
Laborers Union	2,045,500	96	4
Carpenters & Joiners Union	2,033,375	87	13
American Crystal Sugar	1,962,500	68	32
International Association of Fire Fighters	1,960,000	83	16
Plumbers/Pipefitters Union	1,958,350	96	2
Machinists/Aerospace Workers Union	1,958,000	98	2

Source: "Top PACs," The Center for Responsive Politics.
Accessed at: www.opensecrets.org/pacs/toppacs.php?Type=C&cycle=2010

20 largest PACs from 2009 and 2010, along with how much money they raised and which party the money went to.

PACs give money to candidates because they want a say in shaping public policy. Business groups, for example, want policies that help them make a profit, environmental PACs want policies that help protect the natural world, and labor PACs seek policies that help working men and women. But do these groups "buy" policies with their contributions? This is a hotly debated issue. Some suggest the connection between contributions and policy is direct—that contributors are rational and not inclined to spend their money without a direct payback. This is the implicit—and sometimes explicit—assumption of a number of "good government" or "watchdog" organizations. For example, the Center for Responsive Politics is a non-partisan organization that tracks the flow of money in elections and the development of public policy. Its website boasts detailed information on who gives and who receives campaign money. On one of its pages, called "Tracking the Payback," users can explore possible links between how a member of Congress votes on a given policy matter, and the sources of his or her contributions in previous elections.[9] Once again, the assumption is that money can buy policies.

Most scholars suggest that the link between contributions and policies is much less direct. Election officials often point to the difference between "lead and follow." Public perception is that money leads elected officials in a particular policy direction, perhaps a direction they would not likely take if not for the money. Yet, it may be that money follows acts; contributions are essentially rewards for supporting a policy choice. Contributions often come *after* the candidate has supported a policy or, at the very least, he or she has proclaimed a clear policy preference. PACs support candidates who agree with them on

---

[9]See "Tracking the Payback." Accessed at: www.opensecrets.org/payback/index.asp

policy already. Instances where one contribution or a host of contributions changed a member's vote are extremely rare.

Another perspective, perhaps the most likely, is that campaign contributions buy access. Elected officials are busy and have to make tough choices about how they spend their time. A major hurdle for those interested in persuading the elected official to support their cause is simply to gain an audience—a meeting. Campaign contributions help open the door and give the contributor a few moments of time with the elected official. As noted by one PAC officer, "[Contributions] give you access. It makes you a player." Another way of thinking about access is to imagine two groups each wanting a moment of a legislator's time. The first group contributed $5,000 in the last election and the second provided nothing but lip service. Which of the two groups would likely get its brief meeting?

Again, precisely what PACs buy with their contribution is unclear and contested—and political scientists have been unable to settle the matter. What is clear, however, is that the public perceives a problem. An oft-heard remark is that Americans have "the best Congress money can buy!" Numerous public opinion polls confirm that regardless of what actually transpires between contributors and public officials, average Americans see the money flowing from PACs to candidates as a threat to the democratic process. Figure 9.2 shows voters' perceptions on the level of corruption in Congress and the importance of those perceptions in their voting decisions.

The Incumbent Fund-Raising Advantage

There are important differences between the three types of candidates (incumbents, challengers, and open-seat candidates). Incumbents are candidates who already hold the office that is being contested (they are running for reelection), challengers are those opposing incumbents, and open-seat candidates are found when there is no incumbent seeking reelection. PACs hope that their money will somehow lead to support for their policies, which means they hope their money will be given to the candidate who is the eventual winner. (What can a defeated candidate do to shape public policy?) Accordingly, they prefer to send their funds to incumbents, because those already in office have a head start when it comes to reelection, dubbed the incumbent advantage. By sending their money to incumbents, PACs increase the incumbent advantage (Table 9.2).

As shown in Figure 9.3, in most elections, the percentage of successful U.S. House reelection campaigns extends well beyond 90 percent. This occurs even though many Americans seem frustrated with "business as usual politics" and seem anxious to "throw the bums out." Incumbents have always had an advantage, but recent changes have made matters even worse. Yale University scholar David Mayhew was one of the first to draw people's attention to the problem.[10] In his seminal book *Congress: The Electoral Connection*, Mayhew argues that nearly all legislative activity is now

---

[10] There has been a great deal written on the incumbent advantage. The work that kicked it all off, however, was penned by David Mayhew in 1974. See David Mayhew, *Congress: The Electoral Connection* (New Haven, CT: Yale University Press, 1974).

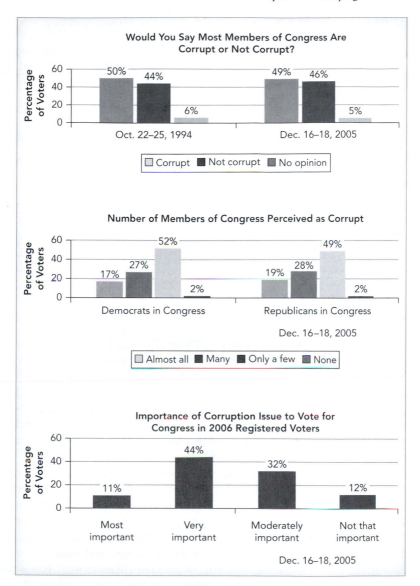

FIGURE 9.2 Public Opinion on Campaign Finance and Congressional Corruption

Source: Lydia Saad, "Political Corruption Is Bipartisan PR Problem," Gallup (January 5, 2006). CNN/*USA Today*/Gallup Poll taken during December 16–18, 2005.
Accessed at: www.gallup.com/poll/20731/Political-Corruption-Bipartisan-Problem.aspx

TABLE 9.2	The Incumbent Advantage in Fund-Raising in 2010		
Type of Candidate	Total Raised ($)	Number of Candidates	Average Raised ($)
Senate			
Incumbent	342,898,037	31	11,061,227
Challenger	141,118,941	152	928,414
Open Seat	355,866,601	122	2,916,939
Grand Total	839,883,579	305	2,753,717
House			
Incumbent	632,071,537	420	1,504,932
Challenger	293,365,660	1,113	263,581
Open Seat	154,306,539	354	435,894
Grand Total	1,079,743,736	1,887	572,201

Source: "Incumbent Advantage," The Center for Responsive Politics.
Accessed at: www.opensecrets.org/overview/incumbs.php

geared toward securing the next reelection. These efforts fall within three categories: *credit claiming*, which is receiving praise for bringing money and federal projects back to the district; *position taking*, which is positioning on the popular side of issues; and *advertising*, which includes constituent outreach through mailings (when paid for by the government, this is called franking) and other means. Others have pointed to additional sources of incumbent support, such as ongoing, frequent media attention— which challengers rarely get. Many agree that things have gotten out of control and that the nature of the electoral process is threatened.

Can anything be done about the incumbent advantage? Numerous reforms have been suggested to reduce this phenomenon. One proposal that jumped to the forefront was term limits. Simply put, if Americans are worried about an unfair advantage given to those already in office, why not mandate more open-seat contests? Limiting the number of times legislators can be reelected, as with the presidency, would guarantee turnover—a stream of new faces, energy, and ideas in Congress. Representatives should know the concerns of average citizens; what better way of ensuring this connection than by forcing entrenched legislators to step aside after a fixed period? Opponents of term limits argue that the legislative process is complex, especially these days, and that it takes time to become familiar with it. Term limits remove experienced legislators and replace them with green ones. Moreover, term limits deny voters an option that many of them would likely choose: the option of reelecting their current representative.

By the early 1990s, roughly half of the states had adopted term limits for state legislators *and* for federal office candidates. Public opinion polls suggested a majority of Americans favored these new restrictions. But many legal scholars wondered if states had the power to limit the terms of U.S. House and Senate members. The issue came to a head in the Supreme Court case of *U.S. Term Limits, Inc., et al.*

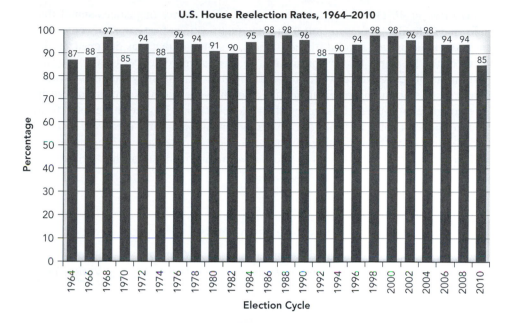

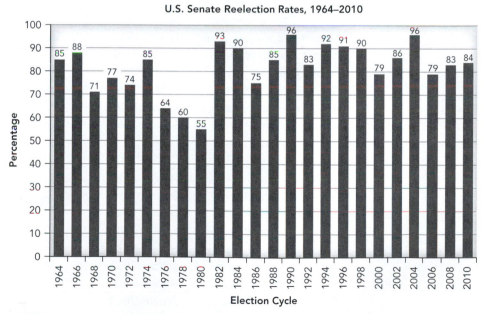

FIGURE 9.3 Incumbent Reelection Rates: 1964–2010

Source: "Reelection Rates Over the Years," The Center for Responsive Politics. Accessed at: www.opensecrets.org/bigpicture/reelect.php

v. Thornton et al. (1995). In a 5–4 decision, the majority of justices stated that "allowing individual States to craft their own qualifications for Congress would thus erode the structure envisioned by the framers, a structure that was designed, in the words of the Preamble to our Constitution, to form a 'more perfect Union.'"[11] This case essentially ended the drive for federal term limits, as the only alternative would be to pass a constitutional amendment. It did not, however, stop reformers from pushing through term limits at the state legislative level. Today, 16 states have some form of term limits, as noted in Table 9.3. Several organizations—most notably U.S. Term Limits, Inc.—have been fighting for their adoption in other states. They have also pushed federal office candidates to adopt a voluntary pledge that they would step

TABLE 9.3	**State-Level Legislative Term Limits**			
State	**Year**	**Limited Terms (Total Years Allowed)**	**Year Law Takes Effect**	**Percentage Voting Yes**
Arizona	1992	House: 4 terms (8 years)	House: 2000	74
		Senate: 4 terms (8 years)	Senate: 2000	
Arkansas	1992	House: 3 terms (6 years)	House: 1998	60
		Senate: 2 terms (8 years)	Senate: 2000	
California	1990	Assembly: 3 terms (6 years)	House: 1996	52
		Senate: 2 terms (8 years)	Senate: 1998	
Colorado	1990	House: 4 terms (8 years)	House: 1998	71
		Senate: 2 terms (8 years)	Senate: 1998	
Florida	1992	House: 4 terms (8 years)	House: 2000	77
		Senate: 2 terms (8 years)	Senate: 2000	
Louisiana†	1995	House: 3 terms (12 years)	House: 2007	76
		Senate: 3 terms (12 years)	Senate: 2007	
*Maine**	1993	House: 4 terms (8 years)	House: 1996	68
		Senate: 4 terms (8 years)	Senate: 1996	
Michigan	1992	House: 3 terms (6 years)	House: 1998	59
		Senate: 2 terms (8 years)	Senate: 2002	
Missouri	1992	House: 4 terms (8 years)	House: 2002	75
		Senate: 2 terms (8 years)	Senate: 2002	
Montana	1992	House: 4 terms (8 years)	House: 2000	67
		Senate: 2 terms (8 years)	Senate: 2000	
Nebraska	2000	Unicameral: 2 terms (8 years)	Senate: 2008	56
Nevada	1994	Assembly: 6 terms (12 years)	House: 2006	70
		Senate: 3 terms (12 years)	Senate: 2006	

(*continued*)

---

[11]*U.S. Term Limits, Inc. et al. v. Thornton et al.*, 63 U.S. Law Week 4413, 4432 (May 22, 1995).

State	Year	Limited Terms (Total Years Allowed)	Year Law Takes Effect	Percentage Voting Yes
Ohio	1992	House: 4 terms (8 years)	House: 2000	66
		Senate: 2 terms (8 years)	Senate: 2000	
Oklahoma	1990	12-year combined total for both houses	State Legislature: 2004	67
South Dakota	1992	House: 4 terms (8 years)	House: 2000	64
		Senate: 2 terms (8 years)	Senate: 2000	
Wyoming‡	1992	House: 6 terms (12 years)	House: 2004	77
		Senate: 3 terms (12 years)	Senate: 2004	
Average Percentage of Vote				67

Note: Italics indicate states limited by statute. All others are limited by state constitutional amendment.
* Maine's law is retroactive.
† Law in Louisiana was passed by the state legislature.
‡ Wyoming's law was originally passed by initiative in 1994. The legislature amended the law to allow members of the House to serve 12 years. A referendum to return to the original six-year House limits garnered 54 percent of the vote but failed to get 50 percent plus one of all voters needed to veto the legislature.
Source: "State Legislative term Limits," U.S. Term Limits.
Accessed at: http://termlimits.org/content.asp?pl=18&sl=19&contentid=19

aside after a set number of terms. Many candidates have done so, but a good many have also reneged on their promise once in office.

REFORMING THE REFORMS: BCRA

By the turn of the 21st century, most Americans had grown cynical about the election process. A 1994 survey found that 75 percent agreed (39 percent agreeing "strongly") that "our [American] present system of government is democratic in name only. In fact, special interests run things."[12] Another poll, conducted in 2001, found that 80 percent of Americans felt that politicians often "did special favors for people or groups who gave them campaign contributions."[13] Something needed to be done; the reforms of the early 1970s had done little to halt the flow of big money into elections and, if anything, had made matters worse by giving the impression that money was limited, when in fact the loopholes were both numerous and gaping.

Any time legislators are called upon to reform the system that put them in office, the process of change is slow, at best. The benefits of reform must be weighed against other issues, namely partisan advantages. Which party gains an advantage with a more restrictive campaign finance system? There is no clear answer to this question. Each party has its own advantages and is not inclined to reform the aspects of the system

[12] Roper Center for Public Opinion Research, 1994, as cited in the Center for Responsive Politics, *The Myths about Money in Politics* (Washington, DC: Center for Responsive Politics, 1995), 19.
[13] Bloomberg News Poll, conducted by Princeton Survey Research Associates, July 31–August 5, 2001.

John McCain and Russ Feingold.   *Source:* Douglas Graham/Roll Call Photos/Newscom

it finds beneficial. So while calls for reform echoed across America, measures in the legislature stalled. By the start of the 21st century, many state and local governments moved to restrict the flow of big campaign money, but at the federal level, the prospects of real change generally seem grim.

In 2002, two forces were able to overcome the stalemate. Leading a bipartisan call for reform were Senators John McCain (R, AZ) (the 2008 Republican presidential nominee), and Russ Feingold (D, WI). Both were significant players in national politics, but it was McCain who drew the most attention. He had run for the presidency in 2000, and although he was defeated for the Republican nomination by George W. Bush, McCain had become the darling of the media and the leader of a growing number of reformers across the nation. As McCain spoke frequently and passionately about the growing corruption in the election process, more and more Americans were drawn into the controversy. Furthering the drive for reform, campaign finance became a big issue in many of the congressional elections in 2000, and most of the successful candidates had pledged to do something about the problem. After much debate and maneuvering by both parties, the Bipartisan Campaign Reform Act (BCRA) was passed and signed into law by George W. Bush in February of 2002.

The new law was sweeping and its effects on contributions in 2009–2010 election cycle are highlighted in Table 9.4. In brief, it outlaws soft money contributions to the national political organizations and bans group-sponsored advertisements 30 days before primary elections and 60 days before general elections. Most observers agree that these limits are dramatic. Yet the law also raises the contribution limits to $2,000 for individuals and $10,000 for groups, and leaves open the ability for wealthy

| TABLE 9.4 | Contribution Limits for 2009–2010 |

Donors	Recipients				Special Limits
	Candidate Committee	PAC[a]	State, Districts, and Local Party Committee[b]	National Party Committee[c]	
Individual	$2,400* per election[d]	$5,000 per year	$10,000 per year combined limit	$30,400* per year	Biennial limit of $115,500* ($45,600 to all candidates and $69,900[e] to all PACs and parties)
State, District, and Local Party Committee	$5,000 per election combined limit	$5,000 per year combined limit	Unlimited transfers to other party committees		
National Party Committee	$5,000 per election	$5,000 per year	Unlimited transfers to other party committees		$42,600* to Senate candidate per campaign[f]
PAC Multicandidate[g]	$5,000 per election	$5,000 per year	$5,000 per year combined limit	$15,000 per year	
PAC Not Multicandidate	$2,400* per election[h]	$5,000 per year	$10,000 per year combined limit	$30,400* per year	

Note: * These limits are indexed for inflation in odd-numbered years.

[a]These limits apply both to separate segregated funds and PACs. Affiliated committees share the same set of limits on contributions made and received.

[b]A state party committee shares its limits with local and district party committees in that state unless a local or district committee's independence can be demonstrated. These limits apply to multicandidate committees only.

[c]A party's national committee, Senate campaign committee, and House campaign committee are each considered national party committees, and each have separate limits, except with respect to Senate candidates—see Special Limits column.

[d]Each of the following is considered a separate election with a separate limit: primary election, caucus, or convention with the authority to nominate; general election; runoff election; and special election.

[e]No more than $45,600 of this amount may be contributed to state and local parties and PACs.

[f]This limit is shared by the national committee and the Senate campaign committee.

[g]A multicandidate committee is a political committee that has been registered for at least six months, has received contributions from more than 50 contributors and—with the exception of a state party committee—has made contributions to at least five federal candidates.

[h]A federal candidate's authorized committee(s) may contribute no more than $2,000 per election to another federal candidate's authorized committee.

Source: "Contribution Limits for 2009–10," Federal Election Commission. Accessed at: www.fec.gov/info/contriblimits0910.pdf

individuals to donate soft money to state and local party organizations. The ban on soft money does not apply to PACs, which are still free to raise unlimited amounts of money.

Court Challenges to BCRA

The BCRA took effect the day after the 2002 midterm election and had a controversial beginning. The very same day that the BCRA was signed into law, Senator Mitch McConnell (R, KY), a strong opponent of campaign finance restrictions, and a host of other legislators, interest groups, and minor parties sought to nullify the measure by using a court-centered approach. The core of their argument was that the BCRA represents an assault on free speech. Constitutional arguments in support of the law were that contributions may be regulated without being a burden on the First Amendment because contributions are indirect, rather than direct, speech.

By the end of 2002, all of the complaints had been merged into one case, dubbed *McConnell v. The Federal Election Commission*, which was heard in the Supreme Court in the fall of 2003. A decision was handed down on December 10, 2003. In a 5–4 decision, the Court upheld the most important elements of the law. It was, according to a *New York Times* account, a "stunning victory for political reform."[14] The Court reasoned that Congress has a "fully legitimate interest in . . . preventing corruption of the federal electoral process through the means it has chosen." Moreover, the majority of justices suggested that the problem with big, unregulated contributions was preferential access and the influence that comes with it. It was, they noted, not simply an issue of the "appearance of corruption," but there were, rather, volumes of data strongly suggesting the existence of real problems. In short, where the majority of justices in the *Buckley* case seemed anxious to protect individual rights (treating money as akin to free speech), the majority of the Court in *McConnell* was anxious to protect the dignity of the American electoral system.

Since *McConnell*, there have been several other legal challenges to the law. In June 2007, the U.S. Supreme Court ruled that provisions in BCRA that banned ads funded by corporations or labor unions from being broadcast within 60 days of a general election and 30 days of a primary were unconstitutional if applied to ads that could reasonably be interpreted in ways other than directing a vote for one candidate or against another. The Supreme Court also overturned what was called the "Millionaire's Amendment" to the law, which increased contribution limits for candidates in races where an opponent spends a large amount of personal funds on the campaign.

The *Citizens United* Bombshell

The most recent chapter in the story of money in American elections was a decision handed down by the Supreme Court on January 21, 2010. The case was *Citizens United v. Federal Elections Commission,* and it dealt with a provision of BCRA that outlawed explicit campaigning by non-partisan groups within 60 days of a general election and 30 days prior to a primary election. Citizens United, a conservative

---

[14] Editorial Desk, "A Campaign Finance Triumph," *New York Times* (December 11, 2003), 42.

nonprofit corporation, produced a 90-minute documentary called *Hillary: The Movie*, which was highly critical of the New York senator. Citizens United was anxious to distribute it throughout the fall of 2007 and spring of 2008, even though Clinton was running in a series of primaries and caucuses for the Democratic nomination for the presidency. Because it was barred from doing so, and because it thought this was a violation of its First Amendment rights, the group took the issue to the federal courts.

When the case was first heard by the Supreme Court, the issue seemed to center on the prohibitions stipulated in BCRA. But when the justices heard arguments a second time, the topic appeared to be much broader: whether prohibitions on corporations and unions from directly spending in campaigns, established a half century before and upheld in several prior cases, were constitutional.

In a 5–4 decision, the Court ruled that unions and corporations were entitled to spend money from their general treasuries (without the use of PACs) on federal elections. They could not give directly to candidates, but they were free to spend lavishly on their behalf. This might imply, for example, that a large multinational corporation could spend $100 million, only a fraction of its budget, toward the election of a handful of members of Congress. Unions could do likewise.

The decision sent shockwaves across the political system. What would this mean? One commentator, writing for the *National Review Online*, suggested, "The ruling represents a tremendous victory for free speech . . . The ruling in *Citizens United* is a straightforward application of basic First Amendment principles."[15] But others feared that the decision would set loose a flood of money and lead to greater corruption. The *New York Times* editorialized, "With a single, disastrous 5-to-4 ruling, the Supreme Court has thrust politics back to the robber-baron era of the 19th century."[16]

While firm conclusions are somewhat elusive, evidence from the 2010 election seems to suggest the *Citizens United* ruling resulted in significantly more money in the election process. The Campaign Finance Institute (CFI), a lead scholarly organization in the study of money in elections, has estimated that spending by nonparty independent organizations increased by 70 percent in 2010, compared to 2008 levels. A vast majority of these funds were spent by Republican-leaning organizations. Figures 9.4 and 9.5 show districts targeted by party funds and independent, outside money in the 2010 mid-term elections. It is easy to see which type of spending had a wider influence. Many believe that this massive influx of "outside money" played a big role in the massive Republican sweep in the 2010 election. Yet CFI scholars caution to not automatically attribute this change to the Court ruling. They write, "Rather than seeing new money, it is at least theoretically possible that money is simply moving from one activity to others closely related: old wine in new bottles."[17] Although this theory is difficult to completely rule out, the sheer amount of money spent

---

[15] Paul Sherman, "*Citizens United* Decision Means More Free Speech," *National Review Online* (January 21, 2010). Accessed at: http://bench.nationalreview.com/post/?q=MGVlYzczZjZlMTM1YWVlYjJhMzA3NzJjMTVhYmUwZDg=

[16] Editorial, "The Court's Blow to Democracy," *New York Times* (January 21, 2010), A 30.

[17] Campaign Finance Institute, "Election Related Spending by Political Committees and Non-Profits Up by 40% in 2010," press release, CFI (October 18, 2010).

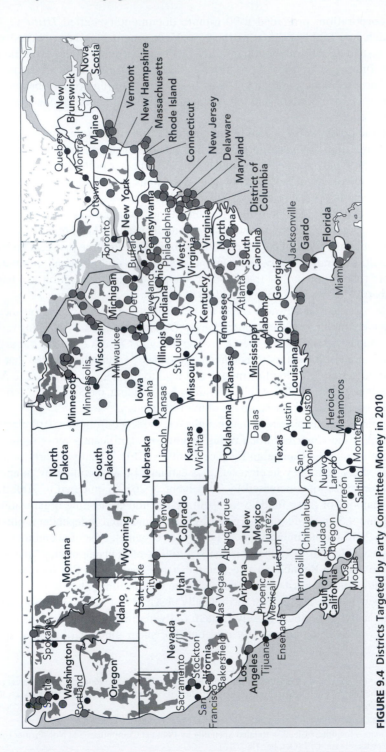

FIGURE 9.4 Districts Targeted by Party Committee Money in 2010

Source: Bob Biersack, FEC Presentation, Southern Political Science Association Annual Conference, New Orleans, LA, January 2011.

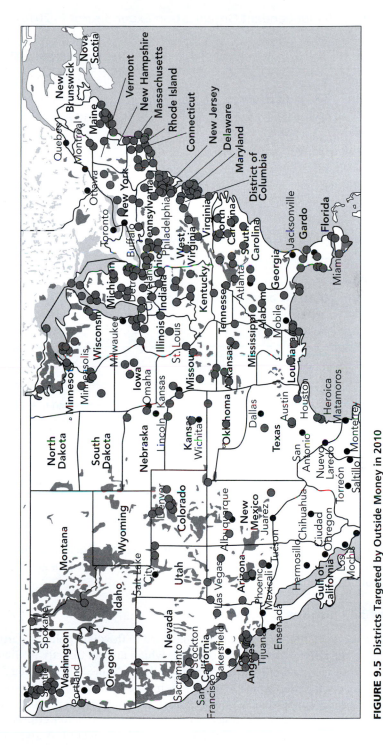

FIGURE 9.5 Districts Targeted by Outside Money in 2010

Source: Bob Biersack, FEC Presentation, Southern Political Science Association Annual Conference, New Orleans, LA, January 2011.

| TABLE 9.5 | Top 20 Independent Organization Expenditures in 2010 |

Spender Name	Total Independent Expenditures ($)
American Crossroads	21,553,272.68
Crossroads Grassroots Policy Strategies	15,556,202.09
SEIU COPE (Service Employees International Union Committee on Political Education)	10,000,241.73
American Federation of State County and Municipal Employees	7,909,582.07
American Future Fund	7,397,831.00
National Rifle Association of America Political Victory Fund	6,729,947.75
The 60 Plus Association Inc.	6,698,293.12
National Association of Realtors Political Action Committee	6,028,285.36
America's Families First Action Fund	5,878,743.10
Club for Growth Action	4,996,970.52
American Federation of State County & Municipal Employees PEOPLE	4,685,512.67
Americans for Job Security	4,406,901.63
NEA Advocacy Fund	4,200,000.00
Americans for Tax Reform	4,198,044.57
League of Conservation Voters Inc	3,923,639.76
American Action Network Inc	3,540,079.35
Women Vote!	3,323,630.91
Our Future Ohio PAC	3,319,530.58
Commonsense Ten	3,257,031.85
Rightchange.Com Inc (527 organization)	3,171,608.55

Source: Bob Biersack, FEC Presentation, Southern Political Science Association Annual Conference, New Orleans, LA, January 2011.

by these organizations makes it seem rather unlikely. Table 9.5 displays the top out-side contributors for the 2010 midterms. Scholars will no doubt spend a good bit of time sorting out this issue in the years to come.

The Rise of 527 Groups

Since BCRA was signed into law, soft money that used to flow into political parties has increasingly been given to 527 organizations, which are not directly affiliated with political parties but quite interested in certain policies. Named after Section 527 of the Internal Revenue Code, which regulates their practices, these organizations are allowed to raise unlimited sums of money. Most 527s are advocacy groups that try to influence the outcome of elections through voter mobilization efforts and television advertisements that praise or criticize a candidate's record. A great deal of the funds now flowing to 527s previously went to the parties in the form of soft money.

Two prominent examples of 527s in the 2004 election were the Swift Vets and POWs for Truth and MoveOn.org. The "Swift Boat Veterans" was set up with the intention of portraying Democratic candidate John Kerry's past military service in a negative light. MoveOn.org, by contrast, was created during the Clinton years, but saw a surge in energy because of anger toward George W. Bush. The 2008 elections also saw 527s play a significant role, although they received less media attention than the highly controversial 2004 groups. Table 9.6 shows the largest 527s in the 2010 election cycle. What is most impressive about this list is the massive sums that these organizations were able to raise. As one observer noted, "Although BCRA cracked down on soft money spending by the political parties, it did nothing to constrain spending by outside groups."[18]

Are 527s the latest loophole in campaign finance law, and do they corrupt the election process? Or are they simply a way for Americans to support candidates and to speak out during elections? If the latter, perhaps they are protected by the Constitution. The future of 527 organizations remains unclear, but their role in the past two presidential elections has been significant.

Super PACs, Too!

The "newest" kid on the block is the super PAC. Officially known as "independent expenditure-only committees," super PACs grew like mushrooms after a summer rain in the wake of recent federal court rulings. These groups are allowed to raise

TABLE 9.6 Top Federally Focused 527 Organizations		
Committee	**Total Receipts ($)**	**Expenditures ($)**
American Solutions Winning the Future	24,416,928	24,464,637
Service Employees International Union	14,923,663	15,489,280
America Votes	8,883,561	11,165,629
Citizens United	8,883,504	8,787,639
EMILY's List	8,710,109	10,137,163
College Republican National Committee	7,984,152	7,918,571
National Education Association	7,217,775	7,453,056
Citizens for Strength & Security	7,127,814	7,216,163
American Crossroads	6,700,312	1,408,323
GOPAC	5,436,751	4,982,268

Source: "Top 50 Federally Focused Organizations," The Center for Responsive Politics. Accessed at: www.opensecrets.org/527s/527cmtes.php?level=C&cycle=2010

---

[18]Marian Currinder, "Campaign Finance: Funding the Presidential and Congressional Elections," *The Elections of 2004*, Michael Nelson, ed. (Washington, DC: CQ Press, 2005), 122.

unlimited sums from unlimited sources, including corporations, unions, and other groups, as well as from wealthy individuals. "With the money they raise, super PACs may overtly advocate for the defeat or election of federal candidates in various communications, including television, radio, print, and online advertisements." Traditional PACs were used, for the most part, by corporations and labor unions. They would collect contributions within prescribed limits ($5,000 or less, in 2008), and spend that money within strict limits (also $5,000). Super PACs, on the other hand, confront few constraints. The one exception is that they are not allowed to coordinate their campaign activities with the candidates they are trying to help. Stated a bit differently, traditional PACs would send checks to candidates, but Super PACs can spend as much as they would like to get a candidate elected so long as they do not coordinate their activities with the candidates, hence the term "independent expenditure-only committee." They might run television advertisements, send direct mail, and conduct polls for an individual candidate or a group of candidates, so long as they played no role in the process.

An illustration might prove helpful. Let us imagine a group of citizens deeply concerned with limiting the sale of hand guns. They learn about super PACs and begin collecting funds. They might collect some small donations, but they might also accept a $1 million or more from an individual citizen, and perhaps another $2 million from a corporation. They would have to disclose where this money came from, but they could spend it as they would like so long as they did not coordinate that spending with candidates. They might spread it around between numerous races, or they could dump all of it on a single election.

Given this flexibility, it should not come as a surprise to hear that by 2010 super PACs had become all the rage. In the 2010 midterm elections, some 74 of these organizations raised and spent just under $84 million. Leading the way was a unit called American Crossroads, which was created by Karl Rove, a key advisor to President George W. Bush. It supported 10 Republican Senate candidates and 30 Republican House candidates. Another massive conservative super PAC in the 2010 election was the Club for Growth.

As is always the case, it takes an election cycle or two for innovative campaign finance approaches to spread throughout the system. By the summer of 2011, it has become clear that super PACs would be the 800-pound gorillas in the following year's congressional and presidential election. Over 100 of these organizations were created, with many more on the way. Democratic-leaning organizations were being formed at a dizzying pace, and many of the conservative groups that proved effective in 2010 were recharging their war chests. For example, Rove's group collected millions from three billionaires in June of that year: $2 million from Jerry Perenchio, the former Hollywood talent agent and ex-chairman of the Spanish language television network Univision; $1 million from Dallas area hotel magnate Robert Rowling; and $5 million from Texas homebuilder Bob Perry. Clearly, these units will reshape the campaign finance terrain for years to come. According to Michael Beckel of the Center for Responsive Politics, super PACs are blazing "new territory" that effectively undoes BCRA. "They now have the freedom to say pretty much whatever they want, whenever they want, and pretty much as loudly as they want."

Conclusion

During every election, a few candidates run for office on a shoestring budget, overcome the odds, and are sent into public life. Americans relish stories in which candidates with guts, determination, and grassroots support bring down the overconfident, wealthy Goliath. Maybe it is not money that wins elections, they ponder, but ideas and character. Unfortunately, elections of this sort are few and far between. Money plays a powerful role in today's American electoral system; a former California politician accurately proclaimed that "money is the mother's milk of politics."[19] Optimistically, perhaps fund-raising is simply a measure of public sentiment—some candidates raise more than others because they are more popular, thus more likely to win on Election Day. Moreover, citizens might applaud the flow of money into campaigns as it is a form of speech. In a democracy, the more political speech, the better—right?

To most, the role of big money in elections is troublesome. It gives some candidates an unfair advantage and it spills past the election into the policy process. Surely contributors expect something for their investment. Should the citizens feel assured that the contributors' only demand might be access? The idea of shifting the balance of the policy process in the direction of those who can give—and give big—during elections is surely contrary to the theory of "democracy through elections." It is one of the many ironies of an open political process: Individuals and groups are encouraged to vigorously back political candidates, but in doing so their efforts create a distorted playing field. The freedom to participate may create a system that is inherently unfair.

Critical Thinking

1. Has the growth in campaign spending altered the democratic nature of the election process?
2. Do you think that campaign contributions are a form of speech that is protected by the First Amendment? If so, do you agree with the Supreme Court that "the quantity of communication by the contributor does not increase perceptibly with the size of his contribution," meaning that, while people have a right to contribute, the amount they may contribute can be limited?
3. With many current presidential candidates opting out of public finance for their campaigns, is that system still a relevant option?

On the Web

If you are interested in reviewing the laws involved with campaign finance or are interested in searching the government's disclosure database, visit the Federal Election Commission's website at www.FEC.gov.

---

[19]This remark was made by California State Treasurer Jesse Unruh. See White and Shea, *New Party Politics*, 95.

Referenda, Initiatives, and Recall

KEY TOPICS

After reading this chapter, you should be able to understand these core concepts and explain their significance:

- Direct Democracy
- Indirect Ballot Initiatives
- Direct Ballot Initiatives
- Referenda
- Recalls

Many Americans believe that elections are used only to select public officials. However, this is not the case, as about half the states allow voters to use elections to directly affect the policy process. (The Constitution does not allow this at the federal level.) This is a vestige of the Progressive Era, when reformers were frustrated with the lack of change resulting from the legislative process. They devised numerous schemes to allow voters a direct say in creating new laws and regulations. These changes stuck, and today are key mechanisms for allowing citizens to alter government policies. Initiative, referendum, and recall are methods collectively referred to as "direct democracy." These processes allow citizens to become directly involved in their government by drafting and voting on laws or by directly removing an elected official from office.

A BRIEF HISTORY OF DIRECT DEMOCRACY

Direct democracy is an American tradition that can be traced to civilization's earliest roots—indeed, back as far as the genesis of democracy itself in Athens, Greece. In colonial New England, citizens did not typically elect others to represent them. Instead, eligible voters themselves debated and decided issues, and each had the opportunity to have his voice and concerns heard in the capital. Direct democracy of this kind, of course, was far more feasible then—only upper-class white male landowners, a small percentage of the population, had voting rights.

The direct democracy of New England was gradually displaced, first by the tightening grasp of the British monarchy, and later by the representative democracy instituted by the framers of the Constitution. Universal enfranchisement and population growth have made New England–style direct democracy largely unworkable, although the practice lives on in some parts of the United States in the form of town hall meetings.

It was the Progressive Era that granted new life to direct democracy. Populists and progressives, tired of having their reform efforts constantly stymied by resistant state legislatures, united around the turn of the 20th century in their desire for a more responsive and accountable government. The first state to adopt an initiative process was South Dakota in 1898, and the first to use referenda was Oregon in 1902. The movement quickly spread, particularly in the Western part of the United States, where party machines were less entrenched. California and Oregon have been the biggest users of initiatives and referenda, averaging roughly three per year since the turn of the 20th century. The latest state to adopt this type of process was Mississippi in 1992. Table 10.1 lists the methods of direct democracy available in each state, and details each process; Figure 10.1 highlights some interesting disparities in initiative use between selected states.

BALLOT INITIATIVES

Ballot initiatives, one of several forms of direct democracy, are used in two ways. The direct initiative approach allows voters the option to decide a policy matter themselves; it allows citizens of a state to bypass their state legislature and place proposed statutes on the ballot to be voted on. Supporters of a measure gather a requisite number of signatures (see Table 10.2) to have the question listed on the ballot. On Election Day, citizens vote either for or against the measure, and if a majority agrees, it becomes the law of the land. In 2010, for example, California voters confronted whether to legalize recreational marijuana. After a high-profile, expensive battle, this move was rejected by 55 percent of the voters.

The second approach, dubbed the indirect initiative, lets voters call upon lawmakers to consider a piece of legislation. This does not guarantee the measure's passage, but rather requires elected officials to confront the issue during the next legislative session. "Referendum" is a term often used to describe the process through which average citizens are given the right to decide a policy issue. The more traditional meaning of the term, however, is a process by which average citizens, through elections, can veto a piece of legislation. For most Americans—and indeed the media as well—the terms "initiative" and "referendum" are interchangeable.

TABLE 10.1 State-by-State List of Initiative and Referendum Provisions

State	Date Adopted	Type of Process Available		Type of Initiative Process Available		Type of Initiative Process Used to Propose Constitutional Amendments		Type of Initiative Process Used to Propose Statutes (Laws)	
		Initiative	Popular Referendum	Constitutional Amendment	Statute	Direct (DA)	Indirect (IDA)	Direct (DS)	Indirect (IDS)
Alaska	1956	Yes	Yes	No	Yes	No	No	No	Yes
Arizona	1911	Yes	Yes	Yes	Yes	Yes	No	Yes	No
Arkansas	1910	Yes	Yes	Yes	Yes	Yes	No	Yes	No
California	1911	Yes	Yes	Yes	Yes	Yes	No	Yes	No
Colorado	1912	Yes	Yes	Yes	Yes	Yes	No	Yes	No
Florida	1972	Yes	No	Yes	No	No	No	No	No
Idaho	1912	Yes	Yes	No	Yes	No	No	Yes	No
Illinois	1970	Yes	No	Yes	No	Yes	No	No	No
Kentucky	1910	No	Yes	No	No	No	No	No	No
Maine	1908	Yes	Yes	No	Yes	No	No	No	Yes
Maryland	1915	No	Yes	No	No	No	No	No	No
Massachusetts	1918	Yes	Yes	Yes	Yes	No	Yes	No	Yes
Michigan	1908	Yes	Yes	Yes	Yes	Yes	No	No	Yes
Mississippi	1914/92	Yes	Yes	Yes	No	No	Yes	No	No
Missouri	1908	Yes	No	Yes	Yes	Yes	No	Yes	No
Montana	1904/72	Yes	Yes	Yes	Yes	Yes	No	Yes	No

Nebraska	1912	Yes	Yes	Yes	Yes	Yes	No	Yes	No
Nevada	1905	Yes	Yes	Yes	Yes	Yes	No	No	Yes
New Mexico	1911	No	Yes	No	No	No	No	No	No
North Dakota	1914	Yes	Yes	Yes	Yes	Yes	No	Yes	No
Ohio	1912	Yes	Yes	Yes	Yes	Yes	No	No	Yes
Oklahoma	1907	Yes	Yes	Yes	Yes	Yes	No	Yes	No
Oregon	1902	Yes	Yes	Yes	Yes	Yes	No	Yes	No
South Dakota	1898/72/88	Yes	Yes	Yes	Yes	Yes	No	Yes	No
Utah	1900/17	Yes	Yes	No	Yes	No	No	Yes	Yes
Washington	1912	Yes	Yes	No	Yes	No	No	Yes	Yes
Wyoming	1968	Yes	Yes	No	Yes	No	No	No	Yes
Total	27 states	24 states	24 states	18 states	21 states	16 states	2 states	14 states	9 states

This list does not include the states with legislative referendum (LR). Legislative referendum is when a state legislature places an amendment or statute on the ballot for voter approval or rejection. The legislative referendum process is available in every state.

Direct initiative amendment (DA) is when constitutional amendments proposed by the people are directly placed on the ballot and then submitted to the people for their approval or rejection.

Indirect initiative amendment (IDA) is when constitutional amendments proposed by the people must first be submitted to the state legislature during a regular session.

Direct initiative statute (DS) is when statutes (laws) proposed by the people are directly placed on the ballot and then submitted to the people for their approval or rejection.

Indirect initiative statute (IDS) is when statutes (laws) proposed by the people must first be submitted to the state legislature during a regular session.

Popular referendum (PR) is the power to refer to the ballot, through a petition, specific legislation that was enacted by the legislature for the public's approval or rejection.

This list does not include the states with legislative referendum, when a state legislature places an amendment or statute on the ballot for voter approval or rejection. Every state but Delaware requires state constitutional amendments to be placed on the ballot for voter approval or rejection.

In 1996, California repealed indirect initiative for statutes.

In Illinois, the subject matter of proposed constitutional amendments is severely limited to legislative matters. Consequently, initiatives seldom appear on the ballot.

Mississippi first adopted the initiative process in 1914, but a Supreme Court ruling voided the election. The process was readopted in 1992.

In 1972, Montana adopted a provision that allows for directly initiated constitutional amendments.

In North Dakota prior to 1918, constitutional amendments could be initiated only indirectly.

In 1972, South Dakota adopted a provision that allows for directly initiated constitutional amendments. In 1988, South Dakota repealed indirect initiative for states.

Source: "Comparison of Statewide Initiative Processes," Initiative & Referendum Institute, 2–3.
Accessed at: www.iandrinstitute.org/New%20IRI%20Website%20Info/Drop%20Down%20Boxes/Requirements/A%20Comparison%20of%20Statewide%20I&R%20Processes.pdf

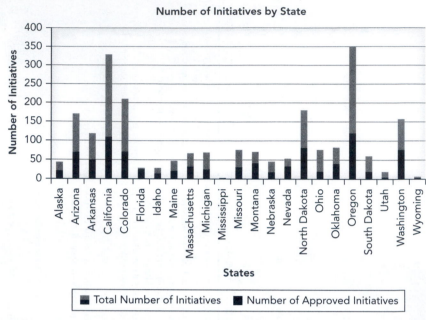

FIGURE 10.1 Number of Initiatives by State: 1904–2008 *Source:* "Initiative Use," Initiative & Referendum Institute (February 2009).
Accessed at: www.iandrinstitute.org/IRI%20Initiative%20Use%20(1904–2008).pdf

TABLE 10.2	Net Number of Signatures Required for Initiatives			
State	**Net Signature Requirement for Constitutional Amendments**	**Estimated Net Number for 2002 Election**	**Net Signature Requirement for Statutes**	**Estimated Net Number for 2002 Election**
Alaska	Not allowed by state constitution	N/A	10% of votes cast in last general election	28,782
Arizona	15% of votes cast for governor	152,643	10% of votes cast for governor	101,762
Arkansas	10% of votes cast for governor	70,602	8% of votes cast for governor	54,481
California	8% of votes cast for governor	670,816	5% of votes cast for governor	419,094
Colorado	5% of votes cast for secretary of state	80,571	5% of votes cast for secretary of state	80,571
Florida	8% of ballots cast in the last presidential election	488,722	Not allowed by state constitution	N/A
Idaho	Not allowed by state constitution	N/A	6% of registered voters	43,685
Maine	Not allowed by state constitution	N/A	10% of votes cast for governor	42,101

(continued)

State	Net Signature Requirement for Constitutional Amendments	Estimated Net Number for 2002 Election	Net Signature Requirement for Statutes	Estimated Net Number for 2002 Election
Massachusetts	3% of votes cast for governor	57,100	3½% of votes cast for governor	57,100
Michigan	10% of votes cast for governor	302,710	8% of votes cast for governor	242,169
Mississippi	12% of votes cast for governor	91,673	Not allowed by state constitution	N/A
Missouri	8% of votes cast for governor	120,571	5% of votes cast for governor	75,356
Montana	10% of votes cast for governor	41,019	5% of votes cast for governor	20,500
Nebraska	10% of registered voters	108,500	7% of registered voters	76,000
Nevada	10% of registered voters	61,366	10% of votes cast in last general election	61,366
North Dakota	4% of population	25,552	2% of population	12,776
Ohio	10% of votes cast for governor	334,624	6% of votes cast for governor	200,774
Oklahoma	15% of votes cast for governor	185,135	8% of votes cast for governor	98,739
Oregon	8% of votes cast for governor	89,048	6% of votes cast for governor	66,786
South Dakota	10% of votes cast for governor	26,019	5% of votes cast for governor	13,010
Utah	Not allowed by state constitution	N/A	Direct statute: 10% of votes cast for Governor; Indirect statute: 10% of votes cast for governor	76,181
Washington	Not allowed by state constitution	N/A	8% of votes cast for governor	197,588
Wyoming	Not allowed by state constitution	N/A	15% of votes cast in the last general election	33,253
Total	————	2,906,671	————	2,002,074

Source: "Comparison of Statewide Initiative Processes," Initiative & Referendum Institute, 17–18.

Accessed at: www.iandrinstitute.org/New%20IRI%20Website%20Info/Drop%20Down%20Boxes/ Requirements/A%20Comparison%20of%20Statewide%20I&R%20Processes.pdf

222 Chapter 10 • Referenda, Initiatives, and Recall

The questions that voters are asked to decide in initiative and referendum elections vary widely. A sampling from recent elections includes the medical use of marijuana, doctor-assisted suicide, English-only measures for schools, pay raises for public school teachers, the protection of wetlands and forests, outlawing the hunting of mountain lions, legislative term limits, prohibition on the trapping of bobcats and bears, permitting some forms of gambling, providing vouchers for students to attend schools of their choice, and so on. In 2002, cockfighting was banned in Oklahoma, but voters rejected efforts in Nevada to legalize recreational use of small amounts of marijuana. Table 10.3 lists a selection of ballot initiatives and referenda from the 2008

TABLE 10.3	A Sampling of Ballot Initiatives and Referenda in 2008 and 2010	
Arizona	2008	Proposition 101. Prohibition of universal health care programs. *FAILED 49.7–50.3*
		Proposition 200. *Payday loans.* Allows payday loan industry to exist after 2010. *FAILED 40–60*
	2010	Proposition 109. Constitutional right to hunt. *FAILED 44–56*
California	2008	Proposition 2. Animal living space. Requires minimum space for farm animals. *APPROVED 63–37*
		Proposition 4. Abortion parental notification. Requires parental notification and waiting period before minor can have abortion. *FAILED 48–52*
		Proposition 8. Marriage. Bans same-sex marriage. *APPROVED 52–48*
		Proposition 9. *Victim rights.* Victims given input during trial process. *APPROVED 53–47*
	2010	Proposition 19. Marijuana legalization initiative. *FAILED 45–55*
Colorado	2008	Amendment 46. Civil rights/affirmative action. Prohibits government from discriminating or giving preferential treatment on the basis of race, sex, ethnicity, and national origin. *FAILED 49–51*
		Amendment 47. *Right to work.* Prohibits requiring union membership/dues. *FAILED 44–56*
		Amendment 54. *Campaign contributions.* Prohibits unions and persons doing business with state from contributing to campaigns. *APPROVED 51–49*
		Amendment 59. *Budget windfalls.* Dedicates to education not tax rebates. *FAILED 45–55*
Florida	2008	Amendment 2. Marriage. Bans same-sex marriage (requires 60 percent). *APPROVED 62–38*
	2010	Amendment 6. Congressional redistricting reform. *PASSED 63–37*
Massachusetts	2008	Question 1. Repeals state income tax. *FAILED 30–70*
		Question 2. Bans commercial dog racing. *APPROVED 65–35*
		Question 3. Decriminalizes marijuana. *APPROVED 56–44*

(continued)

Michigan	2008	Proposition 1. Medical marijuana. Statute allowing medical use. *APPROVED 63–37*
		Proposition 2. Stem cell research. Amendment removing restrictions. *APPROVED 53–47*
North Dakota	2008	Statutory Measure 2. Income tax. Lowers personal and corporate income tax rates. *FAILED 30–70*
		Statutory Measure 3. Tobacco settlement revenue dedicated to antismoking. *APPROVED 54–46*
		Statutory Measure 4. Admin appointment. Allows governor to appoint director of workplace safety. *APPROVED 67–33*

Source: "Ballot Watch," Initiative & Referendum Institute (November 2008).
Accessed at: www.iandrinstitute.org/BW%202008-3%20Results%20v4.pdf

election, as well as a sampling from the 2010 midterm elections. The most notable was the move in California, Proposition 8, to restrict gay marriages.

In 2004, voters in 34 states faced 162 ballot propositions. They approved 108 measures—a 67-percent approval rate. In 2006, 204 ballot propositions were placed before voters in 27 states, an increase of 25 percent over 2004. That year, 137 measures were approved and 67 rejected—a similar 67-percent approval rate. Seventy-six of these measures were initiatives, four were referenda, one was placed on the ballot by a commission, and the rest were legislative measures.[1] In 2008, 153 ballot propositions in 36 states succeeded with a 59-percent approval rate.[2] Figure 10.2 details the rate of initiative use and success during 1904–2008; initiative use appears to have barely fallen from the peak it reached during the 1990s.

Same-Sex Marriage Initiatives in Recent Elections

In 2004, the most popular and possibly deciding factor in the election was gay marriage. Activists and state legislators placed antigay marriage proposals on the ballot in 11 states. Voters in all 11 states voted in favor of amendments that defined marriage as only between one man and one woman. Arguably, the marriage measures on the ballot became a huge motivating factor in the 2004 election and helped to ensure George W. Bush's reelection by attracting religious groups, especially evangelicals, to the polls. Exit polls showed "22 percent of voters named 'moral values' as the most important issue to them—ranking it higher than the economy and the Iraq war."[3] Of this group, 79 percent voted for George W. Bush. Ohio became the major battleground in that presidential race. It had a constitutional amendment on

---

[1]"Ballot Watch," Initiative & Referendum Institute. Accessed at: http://iandrinstitute.org/ballotwatch.htm

[2]"Ballot Watch—Election 2008: Mixed results," Initiative & Referendum Institute. Accessed at: www.iandrinstiture.org/BW%202008-3%20Results%20v4.pdf

[3]Debra Rosenberg and Karen Breslau, "Winning the Values Vote," *Newsweek* (November, 15, 2004). Accessed at: www.newsweek.com/id/55717

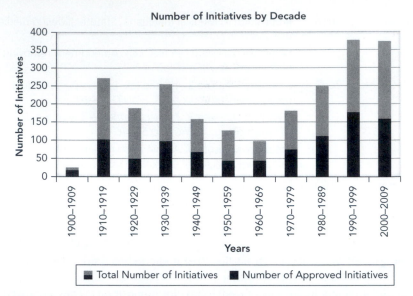

FIGURE 10.2 Overview of Initiative Use, 1904–2009 *Source:* "Initiative Use," Initiative & Referendum Institute (September 2010).
Accessed at: www.iandrinstitute.org/IRI%20Initiative%20Use%20(2010-1).pdf

the ballot that banned same-sex marriage. The law passed overwhelmingly, bringing out to the polls thousands of Christian voters who had never or rarely voted. Some 24 percent of those surveyed branded themselves as "white evangelical/born-again Christians."[4] Most pundits and social scientists agree that the gay marriage ballot measure in Ohio changed the scope of the electorate in 2004, resulting in the reelection of George W. Bush.

Same-sex marriage did not disappear from the ballot after this election, however. In 2006 initiatives, referenda, and constitutional amendments proposing a ban on same-sex marriage appeared in eight states. These measures passed in seven of those states, with Arizona the sole exception by a small margin.

The 2008 election saw its own same-sex marriage controversies. This time, California was the battleground. Proposition 8 sought to reverse a state court decision to allow same-sex marriage. Spending for and against the initiative totaled $83.2 million, a sum higher than every 2008 candidate election other than the presidential race.[5] It was a tumultuous process, with tempers running high on each side of the issue. In the end, Proposition 8 passed by a whisker; 52–48 percent.

Passage of Proposition 8 highlighted much of the controversy surrounding ballot initiatives. For one, some doubted the wisdom of placing questions dealing with individual rights and liberties before the public for a vote. It is an old story in American

---

[4]Ibid.

[5]"Cleary Comments, Williams Institute Estimates Passage of Proposition 8 Will Cost California More Than $800 Million in the Next 3 Years," MarketWatch (June 24, 2009). Accessed at: www.marketwatch.com/ story/cleary-comments-williams-institute-estimates-passage-of-proposition-8-will-cost-california-more-than-800-million-in-the-next-3-years

history that public opinion can often run counter to some of its most basic liberties. For example, a strong majority of Americans opposed allowing a white and black couple to marry even into the 1960s. Most Americans similarly disapproved of the federal government's actions to eliminate racial discrimination in schools. Many would argue that issues of this sort—issues that deal with individual liberties and freedoms—should not be decided by public opinion.

Second, direct democracy of this type—especially in large states such as California—is extremely expensive, leading some critics to contend that ballot initiatives grant undue power to interests wealthy enough to bankroll a statewide effort. Are ballot initiatives decided based upon the wisdom of the measure or the war chests of each side? An additional point is the fact that money may well come from outside the state where the issue is to be decided; indeed, the pro-Proposition 8 campaign received as much as $20 million from out-of-state Mormons (with 45 percent of donors based in Utah) and the Mormon Church.[6]

RECALL

Yet another progressive measure designed to pull the policy process back to the will of the people is the recall. Here, citizens are allowed to vote an officeholder out of office prior to the regularly scheduled election. In other words, recalls allow voters to change the personnel of government without waiting until the next election. Petitions are circulated, and if enough signatures are collected, a date is set for an election. The sitting politician is generally automatically listed on the ballot, but is sent back to private life if he or she receives fewer votes than another candidate.

It is very rare for recall elections to take place. Most of the time, even if people become dissatisfied with elected officials, they simply bear it until the next election. After all, it is the voters themselves who elected the person to office, and it has become part of American political culture to bide time and wait until the next election. Very few recall efforts have been successful. The voters of California, though, made history in the fall of 2003 when they made Democratic Governor Gray Davis the second governor ever to be recalled.

Many Californians, especially Republicans, had grown increasingly dissatisfied with Davis's performance as governor. Their discontent stemmed from, among other things, the governor's handling of California's fiscal problems. In particular, the state had a $38 million deficit, and there was great speculation that Davis was trying to conceal the problems in an effort to protect his reelection campaign.[7] The governor's approval ratings shrank to historic lows: Fewer than one in five Californians believed he was doing a good job. Congressman Darrell Issa (R) seemed to speak for many in the state when he claimed, "Every governor we've ever had in California has been better than Gray Davis."[8]

---

[6]Shane Goldmacher, "Mormon Church Reveals Deeper Involvement in Proposition 8," *Sacramento Bee* (February 1, 2009). Accessed at: www.sacbee.com/capitoland California/story/1589451.html

[7]Judy Woodruff, Candy Crowley, and John Mercurio, "California Governor to Face Recall Vote," CNN.com "Inside Politics" (July 25, 2003). Accessed at: http://edition.cnn.com/2003/ALLPOLITICS/07/24/davis.recall/

[8]Ibid.

Using funds from his own campaign treasury, Issa kicked a recall initiative into gear. The idea of replacing Davis seemed to spread like wildfire, and soon talk of recall spread across the Golden State, and indeed the national media. But if Gray Davis was going to be recalled, who would take his spot? With a minor threshold of signatures to be collected and a nominal fee, anyone could be listed on the ballot. Soon 135 candidates joined the fray, a list that included attorneys, business owners, physicians, firefighters, teachers, college students, publishers, and a porn star, to name a few. The candidacy that drew the most interest came on August 6, when actor Arnold Schwarzenegger, a Republican, told America, via talk show host Jay Leno, that he was going to run for governor in the recall. Overnight, the man who will be forever known from his acting days as the "Terminator" became the leading contender for the position. Toward the end of the campaign, the five leading candidates were Democratic Lieutenant Governor Cruz Bustamante, Republican state senator Tom McClintock, Green Party member Peter Camejo, independent Arianna Huffington, and Schwarzenegger. But it was Schwarzenegger's fame and fortune that helped ignite his campaign.

On October 7, 2003, the voters of California went to the polls to decide two issues. Their first vote was on whether or not Davis should be recalled; the second was to decide—if the first was successful—who would replace him. When it was all totaled, a strong majority agreed that Davis should be sent back to private life and that Schwarzenegger be given the reins of power. The "Terminator" became the "Governor"—the man who once ruled the movie box office found himself at the helm of the largest, and in many ways most complex, state in the Union.

More recently, recall elections were held for 9 Wisconsin state senators in the summer of 2011. Anger over Republican Governor Scott Walker's proposed budget mobilized labor groups and many Democratic organizations. The quickly moved to gather recall petitions in order to oust six key GOP lawmakers. In response, petitions were collected by Republican operatives to recall three Democratic senators. It was a battle of recalls! It was one of the few times in American history that groups of state legislators in both parties were placed into recall elections in the same year. When it was all said and done, none of the Democratic senators were defeated, but two of the Republican legislators lost their jobs. In the fall of that same year, labor and Democratic activist began circulation petitions to oust Walker. Given their success during the summer, these groups no doubt felt as though they had the wind at their backs.

Conclusion

Direct democracy has many implications and impacts on political representation. Initiatives, referenda, and recall elections represent democracy at its best: average citizens proposing changes in government, working to build support, and allowing the

---

[9]Editorial, "Bubble-Up Democracy," *Christian Science Monitor* (November 8, 2002), 10.

[10]Jack Citrin, "Who's the Boss? Direct Democracy and Popular Control of Government," *Broken Contract?*, Stephen C. Craig, ed. (Boulder, CO: Westview, 1996), 271, as cited in Kenneth Janda, Jeffrey M. Berry, and Jerry Goldman, *The Challenge of Democracy: Government in America,* 7th ed. (Boston, MA: Houghton Mifflin, 2002), 40.

majority of the community to decide its own fate. As noted in an editorial from the *Christian Science Monitor* in the fall of 2002, "Such grass-roots efforts can help re-energize voters and preserve an outlet for direct democracy if entrenched interests control the legislature. Research shows that when there is an initiative on the ballot, voter turnout increases 3 to 7 percent."[9] If ballot initiatives prove to enhance citizens' participation and political knowledge, the implication is that participatory models of governance should be bolstered. Polls suggest that roughly two-thirds of Americans believe that they should have some say in policy matters.[10] One study found that ballot initiatives may "indirectly serve to strengthen American democracy, at least with respect to civic engagement."[11] But political observers note that this form of direct democracy can be problematic. For one, government policy is often quite complex—maybe too complex for average citizens. Indeed, many of the initiatives are lengthy, and polling data also suggest that only about 26 percent of Americans pay close attention to what is going on in public affairs.[12] Average folks might find it harder to consider long-term ramifications and to step beyond their own self-interest. More significantly, many suggest the process has been changed and no longer represents "democracy in action." For example, wealthy individuals and groups are able to employ workers to collect signatures and to flood the airways with misleading commercials. Poorly funded groups face a tougher struggle in both building support for their measures and in defeating others. In 2002, public interest groups sponsored a measure in Oregon to provide comprehensive health care for residents of the state, for instance. The motion was defeated due in no small measure to the multimillion-dollar campaign waged against it by the medical/pharmaceutical industry.

Critical Thinking

1. Do initiatives and referenda encourage democracy, or do they grant unprecedented power to the moneyed interests that can afford paid canvassers and large advertising budgets to influence voters?
2. Is direct democracy a good thing? Or is it an example—as might be the case for efforts like California's Proposition 8—of "tyranny of the majority"?
3. How might the framers of the Constitution have felt about direct democracy? One could make the case that the framers deliberately worked *against* direct democracy: Senators were originally chosen by state legislatures rather than voters, and the electoral college selected the president, to name a few examples. Did the framers disdain direct democracy? Or were they merely trying to avoid the sort of mob rule that France experienced during its revolution?

On the Web

To check out ballot measures within your state, go to www.ballotpedia.org, where you can find an interactive map that will lead you through initiatives and more at the state level.

---

[11]Caroline J. Tolbert, Ramona S. McNeal, and Daniel A. Smith, "Enhancing Civic Engagement: The Effect of Direct Democracy on Political Participation and Knowledge," *State Politics & Policy Quarterly* 3, no. 1: 23–41.

[12]The American National Election Studies, Cumulative Data File, 1956–2004, "General Interest in Public Affairs 1960–2004." Accessed at: www.electionstudies.org/nesguide/toptable/tab6d_5.htm

CHAPTER

11

New Media and the Changing Nature of Campaigns

KEY TOPICS

After reading this chapter, you should be able to understand these core concepts and explain their significance:

- Candidate Websites
- Political Blogs
- Online Fund-Raising

- Use of Social Networks
- Online Videos

Technological innovation has always had an impact on American campaigns. Constantly looking for a competitive edge, campaign strategists often embrace new technology ahead of the curve in the hope that it will make the difference between a victory celebration and a concession speech. The railroad-initiated whistle-stop tours allowed candidates to cover more territory and see more voters than ever before. Radio and television put candidates into millions of homes with debates, speeches, and political advertisements. Celebrities and well-known political figures leave messages on millions of answering machines each election cycle. Mass mailing systems allow campaigns to target tightly defined groups of voters. Satellites can place candidates in front of local news anchors at a rate of to 20–30 interviews per day. Full 3-D holograms of guests and correspondents are beamed to Wolf Blitzer's Situation Room. Technology is constantly changing how we elect our public officials.

The Internet has revolutionized life as we know it in too many ways, To fully detail here: It has changed the manner in which we communicate and correspond; it has altered the methods we use to organize our lives and relationships; it has opened up a broad new avenue for commerce. Naturally—inevitably—it has transformed our elections, too. It has become a permanent and significant resource in contemporary campaigns, and this in itself makes for interesting analysis and discussion. This final chapter highlights some of the significant intersections between traditional campaigns in the United States and the evolving applications of the World Wide Web.

ONLINE COMMUNICATIONS

The Internet and its applications constitute the most powerful communications tool known to humans. Through the medium, individuals can communicate with millions—almost instantaneously. Groups organically emerge and facilitate complex social networks. The nature of these communications can take the shape of nearly all known media—text, video, graphics, audio, and so on. Obviously, this capability alone makes the Internet a campaign manager's dream tool. However, figuring out how to effectively use this resource has not been easy or immediate.

Campaign Websites

One of the most important and basic elements of Internet-based campaigns is the use of candidates' websites. Websites first appeared as campaign communications tools in the 1996 presidential election and have since proliferated in terms of their presence and strategic importance. In the early iterations of campaign web design, very few resources were devoted to developing and sustaining the sites. In fact, it was common for candidates to just ask tech-savvy relatives, friends, or students to design and maintain the entire website. In little more than a decade, the volunteer webmaster has now been supplanted by professional web design firms that specialize in online campaigning. According to two scholars of modern campaign practices,

> A candidate without a website appears less than serious, and a disheveled site hints at a disorganized campaign. A visually attractive, user-friendly website that offers an abundance of informational content, tells a different story.[1]

Running for president presents significant communication challenges, and presidential candidates' websites have become essential to helping meet these challenges. Websites establish 24/7 information resources for nearly all constituents of the campaign. Prospective voters browse for information to help make up their minds about the candidates. Volunteers access key resources to help organize their work. "Because candidates can buy ads linked to web searches, they can be reasonably certain that their pitch is reaching people who are somehow interested in the message, and who are, to use the language of commercial marketing, in 'buy mode.'"[2] Reporters find critical information and photos needed to help fill candidate-related stories. Potential

---

[1]Michael John Burton and Daniel M. Shea, *Campaign Craft: The Strategies, Tactics, and Art of Political Campaign Management*, 4th ed. (Westport, CT: Praeger, 2010), 165.
[2]Ibid.

campaign contributors find answers to last-minute questions before they submit donations. In addition to maintaining communications with core constituents, campaign websites typically provide a comprehensive calendar, endorsement-gathering tools, position papers, ways to collect public comments, assistance with organizing blogs, an online campaign store for paraphernalia, contact information for all campaign offices, and—perhaps most importantly—online fund-raising systems.

Online News

Trends suggest voters are moving away from traditional newspapers and toward online news sources for campaign information. This began in the mid-1990s, when independent websites emerged to present campaign information. At the time, these sites were particularly interesting because they were not developed or supported by traditional news providers like CNN or ABC News. They were often the work of fringe groups with no other publishing outlet or early Internet adopters who found the medium to be an interesting information source. One of the most prominent early endeavors in this area was Web White and Blue (WWB). WWB was an online knowledge network that was in many ways university based. At one point, 17 charters at various colleges and universities contributed information to the network. It was similar in concept to a wiki environment where independent writers submit content. As general Internet usage in the United States swelled to numbers that make the World Wide Web a common resource for many Americans, traditional news sources began repurposing their content to online sites. As CNN.com, MSNBC.com, CBSNews.com (and more) began to establish their online resources, they soon overwhelmed the nonprofit and independent websites with their content and general information capacity.

The presence of comprehensive and immediate online news sources and the development of news-aggregating engines (e.g., Google News) have caused a shift in the electorate that was identified as early as 2000. In conducting a survey of WWB users, one scholar found that the group had in general *"substituted* the Internet for newspapers as one of its two main election news sources."[3] He found that television news was the most common news source, followed by the Internet. This supports more general findings from Pew's ongoing study, the Pew Internet and American Life Project.[4] This report found that U.S. citizens who noted the Internet as a "main source of political campaign news" rose 18 percent between 2000 and 2004. According to a 2008 Pew Research Center survey, 40 percent of Americans now depend on the Internet as their primary source of most national and international news—higher, for the first time, than newspapers' share, which stood at 35 percent. Furthermore, this percentage is even higher among people under 30—nearly 60 percent of this demographic gets most of its news from the Internet.[5]

---

[3]Arthur Lupia and Zoë Baird, "Can Web Sites Change Citizens? Implications of Web, White, and Blue 2000." *Political Science and Politics* 36, no. 1 (January 2003): 77–82.

[4]The Pew Research Center funds the Pew Internet and American Life Project. The project "produces reports that explore the impact of the internet on families, communities, work and home, daily life, education, health care, and civic and political life." Reports can be found at www.pewinternet.org

[5]"Internet Overtakes Newspapers as News Outlet," Pew Research Center for the People and the Press (December 23, 2008). Accessed at: http://pewresearch.org/pubs/1066/internet-overtakes-newspapers-as-news-source

Blogging

An online information source and cultural phenomenon that has attracted a great deal of voter interest in recent elections is blogging. Blogs (a group of "web logs") are constantly updated journal-style websites maintained by individuals (bloggers) and are typically devoted to particular topics (e.g., the 2012 campaign). They usually contain personal observations and tend to be opinionated—and are often quite visceral. Blogs have achieved widespread popularity for perhaps the same reason that reality television shows are popular: They are, by and large, written by average individuals from literally every social stratum and are thus considered more "honest" and relatable. According to a recent Technorati Report,[6] the blogosphere (the collective "network" of all blogs) has grown rapidly over the last decade. The first blogs were recorded in 1997, and it took a few years for them to become common enough to register any kind of campaign effect—and indeed for the term "blog" itself to be coined. In August 2004, for example, there were approximately 3 million blogs online. One year later, the number grew to 12 million. In August of 2006, Technorati indexed approximately 50 million blogs, and as of 2008, (only 11 years after their origination), the web hosted at least 133 million blogs.[7]

Although not all of the 133 million blogs participated in the 2008 election, a substantial number did. For example, TechPresident reports that within a one-month period (September 15–October 14, 2007), the blogosphere mentioned Hillary Clinton more than 3,000 times on busy days and around 1,000 times on normal days. During this time period overall, her name was mentioned on average approximately 1,400 times per day.[8] This phenomenon has, unsurprisingly, received national attention from major political strategists. The consequence is that campaign volunteers and staff are now being asked to initiate and maintain blogs that speak favorably of their candidates. Nearly all of the 2008 presidential campaign websites encouraged voters to establish blogs, and thousands of volunteers rose to the occasion. Many believe that this has become a defining element of modern electioneering.

Finally, and perhaps most importantly, a powerful connection has emerged between blogs and traditional media. Very often campaign topics are first raised on blogs and later by the mainstream media. Mark Halperin and John Harris write about this phenomenon in their book *The Way to Win: Taking the White House in 2008*. Discussing the power of the Drudge Report (a popular political site and blog), they note, "Drudge's power derives only in part from the colossal number of people who visit his site . . . His power comes from his ability to shape the perceptions of other news media—Old and New alike."[9]

---

[6]Technorati (www.technorati.com) is a search engine similar to Google; however, it is exclusively devoted to blogs. It produces a regular industry report, "State of the Blogosphere," based on its total indexed blogs.

[7]Phillip Winn, "State of the Blogosphere: Introduction," *Technorati State of the Blogosphere 2008* (August 21, 2009). Accessed at: http://technorati.com/blogging/article/state-of-the-blogosphere-introduction/

[8]"Blog Mentions via Technorati," TechPresident.com. Accessed at: http://techpresident.com/scrape_plot/technorati

[9]Mark Halperin and John F. Harris, *The Way to Win: Taking the White House in 2008* (New York: Random House, 2006), 54.

ONLINE FUND-RAISING

Jesse Unruh, a former California state assemblyman and state treasurer, often said that money is the mother's milk of politics. This has been the case from the inception of the American republic, and the Internet is the latest tool candidates have been using to raise money. The Internet has been used as a fund-raising tool since the development of ecommerce technology in the mid- to late 1990s. John McCain surprised many when he raised a modest sum online during his 2000 bid for the Republican nomination. But the Internet did not become a significant and widely recognized fund-raising medium until 2004, when Howard Dean's presidential campaign and groups like MoveOn.org demonstrated that online fund-raising could generate vast amounts of money. In many respects, Dean and his team rewrote the playbook on how to organize, finance, and mold a presidential campaign.[10] After Dean's success with Internet fund-raising, both John Kerry and George W. Bush followed suit—each raising tens of millions of dollars online.

The success of online fund-raising in 2004 in fact startled many observers, but throughout the 2008 campaign, such systems were commonplace. All the presidential campaign sites of 2008, and indeed nearly every congressional and gubernatorial campaign site, displayed a prominent button encouraging visitors to make an online contribution. And while online contributions remain subject to all campaign contribution guidelines enforced by the Federal Election Commission, they have opened up new strategic territory for the ongoing fund-raising needs of politicians. The pace of collecting funds also stunned many observers. In one month alone—January of 2008—Barack Obama's campaign collected $36 million, an unprecedented feat for a single month in American politics that was powered overwhelmingly by small online donations.[11] "The architects and builders of the Obama field campaign . . . have undogmatically mixed timeless traditions and discipline of good organizing with new technologies of decentralization and self-organization."[12] When the media reported that Hillary Clinton had won the Pennsylvania Democratic primary, her online fund-raising site also started to hum. In the next 24 hours, she raised over $3 million, a staggering sum in such a short period given that it came from relatively small donations.

In the Massachusetts special election for the U.S. Senate in 2010, discussed at the start of this book (Chapter 1), Republican Scott Brown began the race as a fund-raising underdog. But as the race grew tighter, online contributions from across the nation flooded his coffers. In the end, Brown raised over $12 million online, with over 157,000 individual donations. This was likely the largest online fund-raising total for

[10]Jim Drinkard and Jill Lawrence, "Online, Off and Running: Web a New Campaign Front." *USA Today*. Accessed at: www.usatoday.com/news/politicselections/2003–07–14-online-cover-usat_x.htm, August 2, 2005.

[11]Michael Luo, "Small On-Line Contributions Add Up to Huge Edge for Obama," *New York Times* (February 20, 2008). Accessed at: www.nytimes.com/2008/02/20/us/politics/20obama.html

[12]Zach Exley, "The New Organizers, What's Really behind Obama's Ground Game," *Huffington Post* (October 8, 2008). Accessed at: www.huffingtonpost.com/zack-exley/the-new-organizers-part-1_b_132782.html, November 20, 2009.

non-presidential candidate in U.S. history.[13] What is also stunning about this total is that some 97 percent came from individual contributions and only 2 percent from political action committees.[14]

SOCIAL NETWORKS

In the 2008 campaign, online social networks emerged for the first time as a key component of campaign strategies. Increasingly, candidates are leveraging social networks as a means to communicate with prospective voters. Online social networks have been around for a while, but they have not been used in presidential campaign politics until recently. These networks bring individuals together in an online environment with the explicit goal of forming groups around common interests. Online tools used in this environment include chat rooms, basic web design, messaging, video and photo posting, blogging and live-blogging, discussion forums, file sharing and more. As Figure 11.1 suggests, Barack Obama gained an advantage over John McCain in the 2008 election by more effectively using new media. Obama's organization maintained profiles on over 15 social networks, and even created its own network called MyBarackObama.com, enabling over 2 million supporters to sign up and connect with each other. Users were able to plan fund-raising events and call supporters and donors.[15] Anyone who chose to "become a fan" of Obama on Facebook or to "follow" Obama on Twitter received constant status updates that also reminded him or

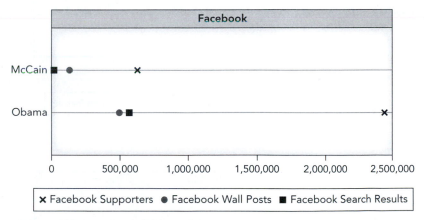

FIGURE 11.1 Obama vs. McCain: New Media.
Source: Peter Quily, "Barack Obama vs. John McCain Social Media and Search Engine Scorecard," Adult ADD Strengths (November 5, 2008).
Accessed at: http://adultaddstrengths.com/2008/11/05/obama-vs-mccain-social-media/

---

[13]Patrick Ruffini, "Scott Brown's Online Fundraising Machine: Inside the Numbers," Engage.Com (January 28, 2010). Accessed at: www.engagedc.com/2010/01/28/scott-browns-online-fundraising-machine-inside-the-numbers/

[14]Center for Responsive Politics, "Scott P. Brown" (March 1, 2010). Accessed at: www.opensecrets.org/politicians/summary.php?cid=N00031174&cycle=2010

[15]J. A. Vargas, "Obama Raised Half a Billion Online," *Washington Post OnLine* (November 20, 2008). Accessed at: http://voices.washingtonpost.com/44/2008/11/20/obama_raised_half_a_billion_on.html. L-N, November 20, 2009.

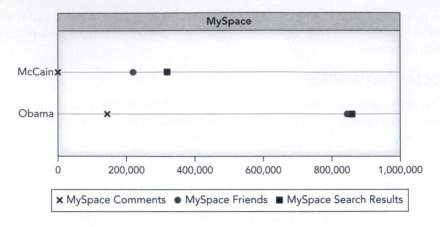

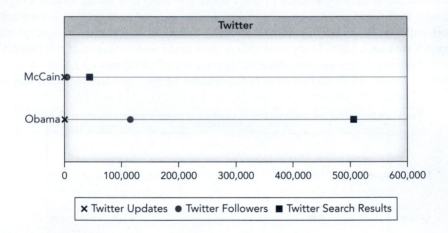

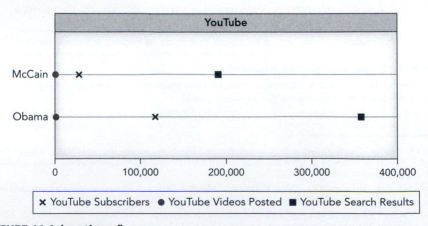

FIGURE 11.1 (continued)

her to donate money to the campaign. Given Obama's overwhelming support among the younger demographics—the very age groups most likely to use services like Facebook, Twitter, and YouTube—these technologies undoubtedly contributed to his victory.

ONLINE VIDEOS/YOUTUBE

In 1960, television exploded onto the presidential campaign scene with the televised Kennedy–Nixon debates. During the 2008 elections, YouTube demonstrated a similar flood of interest with the publication of video streaming from nearly all campaigns. The mention of YouTube as a prominent component of the 2008 campaign is in itself rather remarkable. The online video sharing website started in early 2005. As such, the 2008 presidential election is the first presidential election ever to be held with YouTube in existence—and already some are calling it the "YouTube Election,"[16] implying that the site had a *decisive* role in the first election in which it had *any* role.

But this was surely not the first election influenced by YouTube; it was a prominent feature of the historic 2006 midterm election season. During the midterm election, several Republican seats were in jeopardy, with Democrats experiencing a general popularity upswing due to George W. Bush's falling polling numbers. One of the very tight races was the contest for the Virginia U.S. Senate seat. Incumbent Republican George Allen was running for reelection and in the early stages had a commanding lead over Jim Webb, the Democratic challenger. This lead held steady until one day on the campaign trail when Allen was dramatically tripped up by a new media technology. Allen was at a Republican event in rural Virginia when he noticed a volunteer, a dark-skinned young man of Indian descent, from the Webb campaign filming the event. (This is increasingly common; they are called "trackers.") The GOP (Grand Old Party) candidate lost his cool and began disparaging his opponent and the campaign worker. He called the young man "macaca," twice. This is a racial slur, derived from the macaque, a species of monkey. And of course it was caught on tape and immediately posted on YouTube. Nearly 1 million "views" occurred in the following week and soon Allen was apologizing for the remark on national television and fending off charges that he had made similar racial slurs in his past. Webb ended up closing the gap and ultimately defeated Allen. In previous elections, Allen's comment might have been missed by the media, or perhaps noted as a sidebar story. But posting the clip on YouTube clearly altered the course of the election. Republicans would later send their own trackers into the field hoping to record Democratic blunders.

Early in the 2008 presidential contest, it became clear that candidates and their consultants were thinking formally about how to best utilize the burgeoning power of YouTube. Democratic candidate John Edwards announced his candidacy on the site. YouTube efforts were generally successful because they often heightened an otherwise less-exciting story—the formal announcement of a candidate who had been running for years, for example. When Barrack Obama announced he was running for president, the announcement on YouTube itself was newsworthy.

---

[16]Beth Kowitt, "The YouTube Election: The Obama Campaign Is Taking Its Message Directly to the Internet's Huge Audience," CNN Money.com (July 18, 2008). Accessed at: http://money.cnn .com/2008/07/18/magazines/fortune/kowitt_obamavideo.fortune/.

Beyond official candidacy announcements, candidates routinely produced content for YouTube. Nearly all political ads are now posted on YouTube, many of which never actually run on network or cable television. They are typically played to a specific television market via regional airwaves and then made available to everyone via YouTube. This has allowed campaigns to extend their reach, especially if an ad becomes "viral," meaning that it is shared from one voter to the next via email. It has also given journalists an easier way to monitor political advertisements.

One of the most extraordinary uses of YouTube came about on July 23, 2007. On that date, CNN sponsored a Democratic presidential primary debate in South Carolina where questions were presented by average citizens over YouTube.[17] (The Republican presidential primary CNN/YouTube debate was held on September 14, 2007, in Florida.) The ground-up nature of the event, with average citizens asking questions, gave the debate a greater sense of democratic authenticity.

The use of YouTube on the campaign trail underscores an important relationship that we have discussed a few times already: the relationship between online information and the establishment media. As more and more citizens post videos of campaign events on YouTube, citizens learn new information about candidates—often unflattering information.

In the spring of 2008, as Barack Obama seemed to be sailing to the nomination, posts of Reverend Jeremiah Wright, the senator's pastor, began appearing on YouTube. These clips, containing portions of fiery, controversial sermons, were played and replayed by millions of Americans. What was Obama's precise relationship with this man? Did he share these controversial thoughts? The Wright controversy became Obama's greatest primary election obstacle, and it was perpetuated in no small measure due to YouTube.

Conclusion

Through changes in technology, candidates are able to spread their messages faster and with fewer resources than ever before. Campaign websites give voters a chance to research the candidates, and news stories appear online at any hour of the day. Gone are the days of waiting for the morning edition of the newspaper to arrive. Searchable websites provide detailed, up-to-date information, and online techniques let voters make quick, small financial contributions and to join campaign efforts in a host of ways. Social networks connect candidates with a younger generation of voters, and video-sharing sites go way beyond mere descriptions of events. So much has changed in the past decade.

One of the themes of this text is that candidates, parties, and campaign operatives adjust quickly to changing conditions. With the rise of mass-based newspapers in the 1840s, candidates discovered the power of controlling the media message. This led to the rise of the partisan press. A few generations later, Mark Hanna was able to

[17]"The Skinny on the CNN, YouTube's Presidential Debates," CNN Political Ticker (June 14, 2007). Accessed at: http://politicalticker.blogs.cnn.com/2007/06/14/the-skinny-on-cnn-youtubes-presidential-debates/?fbid=2HSoaN0kf8j

help elect Republican William McKinley to the presidency by ushering in a host of techniques. At the center of this change was money—massive sums of money—and astute campaign advisors (the precursor to today's campaign consultants). A few generations later, candidates came to grips with the decline in local party structures and the importance of television. Nearly overnight, 30-second spot ads transformed voter communication techniques.

Now American politics has entered into another transformative period. It's likely that in a few years, people will no longer marvel at the power of blogs, Twitter, video-sharing sites, and social networks. Candidates will adapt to these changes, and many others, and the texture of American campaigns will change. At the center of all these transformations, however, remains the voter. Those interested in the evolution of the American system of government should monitor closely the role of average voters in the years ahead. As new media transformations plow ahead, what will be the impact on voter knowledge and efficacy? Will voters have more or less trust in the American electoral system? Will they find their role in the process? And will they feel compelled to join others in one of the most basic functions of any democracy: voting?

Critical Thinking

1. Have the changes in technology helped voters know the candidates better or have they cluttered the facts with too many personal opinions?
2. With the success of online fund-raising, particularly in 2008, do you think it will help future unknown primary candidates, challengers, and third-party candidates receive the funds needed to win a campaign, or will incumbents and well-known candidates still receive the advantage?

On the Web

Whether you use Twitter, Facebook, MySpace or YouTube, search for your favorite political candidate or public official—you are sure to find a detailed online following to get involved with.

CONCLUSION

York, Barack, and Voting in the American Experience

As we now know, the power and potential of voting and elections runs deep in the American psyche. A great deal has changed, with new adjustments around the corner. But along the way, there have been countless tales of how voting and elections transformed both public policy and the nature of American democracy. Elections have served in many tangible and indefinable ways as the building blocks of a "more perfect union" of the United States of America. As a conclusion to our exploration of American elections, one such story seems especially significant.

Almost exactly 200 years before Barack Obama's election to the presidency of the United States, Meriwether Lewis, William Clark, and a troop of about 45 men began an epic journey across North America. The Corps of Discovery, as it was called by President Thomas Jefferson, toiled for two-and-one-half years. It was a test of endurance, courage, clear-sightedness, and teamwork. It is one of the great stories of American history, not simply because of the immense obstacles overcome, but because the expedition seemed to define the geographic and economic destiny of the United States.

After more than two years of travel, the corps finally reached the Pacific Ocean. They had paddled up the Missouri River to its source, traversed the massive Rocky Mountains, and navigated the perilous upper waters of the Columbia River basin. They had gone as far from their friends and family as was possible on the continent; they had stepped out of what was then the United States, and in a way they had taken a leap into America's future. Yet their elation at having finally reached the Pacific was tempered by the realization that they would spend another winter in the wilds—and this time in the very wet, hostile climate of the Pacific Northwest. Minds quickly turned to where they would build their winter camp. Each option presented its own difficulties. To decide the matter, Lewis and Clark did the unthinkable: Rather than settle the issue unilaterally, as the leaders of the expedition, they would put the matter to a vote.

On November 24, 1805, each member of the group was asked to cast a ballot on where to spend the winter. One by one the soldiers of the expedition stepped forward to have their choice recorded. But Lewis and Clark went a bit further. Also on the expedition was York, Clark's long-time slave. He was allowed to vote. And there was of course Sacagawea, a young Shoshone woman who had traveled with the expedition for the previous year as an interpreter (all the while carrying her newborn baby on her back). She too was granted a vote.

Many of the white men in the corps would not have had the right to cast a ballot in their native states due to property qualifications, which were not completely abandoned until the 1830s. Black men would not have the right to vote for nearly 70 years—and even after the Fifteenth Amendment, numerous state laws kept African-Americans from the polls. Women would not have suffrage until well into the next century. Native Americans would not be considered citizens until 1924 and would not have the right to vote in all states until 1956. Yet, confronting one of the greatest predicaments of the journey, and as far from the political institutions of the East as one could get, the leaders of the expedition somehow felt compelled to put the issue to a vote of the entire party.

Historians have been baffled by the move. Why would the expedition leaders do such a thing? It was the first vote ever held in the Pacific Northwest. It was the first time in American history that a black slave had voted, the first time that a woman had voted. Their rationale was likely pragmatic. The late Stephen Ambrose, for example, suggests, "Perhaps they felt that, since they were all going to be in this together, they should all have a say . . . maybe they just wanted to involve everyone so that none would have the right to complain."[1]

Maybe it was more than pragmatism. We might imagine that the two leaders shared a cup of tea under the stars during their first night on the Pacific (their rum having run out) and chatted about the difficulties of their journey and about the great land that they had crossed. They would have talked about the many tribes of Indians they encountered and what might be the fate of settlers as they moved West—as they surely would. They would have mused about what Thomas Jefferson, their president, might think of their report.

And maybe, just maybe, the two captains talked about the future of American politics. Lewis and Clark would have chatted about liberty, honor, and respect, and would have fallen asleep dreaming of equality. When they awoke the next morning, a vote on where to build their camp would have just seemed right. Lewis and Clark looked into the future of the nation—its geographic future, its economic future, and indeed its political future. There was no other route than to put the issue to a vote.

If one were to chart the course of American politics from the early 1800s, elections would leap to the fore. Each generation of Americans has seen elections, and the right to vote, as the cornerstone of their democratic rights. Over the years, the right to vote has expanded; today, all citizens over the age of 18 are allowed to "step forward to have their choice recorded," so to speak. On one level, the story of the growing import of elections in America, as with the tale of Lewis and Clark, is nothing short of joyous.

But this story, like most other stories in American history, is more complex. To Native Americans, Lewis and Clark's trek marked the beginning of the systematic destruction of their way of life. Within 80 years, Native American lands, rights, and culture would be stripped—and their population decimated. As the United States rolled West, environmental destruction came, part and parcel. The "Garden of Eden" that Lewis and Clark wrote about in their journal was fleeting. The near-extinction of the buffalo is but one piece of the story. Although York was granted a vote on the Pacific Coast, once he returned to the East he was again Clark's slave and was frequently beaten. According to Clark, York had grown "uppity" after the expedition. Sacagawea remained the property of her husband (who also had another wife) until she died in childbirth a few years later. Lewis, the true genius of the expedition, fell so far into depression after the journey that

---

[1]Stephen E. Ambrose, *Undaunted Courage: Meriwether Lewis, Thomas Jefferson, and the Opening of the American West* (New York: Simon and Schuster, 1996), 315.

his only escape seemed suicide. He died of his own hand on October 11, 1809. One of the greatest stories of American history is also one of the saddest.

The story of elections in America has a sullen side, too. With the Jacksonian democratic movement of the 1830s came aggressive party committees (later dubbed "machines"). They organized the election process, but they also created a barrier between citizens and public policy. They forged a system that aided their own interests, often at the expense of fair public policy. That minor parties have long toiled ineffectively in the United States speaks to the fact that the major parties have rigged the political system to their benefit. Party machines reached their heyday by the end of the 19th century as their corruption spilled in many directions.

It took over 100 years for women to be granted the right to vote, and while African-Americans had been granted suffrage after the Civil War, another 100 years would pass before the right would become a reality. Money played a minor role in the 19th-century elections, but by the midpoint of the 20th century, it had become the principal determinant of election outcomes. Campaign consultants have burst onto the scene in the past few decades, greatly altering the way elections are run. Instead of receiving most of the campaign information from party workers or from the newspaper, 30-second television spots bombard American citizens each night. Perhaps because of these changes, and many others, interest in elections has become modest even when the opportunity to collect and distribute campaign information, via new media, has mushroomed. Many Americans no longer see elections as a viable avenue of change.

Still, Americans celebrate the right to vote and the importance of elections, just as they celebrate the achievement of their forbearers. With all their imperfections, elections remain a powerful pathway for change. Average citizens can use elections to change the outcome of government only if they understand the nature of the process—its power and its limitations. Elections may not be the best route for all political actors—or for even most. But each year, citizens are called upon to help choose the personnel of government. Democracy calls upon citizens to step forward, and elections, with all their limitations, still allow citizens' voices to be heard. Lewis and Clark had indeed stepped into the future—a future Americans are still trying to discover.

We will probably never know what thoughts passed through Barack Obama's mind as he drifted to sleep on the night of his inauguration. One would guess he thought of his mother and retraced his journey from a poor, single-parent household to his post as editor of the *Harvard Law Review*, and ultimately president. Or perhaps he would have thought about his work in Chicago as a community organizer and law professor and his difficult campaigns against Hillary Clinton and John McCain. Surely he would have considered the help of friends, the love of his family, and the sacrifices that Michelle and his daughters had made and that they would endure for his political career. And just maybe Barack Obama included in his grateful musings those who lived too early to realize successes like his. He may have considered the 200-year time span between his inauguration and Lewis and Clark's realization that, though still a slave, York should have his say.

Elections by themselves have not changed American society. But the right to vote, to stand and be counted, has been the trail marker to a more perfect union of the United States of America.

GLOSSARY

527 Organizations Named after Section 527 of the Internal Revenue Code, these units were created in the aftermath of the Bipartisan Campaign Reform Act primarily to influence the selection, nomination, election, appointment, or defeat of candidates to federal, state, or local public office. They first came to light in the 2004 election.

Activism A practice that emphasizes action in support of or opposition of an issue or cause.

Advocacy Spots Advocacy groups that purchase television or radio commercial times to promote a candidate or an issue during political campaigns.

The American Association for Political Consultants (AAPC) A nonpartisan organization of political consultants, media consultants, pollsters, campaign managers, corporate public affairs officers, professors, fund-raisers, lobbyists, congressional staffers, and vendors.

BCRA Also called the McCain–Feingold Law, this measure, passed in 2002, regulates the financing of political campaigns. Its foremost aim was to eliminate the flood of soft money collected and dispersed by party committees.

Bipartisanship A situation where a program or policy garners support from both Democratic and Republican officials. It often implies a compromise position.

Bureaucracy A system of government where most of the important decisions are made by appointed officials (bureaucrats) rather than by elected representatives (legislators).

Campaign/Political Consultant An individual who is hired for his or her skills and knowledge to help a candidate win an election, or to aid in efforts to pass or defeat a ballot initiative.

Candidate Someone who aspires to or is nominated to an elected position. Candidates run for political office.

Census An official count or survey of a population. In the American setting, a census is mandated by the Constitution every 10 years.

Citizens United v. Federal Election Commission The decision made by the U.S. Supreme Court in 2010 stating that corporate and union funding of independent political broadcasts in candidate elections cannot be limited. *Independent* means that direct contributions cannot be made to the candidates.

Civic Duty Those activities deemed to be the responsibility of a citizen in a democracy. Often one's civic duty is defined by custom and tradition.

Civics The study of obligations of citizens in a democratic system.

Closed Primary An election to nominate a candidate for the general election in which only members of that particular party are allowed to vote. You must be registered with a party to vote in that party's closed primary.

Comparative Campaign Ad Advertisements that contrast the views of candidates without being negative about the differences.

Congress The national legislative body of the United States, consisting of the Senate and the House of Representatives. However, members of the House are sometimes called "congressmen" and "congresswomen."

The Delaware Plan Grouping of four "blocks" of states according to population to determine the order of presidential primaries. The smallest 12 states and the District of Columbia would go first, then the next 12, then the 13 medium states, followed by the largest 13 states.

Democracy A system of government where power is vested in the people and is generally exercised through a system of periodically held open elections. The system also ensures citizens the protection of basic civil liberties, such as free speech and the right to assemble.

Direct Democracy A form of democracy where all citizens are allowed to decide policy questions. There are no legislatures in direct democracies. This process is sometimes referred to a "New England Town Hall Democracy," given that there are still a few small towns in that region that use direct democracy.

Disenfranchisement Depriving a citizen from his or her legal right to vote. Many minority groups were disenfranchised throughout much of American history.

District An electorally relevant geographic area defined by the government, such as congressional districts.

FEC (Federal Election Commission) An independent regulatory agency founded in 1975 to regulate the campaign finance legislation in the United States.

Federalism The distribution of power between layers of governmental authority. In the American setting, the layers are the federal government and the state governments.

The Federalist Papers A series of 85 essays promoting the ratification of the U.S. Constitution. They were written by John Jay, James Madison, and Alexander Hamilton in 1787 and 1788.

The Framers Also known as the Founding Fathers of the United States, these are the men who were central to the development of the American system. Sometimes this term also refers to those at the Constitutional Convention, but generally it implies all those at critical moments in the formation period.

Franking When incumbents are provided government-sponsored mailings in order to keep their constituents informed.

Gerrymandering Manipulating the boundaries of a legislative district so as to favor one party or group of people. In the past, this process was done for partisan advantage, but also to minimize the electoral significance of minority groups.

Get Out the Vote A slogan used by political operatives when they refer to programs and activities designed to get citizens to vote.

Grassroots Politics Political movements or activities that rely upon the support of a broad range of average citizens. This is sometimes called "bottom up" political activism.

Incumbent A candidate for office who is occupying a particular position that he or she is trying to keep. Incumbents run for reelection. The "incumbent advantage" refers to the benefits these candidates have when they run for reelection.

Interest Groups A group of people drawn or acting together in support of a common interest or to voice a common concern.

Intra-Party Actions or relations within a political party.

Landslide Elections When a candidate wins an election by an overwhelming margin of votes.

Legislation A law that has been enacted by a legislature or other governing body, or the process of making it. It is synonymous with *statute*.

Legislative Campaign Committees Branch party organizations designed to finance and manage legislative contests at the federal and state levels. At the federal level, they are often called the "Hill Committees."

Lobbying The attempt to influence public officials or members of a legislative body in the development of public policy.

Mandate/Referendum Election When a candidate (or body of candidates) with a similar set of policy positions wins an election by advocating these positions.

Media The main means of mass communication, regarded collectively.

National Primary Day The day when voters from across the country pick their party's nominees. (Not currently used.)

Negative Campaigning Referring to negative aspects of an opponent rather than emphasizing one's own positive attributes or preferred policies. Negative advertising is sometimes called "attack advertising."

New Media The use of the most recent technologies (e.g., YouTube, social networks, blogging, and websites) in mass media and political campaigns.

The Ohio Plan Splitting of states into three tiers—early states, small states, and large states—and voting in that order.

Open Primary An election to nominate a candidate for the general election in which all registered voters are allowed to participate. That is, one need not be a registered member of party to vote in that party's open primary.

PAC Short for political action committee, this is an extension of a special interest group that has a stake in the development of public policy. Often PACs are organized to elect political candidates or to advance the outcome of a political issue or piece of legislation. PACs generally support candidates by contributing funds or by spending on a candidate's behalf.

PAC Kits Tailored appeals for candidates to use when meeting with PAC representatives.

Partisanship An emotional and intellectual connection to a party, faction, cause, or person.

Party Affiliation Membership or affiliation with a political party. This is generally defined as registering oneself with a political party, but often the terms "party affiliation" and "party identification" can be used interchangeably.

Party Presence The level of enthusiasm for a political party within a designated area. This is defined by the strength of the local party organization, often called the party committee.

Polarization When the average policy positions of voters in one party are greatly at odds with the policy positions of average voters in the other party. One might say that the parties are "miles apart." It is also when the extreme factions of a political party gain dominance in a party.

Political Campaign The organized effort to elect an individual to an elected position or to win a ballot initiative.

Political Party A political organization that seeks to influence government policy by nominating candidates and helping them win political campaigns.

Political Platform A document outlining the goals, principles, and policy planks of a political party or candidate.

The Political Spectrum The range of political viewpoints based on ideology and policy positions. We often think of the spectrum as stretching from very liberal to very conservative.

Polling A systematic process of collecting and interpreting information garnered from a randomly selected group of individuals or cases.

Polling Place Locations that are designated for eligible citizens to cast their votes.

Primary Election The means by which a political party selects nominees for the general election.

Rank and File The ordinary members of an organization, often the core support for the group. They are sometimes called "party hacks."

Recall Elections A procedure by which voters can remove an elected official from office through a direct vote. Although rare, recalls can be initiated when sufficient voters sign a petition.

Redistricting The process of changing electoral district and constituency boundaries, usually in response to periodic census results. This happens at both the federal level (House of Representatives) and at the state level (state legislatures).

Republicanism Where the general population elects representatives to government so that they may represent the citizens' views and interests.

Rotating Primary Plan Related to the nomination of presidential candidates, this is where the United States would be split into four regions—Northeast, Midwest, West, and South. The blocks would rotate every presidential election, allowing different regions to be influential each time.

Spoiler Candidate A third-party candidate whose presence in an election draws votes from a candidate similar in ideology to him or her, thereby causing another candidate dissimilar to them to win the election.

Straight-Ticket Voter A citizen who votes for the same party in the same election, as well as in subsequent elections.

Suffrage The right to vote in political elections. Women were granted suffrage, for example, with the passage of the Nineteenth Amendment.

Super PAC Officially known as "independent expenditure-only committees," these groups are allowed to raise unlimited sums from unlimited sources, including corporations, unions and other groups, as well as wealthy individuals. But, they are not allowed to coordinate their campaign activities and spending with the candidates they are trying to help, hence the term "independent expenditure-only committee."

Swing State A state in which no single candidate or party has overwhelming support during elections. Often we think of swing states when considering electoral college votes.

Swing Voter A citizen who may not be affiliated with a particular political party or who will often vote across party lines. He or she may switch from one party to the next in the same election, as well as from one election to the next.

Trackers Operatives hired by political campaigns to follow and record the public actions of their opposition.

Veto The constitutional right of a president or governor to reject a decision or proposal made by the law-making body. Often a veto can be overridden by a supermajority vote in the legislature.

Voter Perception How voters view a particular candidate, policy, or program.

Voter Turnout The percentage of eligible voters who cast a ballot in an election. It is often noted as a percentage. This would be the number of voters in a particular election divided by the total number of citizens who were legally able to vote in that election.

INDEX

Note: Page references followed by "*f*" and "*t*" denote figures and tables, respectively.